Shakespeare and the Denial of Death

Shakespeare

Amherst   1987

& the Denial of Death

James L. Calderwood

University of Massachusetts Press

Copyright © 1987 by
The University of Massachusetts Press
All rights reserved
Printed in the United States of America
LC 87–5922
ISBN 0–87023–582–6 (cloth); 583–4 (paper)
Set in Palatino by Meriden-Stinehour Press
Printed by Cushing-Malloy and bound by John Dekker & Sons, Inc.
Library of Congress Cataloging-in-Publication Data

Calderwood, James L.
  Shakespeare and the denial of death.

  Includes bibliographical references and index.
    1. Shakespeare, William, 1564–1616—Criticism and
interpretation.   2. Death in literature.   3. Immortality
in literature.   I. Title.
  PR3069.D42C35   1987   822.3'3   87–5922
  ISBN 0–87023–582–6 (alk. paper)
  ISBN 0–87023–583–4 (pbk. : alk. paper)

British Library Cataloguing in Publication data are available

Publication of this book has been assisted by a grant from the
University of California, Irvine.

To My Father and Mother

Contents

Acknowledgments   xi

Introduction: Spiritual Highs and Corporeal Lows   3
1. The Denial of Death   4
2. Death and the Elizabethans   9
3. Indirections   13

Part 1. The Denial of Death

I   Cannibalism   17
1. Shylock   17
2. Timon and Coriolanus   19

II   Mana and Money, Feeding and Fasting   23
1. Hotspur   23
2. Falstaff   26
3. Prince Hal   27
4. Prospero, Macbeth, Hamlet   29

III   Disguise, Role-Playing, and Honor   33
1. Falstaff and Coriolanus   33
2. Feminine Disguise in Comedy   35
3. Honor and Honesty   40

IV   Death, Sex, and the Body   46
1. Animals and Death   46
2. Masculine Identity   49
3. Adonis and Bertram   51
4. Sex and Death   53

V   Sacrifice   58
1. *Henry VI*   59
2. *Henry V*   62
3. *A Midsummer Night's Dream*   64

VI   Clothing Mortality   68
1. Custom and Costume   68
2. Styles of Clothing   70
3. Thrice-Gorgeous Ceremony   73

VII   Mortal Clothing in *Hamlet*   77
     1. Readiness   77
     2. Outward Apparel   78
     3. Inward Clothing   81
     4. The Fit of Death   83

VIII   Immortal Money in *The Merchant of Venice*   87
     1. Gold and the Devil   87
     2. Midas and Portia   90
     3. Denying Death by Choosing Death   92
     4. Portia as Apportioner   93
     5. Metaphoric Trade   96

Part 2. Tragedy and Death

IX   Tragedy and the Denial of Death 1   103
     1. Tragedy, Comedy, and Immortality   103
     2. Unfathering in *Romeo and Juliet*   105
     3. Divinity in *Richard II*   109

X   Tragedy and the Denial of Death 2   113
     1. Fathers in *Hamlet*   113
     2. Fetishism in *Othello*   118

XI   Tragedy and the Denial of Death 3   122
     1. Patricide in *Macbeth*   122
     2. Death Devotion in *Coriolanus*   125
     3. Immortality in the Globe   129
     4. Death Demeaned and Dignified   131

XII   *King Lear* 1   136
     1. The Truth—More or Less   138
     2. Poetic Truth—More and Less   144

XIII   *King Lear* 2   146
     1. Abdication and Authority   146

XIV   *King Lear* 3   157
     1. Report   157
     2. Bearing Affliction in the Globe   159
     3. Worse Still   162
     4. Saying the Worst   165

Part 3. Immortality and Art

XV   Immortalizing Art   169
     1. The Body and Breath of Words   171
     2. *Love's Labour's Lost*   173

3. Death in the Dramatic Mode   177
4. *Julius Caesar*   181
5. *Antony and Cleopatra*   184
6. *The Tempest*: Death and Drama   187
7. *The Tempest*: Art and Nature   189
8. Dissolving Art   193

Supplement
The Anti-Immortalists   197
1. Villains   197
2. Fools   203

Notes 207

Index   229

Acknowledgments

My major debt is to Ernest Becker, the title of whose extraordinary book *The Denial of Death*, and many of whose ideas, I have borrowed in the spirit of plagiaristic intertextuality. I have also lifted some of the following material from myself; and I am grateful to Barbara A. Mowat and Willard Spiegelman for permission to reprint in revised form articles previously appearing in the *Shakespeare Quarterly* and the *Southwest Review*. I am grateful to Lawrence Danson, who read and commented helpfully on an early version of the manuscript, and especially to William C. Carroll and Richard Abrams, who were wonderfully generous with suggestions on how to put the book back together again after first subjecting it to the fate of Captain Carpenter. Bruce Wilcox, director of the Press, conducted the manuscript into print with his unusually usual combination of graciousness and efficiency; and Pam Wilkinson was again the ideal managing editor. Finally, I am grateful to the University of California, Irvine, for the sabbatical time in which to write much of the book.

Shakespeare and the Denial of Death

Introduction:
Spiritual Highs and Corporeal Lows

Shakespeare was more than usually aware of man's ironic status as the animal that seeks to deny its mortal limitations by fashioning idealized images of itself. Thus throughout the plays and poems he provides abundant opportunities for man's spiritual highness to come to grief on his corporeal lowness. This tendency may materialize in a passing remark in a comedy, "For there was never yet philosopher / That could endure the toothache patiently," or take more impressive rhetorical form in speeches like Hamlet's "What a piece of work is a man," in which the masterpiece of divine workmanship suffers a sudden fall to "this quintessence of dust." The discrepancy between ideal and real is the governing idea of many a sonnet—Sonnet 129, for instance, where a lustful heaven wastes into hell when put to the test—and it is such stuff as entire play after play is made on, whether a festive comedy like *Love's Labour's Lost*, in which the nobles of Navarre, who would "eternize" themselves in the fame of academic monasticism, are recalled to the mutable world by the French ladies and a messenger of death; a history like *Henry IV*, in which Hotspur's high-flying honor is weighed down by the corpulence of Falstaff; a problem play like *Troilus and Cressida*, in which the twin ideals of honor and love are eaten away by life's cankers; a tragedy like *King Lear*, in which a king who was told he was "everything" makes the long painful discovery that he is not ague-proof; or a romance like *The Tempest*, in which the hero's almost divinely magical powers must be forsworn at the end so he can descend to merely mortal status.

This is hardly surprising. After all, theologians of Shakespeare's time quarreled over many fine and not-so-fine points of religious doctrine, but they all agreed on the binary opposition of heaven and hell, soul and body, and God and Devil, and were confident that in degrees of dubious harmony these all melded to form the *concordia discors* of man himself. For every neoplatonist like Pico who thought man could actually climb the great chain of being and etherealize himself among the angels there was a naturalist like Montaigne who felt that he had a far better chance of growing, like Bottom, marvelous hairy about the face.

My interest, however, is not in documenting an Elizabethan or Shakespearean obsession with contraries but in examining the ways in which

Shakespeare, focusing on the major consequence of our corporeal lowness, the inevitability of death, dramatizes the "spiritual" strategies we employ to transcend this biological embarrassment. In keeping with the views of various modern students of human behavior,[1] I assume that the denial of death is a fundamental motive not merely of individuals but of their cultures as well; and in what follows I attempt selectively to suggest how often and how variously Shakespeare dramatizes the human desire for symbolic immortality.

1. The Denial of Death

Before turning to Shakespeare, however, let me sketch in a background to this immortalizing impulse by referring to some familiar anthropological and psychological notions about man's obligatory acquaintance with death. To begin with, in these postessentialist times it is pretty well accepted that human nature consists largely of human culture. For other creatures sheer survival depends on having an essential nature, a more or less flexible program of instincts that come into play almost at birth—the "more" and the "less" being dependent on the amount of compensatory brains the creature possesses. Man's status is roughly defined, in defiance of a good bit of evidence to the contrary, as much-brains and little-instinct, which means we are either a wonderfully fine or a woefully imperfect animal. In either case, unlike other animals, we are not fully embedded in nature. As Sir Thomas Browne said, "Thus is Man that great and true *Amphibian*, whose nature is disposed to live, not onely like other creatures in divers elements, but in divided and distinguished worlds: for though there be but one [world] to sense, there are two to reason, the one visible, the other invisible."[2] From a modern perspective Erich Fromm regards Browne's great and true Amphibian in a less sanguine light:

> Man transcends all other life because he is, for the first time, *life aware of itself*. Man is *in* nature, subject to its dictates and accidents, yet he transcends nature because he lacks the unawareness which makes the animal a part of nature—as one with it. Man is confronted with the frightening conflict of being the prisoner of nature, yet being free in his thoughts; being a part of nature, and yet to be as it were a freak of nature; being neither here nor there. Human self-awareness has made man a stranger in the world, separate, lonely, and frightened.[3]

Without instinctual programming and cursed therefore with a prolonged infancy and childhood, such a creature cannot survive if left to itself. It must create collective strategies for survival—a cultural library of "how to" books ranging from how to evade saber-toothed tigers to how to build arks.

"Every age," Joseph Conrad said, "is fed on illusions, lest man should renounce life early and the human race come to an end." Perhaps the most basic illusion is the one we share biologically with all other creatures, the instinctive sense that life is worth living and that we are worth preserving. Whatever we may be—mouse, man, or tyrannosaur—we will kill to eat; walk, stagger, or crawl as far as we can to drink; run as fast as we can to escape extinction; and in the ultimate pinch, cornered by something with fangs and claws, fight to the death to avoid dying. This organismic egotism that says the world cannot do without me, is enough to keep all other creatures breathing. But as humans we need a sense of self-esteem that is bred not only in the bone but in the brain, and bred there by the structures of meaning we grow up in and that grow up in us.

Humans, in short, cannot live by survival alone. The self-awareness of which Fromm speaks makes us want not merely to be alive but to be meaningfully alive—to feel that what we do and are makes a difference, inspiring love and respect or, if nothing else, fear and hatred in others. Culture then must not only provide for the survival of the pack but minister to this equally crucial need to live properly and meaningfully. Role prescriptions and status cues, religious ceremonies, arm-wrestling contests, batting averages and professorial pay scales are as crucial to our preservation as instruction manuals on how to plant corn and issue mating calls.[4]

Most fundamentally, we humans feel meaningful when we belong to a meaningful community, which is to say one sired by the gods and situated at the omphalos of the earth. Then like the Israelites we become the Chosen People or, like the immodest Cheyenne, the Human Beings. But when a culture loses its distinctive mana—when the Cheyenne discover the white man's magic is more powerful than theirs—then they shrivel spiritually. They may simply cease reproducing, as Ernest Becker says, or "lie down and die beside streams full of fish."[5] In the words of a Digger Indian chief: "In the beginning God gave to every people a cup, and from this they drank their life. . . . They all dipped in the water . . . but their cups were different. Our cup is broken now. It has passed away."[6]

As this suggests, our need to feel meaningful is complicated by the fact that we are not just another organism in search of a patch of psychic sunlight but also a self-conscious, symbolic animal. In fact the self-consciousness and symbolism were probably coincident. If man is, as Kenneth Burke claims, the "symbol-using, symbol-misusing, and symbol-making animal," he is also the "symbol-made animal."[7] The fact that language is itself so deeply dependent on the concept of negation may account for that particularly negative consequence of self-consciousness, the awareness and fear of death. As far as we know, all other creatures, lacking the negative, experience their bodies as positive entities that simply "are," whereas we register the presence of our bodies against a ground of not-being, as positive-negatives that "are" but ultimately "will not be."

For this one flower of the field to receive its fatal mark so far before its final wilting is, as Hopkins said, a hard and dismal thing. Though no one knows when or how the fear of death arrived on the evolutionary scene, psychologists say that annihilation anxiety afflicts us from infancy, not necessarily because of inherited Oedipal complexes but simply because we are all born prematurely. A tiny, thin-skinned creature without claws or fangs, set down among giants in a world of unknown but sensed dangers where animals are killed and eaten, for some ten years almost wholly dependent for survival on parents who inexplicably appear and disappear and sometimes explode into rage, the child requires no special genetic inheritance in order to fear abandonment, brutality, and death.[8]

No doubt creatures *can* survive in such a state, but not in constant consciousness of their plight. Other animals, mercifully endowed with what Hamlet calls bestial oblivion, live in the immortality of the moment; and child pychologists tell us that by virtue of an undeveloped neocortex children are granted about seven years of Edenic grace during which they do not know they will die, as though they have not yet sufficiently extricated themselves from "lower" nature to take the long view. This immortality of childhood has its parallel in the primitive belief that man is not destined by nature to die, that except for violence and accident there would be no death.[9] In keeping with this, many myths—the story of the Fall, for instance—are attempts to account for this great wrong; and Ernst Cassirer even says "In a certain sense the whole of mythical thought may be interpreted as a constant and obstinate negation of the phenomenon of death."[10] Of course the same may be said of religious thought insofar as it creates immortal gods and construes human death as the gateway to eternal life.

Man's need to deny death is most apparent in myth and religion, and the fact that these are cultural institutions suggests that culture as a whole is in some degree a death-denying agency, a pool of sacred meanings in which we cleanse ourselves of mortality. As mentioned earlier, for about seven years the child abides in a state of grace, unaware that it is personally marked for death: the Id knows only Yes. Then this prelapsarian sense of immortality is lost, only to be recaptured through the good offices of repression and transference, which enable us to go about the daily business of living—astonishingly, as Camus says—"as if no one *knew*." Or as Freud put it,

> We display an unmistakable tendency to "shelve" death, to eliminate it from life. We try to hush it up; indeed we even have the saying, "To think of something as we think of death." That is our own death, of course. Our own death is indeed unimaginable, and whenever we make the attempt to imagine it we can perceive that we really survive as spectators. Hence the psychoanalytic school could venture on the assertion that at bottom no one believes in his own death, or to put the same thing another way, in the unconscious every one of us is convinced of his own immortality.[11]

The source of this conviction lies in what psychoanalysts call the ego ideal, which contains "a core of narcissistic omnipotence" and relies on a "magic belief in one's invulnerability or immortality [to engender] physical courage and counteract realistic fears of injury and death."[12]

The most familiar form of death denial is simply life-involvement. We cannot dwell very deeply on our ultimate extinction while playing chess or break dancing. We may be, as Yeats said, fastened to a dying animal, but while the beast drags us toward the grave it also records each moment of the journey so vividly that we forget where we are headed. In the short run, at least, not even death can compete with such distractions as hay fever and electric guitars.

Nor can it compete with that monster "custom," which Hamlet regards as a cultural version of bestial oblivion. The daily habitualities of dressing and eating and parking-place-hunting draw a film of familiarity over our eyes and keep us from perceiving life's hidden imposthumes. Nevertheless, though they may show no cause without why we will die, the imposthumes are always there—and not so very far below the level of consciousness, as William James argues: "Let sanguine healthy-mindedness do its best with its strange power of living in the moment and ignoring and forgetting, still the evil background is really there to be thought of, and the skull will grin in at the banquet."[13] Such healthy-mindedness seems tied to an understandably near-sighted concern for personal survival which, overdone, is from the purpose of collective living. For a social creature like man, survival as a self-preserving effort must graduate into survival as a cultural project. There is an Arab proverb that says "I against my brother, I and my brother against my cousin, I and my brother and my cousin against the world." Read from left to right, it records at least a crude gesture toward socialization; read from right to left, it returns us to an atavistic narcissism that stubbornly resists all socialization. In this latter sense, it accords with the fact that as self-assertive individuals we can not only endure the deaths of others, we can thrive on them, especially when it is *your* death and not mine: "The moment of *survival* [Elias Canetti writes] is the moment of power. Horror at the sight of death turns into satisfaction that it is someone else who is dead."[14]

Against this we might want to set Donne's famous statement in his *Devotions*, "Any man's death diminishes me, because I am involved in Mankinde." At first glance Donne's view entails great hazard. Having given all mankind as hostages to fortune, I am vulnerable from every direction. Nevertheless, there are compensations. For if I am involved in mankind I am not an isolated creature struggling to survive in an alien world. I am "a part of the main," and the main, though somewhat diminished by individual deaths, has an enduring mass to it, a symbolic immortality I can share in. As René Girard says, "The death of the individual has something of the quality of a tribute levied for the continued existence of the collectivity. A human being dies, and the solidarity of the survivors is enhanced by his death."[15]

From this standpoint we can see that what Cassirer claims about myth, that it is a vast effort to deny death, applies to culture as a whole. This view has been maintained by a number of thinkers. Schopenhauer claims that "all religious and philosophical systems are principally directed to this end, and are thus primarily the antidote to the certainty of death"; Otto Rank says "man creates culture by changing natural conditions in order to maintain his spiritual self" —i.e., to deny death and preserve his own meaning; Becker claims that "each society is a hero system which promises victory over evil and death"; and Norman O. Brown sweepingly announces that "civilization is an attempt to overcome death."[16]

In this light, not just religion but culture as a whole is the opiate of the people. Or, rather, the distinction between the two fades. Culture is itself profoundly religious, reflecting at a secular level the desire to transcend guilt, finitude, and death through communion with the sacred. Becker's notion of a communal "hero system" is an extension of the conquest of death through individual heroics. As a symbol-made creature I need not literally survive death in battle to become immortal. I make a conquest of death symbolically when I win an argument, a chess match, a lucrative contract, or the hand of a fair lady. For I do not merely win in these contests, I kill. Almost every sport thrives on phrases like "kill, slaughter, destroy, annihilate, bury," and so on. Through such killings I grow great. If I kill often enough, I will live forever. In a society in which winning is not everything but the *only* thing, we need merely compare the faces of winners and losers at the end of a Super Bowl, a World Series, or a national spelling bee to realize what the stakes have really been.

Unfortunately, because the world abounds with articulate debaters, master chess players, shrewd businessmen, and irresistible courtly lovers, my chances of killing consistently are not as good as my chances of getting killed rather often. In which case, rather than put up with these lesser deaths I will simply join the higher powers and grow great by proxy. If I cannot play in the Super Bowl or be president of General Motors, at least I can sit in the stands and root for the Chicago Bears or buy GM cars with names like Firebird or Challenger and enter the lists with death on the freeway. Or if I cannot write like Shakespeare or Joyce, or think like Aquinas or Wittgenstein, still I can accumulate a great library and absorb their immortal rays by osmosis. Each new book I place on the shelves is one more gold piece in my strongbox: I grow, I prosper. But of course no immortality system is infallible; even the Chicago Bears can lose Super Bowls and the Boston Celtics, NBA championships. And if they do—or if my stocks fall, my car is totaled, or my library burns up—there is nothing for it: I die.

2. Death and the Elizabethans

To move these issues a little closer to Shakespeare, let me outline all too sketchily some general attitudes toward death in and around his time.

At particular points in history, as the work of Philippe Ariès suggests,[17] man's need to deny death is more acute than at others. On the whole the Middle Ages was not such a time, or if it was, the denial was accomplished so gracefully as to render death somewhat transparent. Transparent but by no means invisible. Death is too culturally useful to be allowed to become, as if it ever really could be, invisible. Socially and theologically death is valuable for its reformative virtue. Only by keeping fearful images of death before our eyes can our spiritual self-interestedness be activated. In this way death ministers to most of the deadly sins, although it is especially sovereign for pride. However, during the Middle Ages the principal cure for sin was hell. On canvas and from the pulpit, the nether regions were painted in such ghastly colors that death paled by comparison. Hell's full assortment of roasting, racking, boiling, flailing, and eviscerating was offered up in words, paint, and sculpture for the edification of those who lusted after sin.

Death, on the other hand, though sometimes associated with Satan, was more often seen as the servant of God, doing his bidding. The specter appeared as part of an inevitable and universal process, fetching Everyman to a final audit and settling of accounts. For the virtuous it was all as natural as the seasons. The notion that we start dying the moment we are born, and hence find our end in our beginnings, is a commonplace from Manilius to Montaigne to Gertrude's observation that "all that lives must die, / Passing through nature to eternity" and Edgar's "Ripeness is all." As a result, death—especially death under the management of the Church—could have its comfortable aspect. You gathered your friends and family about you, received absolution, and prepared to become immortal both in heaven and in the communal memory. One way or the other your spirit flowed gently into a greater sea.

From the thirteenth to the sixteenth centuries, however, death gradually came to appear in a different and more unnerving light. During the fifteenth century in particular, death became an obsession. "The whole fifteenth century," Theodore Spencer says, "was frenzied about death. The *Ars Moriendi* was one of the first examples of printing, and it had appeared everywhere before the fifteenth century had expired."[18] It is not merely that death was universalized, it was also horrified—or "hellified," since it now began to compete with hell as the great scarecrow to fright man into repentance. Choreographed in paintings and murals all over Europe, the rotting mummies of the *danse macabre* promenaded their unbelieving partners toward eternity. Death's role in these dances graduated from gentleness toward increasing violence as the sixteenth century approached. Similarly, the relatively peaceful figures carved on thirteenth-century tombs gradually metamorphosed into decomposing bodies and similarly horrible images of a death that was no longer simply eternity's doorstep but life's grisly terminus. The skeleton now became the universal symbol of man's destination, and no painting of a nobleman was complete without a skull grinning in the corner.

The sixteenth century was a continuation of but also a reaction against this preoccupation with death. The "tame" death of the Middle Ages was still in evidence, but the "invisible" death of the twentieth century—death as the ultimate humiliation to be hidden in hospitals and euphemisms—was making a tentative entrance.[19] Early in the century, in Holbein's famous "Dance of Death," ghastliness and gaiety seem to be in competition; there is a liveliness about Death's cotillion that almost belies its destination. And when Elizabethan painters set a skull at the feet of sumptuously clad nobles, it is a question whether death subsumes life or the magnificence of the great men transcends death. By the same token the popularity of elegies, epitaphs, and ornate monuments and tombs in the sixteenth century raises the question whether words and stone call up grim images of death or replace it in the imagination. Is it the *ars* or the *moriendi* that counts most?

Montaigne is instructive in this regard. In his essay "That to philosophize is to learn how to die" he tells how "even in the most licentious season of [his] life" his imagination dwelled on death. However, instead of envisioning death as a ghastly assault on the body in the fifteenth-century manner, he calls on classical authorities, especially the Stoics, to testify to its natural-ness. "To the man who told Socrates, 'The thirty tyrants have condemned you to death,' he replied: 'And nature them.' " His aim in dwelling so con-stantly on death is to familiarize himself with it in order to become indiffe-rent to it. Whereas a monk of the tenth to fifteenth centuries, told that he was about to die, would abandon his worldly affairs and devote himself entirely to the salvation of his soul, Montaigne is not at all fearful of being taken full of bread. In lines anticipative of Hamlet's "Readiness is all," he says "We must be always booted and ready to go, so far as it is in our power, and take special care to have only ourselves to deal with then."[20]

Montaigne's philosophy, the *ars moriendi*, church ritual, and funerary art were all in some degree a prophylactic against death. Taken institutionally in small doses, death lost some of its sting. Such a strategy was all the more necessary at a time when death was ubiquitous. At any moment you might meet your maker by way of plague or war, syphilis, smallpox, a rowdy's dagger, or, perhaps most deadly of all, a barber-surgeon. The funeral bells of London were always tolling, and, as priests and preachers cried, they tolled for the sinful—that is, for everyone.

A major aim of Lutherans and Calvinists seemed to be to generate guilt by calling on death as the ultimate witness for the prosecution. "Man is conceived in sin and born in corruption, and he passeth from the stink of the didie to the stench of the shroud." The words are Willie Stark's, cynical commentator on Protestant fundamentalism in Warren's *All the King's Men*, but the accent is Luther's.[21] If we are guilty at birth we must be guilty at death, even guilty *of* death, for the fact that we die is, after all, the ultimate proof of our guilt. And if we are guilty, then we must seek forgiveness. We must renounce our narcissistic desire to grow great and transcend death. That is the sin of pride. We must abase ourselves before death, acknowledge its inevitability and our guilt, and yield ourselves to some collective illu-sion—theological or otherwise—that gives the impression of safety. Surviv-ing alone spiritually is as hard as surviving alone biologically. Two quotes are suggestive in this regard, the first from Montaigne, the second from Carl Jung:[22]

Man is possessed by an extreme concern with prolonging his existence; he has provided for it with all his faculties. For the preservation of the body there are sepulchers; for the preservation of the name, glory. Impa-tient with his fortune, he has used all his wits to rebuild himself and prop himself up with his inventions. The soul, through its confusion and weakness being unable to stand on its own feet, goes looking

everywhere for consolations, hopes and foundations in external cir-
cumstances where it clings and takes root; and, flimsy and fantastic as
its imagination may create them, it rests more assured in them than in
itself, and more gladly.

And Jung:

During the past thirty years people from all of the civilized countries of
the earth have consulted me. Among all my patients in the second half
of life—that is to say, over thirty-five—there has not been one whose
problem in the last resort was not that of finding a religious outlook on
life. It is safe to say that every one of them fell ill because he had lost that
which the living religions of every age have given to their followers, and
none of them has been really healed who did not regain his religious
outlook. This of course has nothing to do with a particular creed or
membership of a church.

Montaigne's forlorn soul, unable to "rebuild himself" and find symbolic
immortality among the inventions of his imagination, falls into the sickness
that later fills the Swiss psychoanalyst's waiting room. Of course Montaigne
sees this spiritual impoverishment as a lack of faith in the true religion, but
as Jung indicates it has nothing to do with particular creeds: churches are
where you find them. People fall ill and die when their cultures can no
longer guarantee them access to the sacred fountain, which is equally sacred
whether it flows from god or queen and consists in grace or gold.

In the late sixteenth century the sacred current flowed from both God
and Queen, and it consisted in both grace and gold. But it had many other
sources. And Elizabethans needed all the sources they could find after the
breakdown of religious certainties occasioned by the Reformation. Freed by
Luther from the authority of the Church, Elizabethans no doubt gained an
increased sense of individuality and a more direct contact with God by way
of the Book. But they also lost the comforts of authority—the sense of place
in a fixed hierarchy, the certainty of truth, the psychological protection of
the Roman patriarchy—and discovered that they were alone and borne
down by feelings of insignificance and helplessness.[23] Cast out of the
Church, they rushed to substitute sects like those that formed nationally
around monarchs like Elizabeth, locally around nobles like Essex or adventurers like Frobisher and Hawkins, and domestically around the patriarchal
family.

It is no secret that the late Elizabethans were neurotically obsessed with
power and self-advancement, as if in desperate flight from the repressions

of self demanded by Protestantism and the Elizabethan parental system.[24] For them religious masochism yielded as readily to secular exhibitionism as sackcloth did to cambric and silk. And why not? If the Queen's eye falls with pleasure on my blue beard, dyed to match the blue feathers in my Osric-style bonnet, then surely the music of the spheres will resound in my temple. Instead of pilgrimages to Canterbury or Jerusalem, let me join with Drake in his round-the-world expedition—if not as a buccaneer then, perhaps better yet, as an investor in his seagoing joint stock company. But of course when I sidle up next to the great it is not cash I am after but life, the greater life they possess by virtue of social station, heroism, beauty, power, piety, or on rare occasion even learning. The lines of the Chorus in *Henry V* about "the general of our gracious empress" bringing rebellion home from Ireland "broached on his sword" suggest that Shakespeare himself felt some of the immortalizing magnetism of Essex's mana before the general rode home and burst into one bedroom too many.

Because men care more about their immortality than they do about their lives, as Rank remarked, what impoverished young gentleman would not cast his cuisses aside and ride with Sidney in search of a glorious death at Zutphen, or sail with Ralegh in search of the heavenly albeit malarial El Dorado, or court the princess in her high pavilion? And who would not gladly entertain the court on one of the Queen's progresses, loading the table with exotic foods and the woods with stationary deer, supplying handsome housing and enough pseudomedieval and classical pageantry and ceremonies to make it clear that queen and court and host are all legitimate heirs of the antique world—and all on money borrowed at rates of at least ten percent? Even at this high price it is worth it. In fact *because* of this high price it is worth it. For as in a Kwakiutl potlatch, if I spend much I must be much.[25] And being much was an obsession with the young gallants of Shakespeare's generation.

And where could they be much more than by taking a box at the Globe theater or, even more impressive, wangling a seat at a court performance? In the latter case they could enter the grand ritualized ambience of queen or king, where death clearly had no dominion, and pass from there into the even more deathless world of theatrical illusion where they could be not merely much but all things, like Bottom the would-be player of all parts.

3. Indirections

The art of being much or of acquiring much being is fairly ardently practiced at all times. Certainly it is a passion of Shakespeare's characters, whether they seek to eat their way to greatness like Falstaff, hoard their way to it like Shylock, or slaughter their way to it like Macbeth. By these and many other means, the men and women of the plays heap wood on the sacred bonfire that keeps death at bay.

In the essays that follow I examine some of the ways in which Shakespeare's characters tend that fire. My critical plot consists of a series of interconnected studies, a kind of compound of Aristotle's unity of action and Wittgenstein's notion of family resemblances. Part 1, "The Denial of Death," begins by examining how Shakespeare's characters deny death in the most elementary biological fashion (relying on such strategies for survival as feeding, fighting, fleeing, hiding) and then turns at an indeterminate point—because there is no clear distinction between the bodily and the symbolic—to discuss how characters acquire symbolic immortality by merging with a collective (nation, sex, class, cult). To illustrate this I discuss characters, scenes, and actions in a variety of plays, occasionally pausing to take a longer look at individual texts, especially *Henry V, A Midsummer Night's Dream, Hamlet,* and *The Merchant of Venice.*

As the book proceeds, the essays get more ambitious, certainly more longwinded. Chapters 7 and 8 take a sustained look at the role of clothing in *Hamlet* and of money in *The Merchant of Venice;* and then in Part 2, "Tragedy and Death," three chapters deal at some length with Shakespearean tragedy and symbolic immortality, and three more chapters are devoted to *King Lear* and the ways in which culture mediates between man and the more abrasive aspects of nature. At this point, and in Part 3, the movement turns, like the old king's wheel of fire, from thematic questions of how people survive to metadramatic ones of how plays do so.

Needless to say—sad to say too—in the notion of symbolic immortality I have not discovered the great subplot of Shakespearean drama. However, it does offer a different and perhaps helpful way of looking at the plays, one that suggests that Shakespeare's interest in the denial of death as an abiding motive in human affairs may have some bearing on his own enduring life in the theater.

Part 1
The Denial of Death

I   Cannibalism

1. Shylock

The simplest way to deny death is to stay alive, and the simplest way to stay alive is to eat. Like Polonius every organism on earth must sometimes be at supper—if not where it eats, then where it is eaten—for as Hamlet says "your worm is your only emperor for diet" (4.3). Hamlet's witty line alludes to the famous Diet of Worms in 1521, presided over by the Holy Roman Emperor Charles of Hapsburg, at which Luther was placed under ban after refusing to recant. Hamlet's pun suggests the kind of spiritual-corporeal division dwelled on in the introduction. The Holy Roman Emperor, fatted with pomp, encounters a ruler more sovereign than he, having the imperial power to convene Catholic, Protestant, atheist, and Holy Roman Emperor alike for its dietary purposes. Thus the sacred succumbs to the profane, and man's immortal pretensions yield to his mortal edibility.

The emperor worm will have to cinch in its belt when it comes to Hamlet and Claudius, for the one eats air and the other is fed puns:

KING. How fares our cousin Hamlet?
HAM. Excellent, i' faith, of the chameleon's dish: I eat the air, promise-crammed. You cannot feed capons so.
KING. I have nothing with this answer, Hamlet.   (3.2)

Fed on Claudius's airy promises of Hamlet's being his heir ("You are the most immediate to our throne" [1.2]), the wary Prince adopts not only the chameleon's diet but its cosmetics of disguise as well. Otherwise, like the capon, he may find himself at a dinner where he does not feed but is fed upon.

That is precisely where the sons of Tamora, Queen of the Goths, find themselves at the end of *Titus Andronicus*. Tamora would have done well to listen to Hamlet's remarks on dieting before she sat down with the vengeful Titus and discovered too late that she had dined on her own sons, their bones ground up and their heads baked like two and twenty blackbirds in a pie. Actually Tamora is at a table where she both eats and is eaten, for while she samples her sons her host Titus is dining revengefully on her.

Only in this play does Shakespeare oblige his audience to watch humans eating humans on stage. Yet symbolic cannibalism is ubiquitous. In its most primitive form it occurs in battle where to kill your enemy is to consume him. The object of such consumption is not of course to fill your belly with food but to enlarge your soul with mana, to recharge your spiritual batteries with your enemy's vital principle. Usually Shakespeare deals lightly with this practice, calling on carnivorous terms to ridicule the chivalric ferocity of characters like the Dauphin in *Henry V*, who on the eve of Agincourt "longs to eat the English," as a fatuous follower claims, to the amusement of a skeptic who replies "I think he will eat all he kills" (3.7). Beatrice takes the same view of Benedick's valor in *Much Ado*: "I pray you, how many hath he killed and eaten in these wars? But how many hath he killed? for indeed I have promised to eat all of his killing" (1.1).

In these two scenes war calls forth a kind of ireful hunger that contrasts with the satieties of the table. Before Agincourt, the English are said by the French to be a nation of beef-eaters who because they are currently out of beef will "have only stomachs to eat and none to fight." By the same token, Beatrice derides the claim that Benedick has done "good service" in the wars by saying "You had musty victual, and he hath holp to eat it. He is a very valiant trencherman; he hath an excellent stomach." He who has a stomach for food, like Falstaff, cannot, like Falstaff, have a stomach for war. It is the lean and hungry sorts like Cassius and Coriolanus and Macbeth—and, to be sure, Fluellen—who salivate at the sight of armor. Coriolanus I shall come back to in a moment, but Fluellen deserves special mention. If his military hunger is a consequence of a diet of leeks, one would expect the Welsh to conquer the world. But his greatest conquest is of Pistol, whose appetite for war is no greater than his appetite for leeks. But this is a conquest in reverse. When Fluellen cudgels Pistol about, he does not eat him but feeds him. Instead of consuming Pistol's vital spirit, such as it may or may not be, Fluellen compels him to eat a leek, and hence to ingest the Welsh mana. Henceforth a bit of "Cadwallader and all his goats" will vie inside Pistol with his native ferocity.

Warfare, then, seems an only slightly sublimated version of cannibalism. We don't add much more sublimity to the notion if we turn to *The Merchant of Venice* and Shylock's demand for a pound of Antonio's Christian flesh. Such a demand suggests that if you desublimate the comparatively civilized practice of money-lending what you have is people eating people. Indeed that is what Elizabethan moralists like Thomas Wilson, Gerald de Malynes, and Arthur Warren claimed.[1] In Shylock's case this is a two-step process. When Shylock mentions that Jacob kept sheep for his uncle Laban, Antonio asks sarcastically "Did [Jacob] take interest?" and Shylock replies "No, not take interest, not, as you would say, / Directly interest" (1.3). Instead, by a clever device Jacob made the ewes breed the kind of pied lambs that Jacob had promised he could keep for himself. Antonio replies "Was this [tale] inserted to make interest good? / Or is your gold and silver ewes and rams?"—to which Shylock: "I cannot tell; I make it breed as fast."

Thus "use" is punningly equated with "ewes"; and interest, a sophisticated form of money, parallels animal barter, a primitive form of exchange. Shylock's puns breed even faster than Laban's sheep—and continue to do so when he demands his pound of flesh instead of "use." For ewes are bred ultimately to be eaten, and so, it would seem, is Antonio. In Shylock's culinary hierarchy, the symbolic consumption of your enemy's purse by way of usury rests quite naturally on the universally accepted practice of eating domestic animals. Shylock—or, rather, Shakespeare through Shylock—demystifies the "higher" socio-economics of money-lending by exposing their "lower" cannibalistic intent. He blandly acknowledges that

> A pound of man's flesh taken from a man
> Is not so estimable, profitable neither,
> As flesh of muttons, beefs, or goats
>
> (1.3)

but to seal his bond he will dine both with and upon Antonio and Bassanio: "But yet I'll go in hate, to feed upon / The prodigal Christian" (2.5). When one is famished for revenge, Christian flesh is far more filling than mutton.[2]

2. Timon and Coriolanus

This equation of food and money recurs in *Timon of Athens*, where the over-generous hero is at the same table as Polonius and Antonio, fed upon not by your emperor worm or even by carnivorous enemies but by hordes of flattering friends. Timon's banquets are a bit sumptuous to serve as instances of survival by eating, but the railing Apemantus makes the cannibalistic point clearly enough:

> I scorn thy meat; 'twould choke me, for I should never flatter thee. O you gods, what a number of men eats Timon, and he sees them not! (1.2)

Shylock comes to grief because he demands a bloody return on his loan to Antonio; Timon comes to grief because he refuses to accept a return on his gifts. Timon is the soul of magnaminous idealism. "I gave it freely ever," he says, "and there's none / Can truly say he gives if he receives" (1.2). Here, it seems, is philanthropy at its finest. And yet in the second half of the play we see in Timon misanthropy at its meanest. How does Shakespeare get from the one to the other?

Perhaps by regarding philanthropy and misanthropy not as total opposites but as complements. That is, if we look for incipient misanthropy in the first part of the play, we might argue that in differing degrees lavish giving and bitter hoarding both exemplify antisocial behavior. For pure giving, as opposed to loaning, creates no contract, no bond, no financial reciprocity. It takes place in a social vacuum, and suggests a kind of grand self-sufficiency that sets Timon above the needs of ordinary men who must replenish themselves from time to time. Thus his insistence on being always at the head of the table in Athens implies an isolation from other men that is simply reversed and intensified by his removal to the woods. The man who feeds others and will not be fed in return lays claim to a kind of immortality, an endless repleteness of self.

But of course such a diet can be viciously slenderizing, as Timon discovers when his funds run out. Obliged to appeal to his pseudofriends for aid, he is deprived of his self-sufficient symbolic immortality and reduced to a state of mortal peril. Shakespeare graphically demonstrates that money is not simply a means of economic exchange but a sacred life-giving substance, the symbolic flesh and blood of its owner. As long as money flows in his veins he lives, flourishes, transcends mortality. When it ceases to do so he dies. "Cut my heart in sums," Timon cries to his creditors, "Tell out my blood. . . . Five thousand drops pays that" (3.4). Without money in Athens, Timon is as near starvation as he is without roots in the woods.

The experience of Timon very nearly reverses that of Coriolanus. Where Timon spends, Coriolanus hoards. But their contrasting conduct derives from a common cannibalistic subtext. Coriolanus's refusal to distribute grain to the plebeians is in symbolic effect a refusal to allow them to feed off his body and hence to ingest his mana. He is himself a well-stocked storehouse of cultural foods like constancy, honesty, courage, and nobility. But because he alone eats from this private larder, he is also full of pride, which might be defined in this context as an excessive well-fedness of self. By the same token the unfed plebeians are depicted as hungering for the virtues Coriolanus so abundantly possesses. Unable to feed on him, they remain fickle, untrustworthy, cowardly, and ignoble.

Timon, as Apemantus says, sees not the men who eat him, but Coriolanus is all too concious of the threat of being eaten.[3] His refusal to accept the judgments of others is a form of psychic armor, a declaration of self-sufficiency, as though even honest praise were the flattery that paves

the way to Timon's table. At any rate, when he stands for consul, his chur-
lishness about exposing his scars to the plebeians reminds one of the behavior of a captive who fears being poked and prodded by cannibals. Scars,
after all, are not only marks of supernatural distinction but also signs of
mortal vulnerability.

Timon's magnanimity is in a sense as self-centered as Coriolanus's pride,
because both represent a supreme independence from the world of feeding
men around them. No matter how often Timon is financially fed upon, he
heaps the platter of himself anew until at last he finds, like Mother Hubbard,
that the cupboard is bare. Conversely, no matter how morally and spiritually
famished the plebeians may be, Coriolanus hoards the grain of his virtue
until he must be driven from the city. In Antium where he risks being eaten
as an enemy he is asked rather to join the Volsces at table (4.5), and soon
afterward he resumes and even elevates to a kind of godlikeness his status
as the autonomous individual. Now he will march on Rome with devouring
intent. But after his mother persuades him otherwise, he returns to Corioli
and suffers a species of ritual *sparagmos* as the Volscian citizens—displaced
versions of the Roman plebeians—cry "Tear him to pieces!" At last the grain
god is slain and distributed to the hungering mob.

Coriolanus ends where *Timon* begins, with the hero being torn apart and
eaten. In Timon's case the *sparagmos* is only symbolic, a rending of the hero's
financial body that leaves him still alive to retire to the woods and compete
with Apemantus in misanthropic invective. Now instead of feeding others
he will feed on them. "Destruction fang mankind!" he cries, "Earth, yield
me roots!"—and he immediately discovers gold (4.3). At this point gold
metaphorically becomes the poison and disease that will gnaw away at
human virtue, fanging mankind at its weakest point. "Come, damned earth,
/ Thou common whore of mankind"—from whose womb gold has so poison-
ously issued— "I will make thee do thy right nature." Earth's whorish right
nature is to spread corruption by means of gold, and hence Timon spreads
gold among Alcibiades' whores to encourage them in their profession of
generating not children to preserve but diseases to plague mankind.

Shakespeare seems to be ringing a change on the association of money
and feces popularized by psychoanalysis. Filth, the term he and Apemantus
repeatedly use, is not anal but vaginal. Hence Titus's curse on Athens:

> To general filths
> Convert on the instant, green virginity!
> Do it in your parents' eyes! (4.1.6-8)

"General filths" means whores, but filth also refers to the whore-induced
diseases Timon wishes on mankind (which literally ate away noses in Shake-

speare's day). Apemantus made the same point earlier when a lady at Timon's feast said "My lord, you take us even at the best" and he replied "Faith, for the worst is filthy [i.e., diseased], and would not hold taking, I doubt me" (1.2.151). But the ground (literally) for all disease is the fecund earth that issues infectious gold. In other words Shakespeare is maintaining the equation between money and body established during the philanthropic phase of the play, except that now in the misanthropic phase money is no longer the sacred source of life but the corruptive source of disease and death. At the end, having done what he could to spread death by gold, Timon turns merciless, giving the remainder of his gold to the faithful Flavius on condition that it never be used medicinally on behalf of man. If Timon does not himself "fang mankind" in cannibalistic revenge, he will allow the diseases produced by gold to eat away at them.

Mana and Money,
        Feeding and Fasting

1. Hotspur

The Shakespearean equation of food and money discussed in the last chapter has its parallel in the primitive belief that money, whether dog's teeth, beads, or gold coins, is ultimately, as Norman O. Brown has shown, a form of sacred power.[1] Thus to take a man's money is to confiscate his mana and diminish his life, in the same way that by eating an enemy's body you absorb his sacred significance. This puts a somewhat different light on the cases of symbolic cannibalism we have been looking at. It helps us see for instance that Shylock does not want Antonio's money simply to increase his own wealth, or his flesh to increase his own girth. His hatred includes an element of envy. What he really wants is to deprive Antonio of his sacred status within a predominantly Christian society that spurns the Jew, denying him access to its immortality pool. To eat Antonio, then, is not merely to kill him and rid oneself of an enemy but in some degree to absorb his vital principle. The same motive stimulates the hunger of the plebeians for Coriolanus and of the sycophants for Timon. The killing and consuming aspect of eating is coupled to a desire for what the Greeks called *entheos* and the Christians *communion*—a spiritual participation in the sacred power of the god.

There is of course a more direct way to confiscate your enemy's mana than to take his money: simply take his life. That in itself will make you swell with power whether you also eat his flesh, as Shylock seems inclined to do, or his heart, as some cannibals do, or his liver, as the mountain man Liver-Eating Johnson preferred. In Shakespeare, as I mentioned earlier, the field of battle is compared to the dinner table as a scene of consumption. Men have a natural appetite for fighting and for feeding, but for some reason they cannot have a stomach for both. Falstaff and Hotspur are the classic examples. For Hotspur battle is a way of denying death by inflicting it on others. Killing someone who sought to kill you is a conquest of death and can inspire a sense of symbolic immortality, as Elias Canetti points out: "The man who faces [a danger], and truly survives it; who then faces the next one; who piles up the moments of survival—he is the man who attains the feeling of invulnerability. Only when he has attained it does he actually become a hero, able to take any risk, for by then there is nothing he fears."[2] Hotspur plunging fearlessly into battle at Shrewsbury crying "Die all, die merrily!" fits the description well enough. For the adrenalin in the bloodstream tells Hotspur he cannot die. His followers will die, his enemies will die, but not he. Hence he is less interested in the immortality he may be granted after he has become a corpse than in the symbolic immortality he enjoys while making corpses of others. What intoxicates him is the living sensation of deathlessness as he stands over those he has killed, his lungs swelling as if with the breath they have lost.

If you happen to be a king, what better way to experience this sensation than to send your followers against your enemies and watch both die in the action? "Into the breach, dear friends" as King Harry cries. And indeed they are his dearest friends, his perfect subjects, because they die at his command, and in his cause, and, most significantly, in his stead. All those fallen bodies—enemies who sought his death, dear friends who died for him—testify to his greatness. As Michel Foucault says,

> The sovereign exercised his right of life only by exercising his right to kill, or by refraining from killing; he evidenced his power over life only through the death he was capable of requiring. The right which was formulated as the "power of life and death" was in reality the right to *take* life or *let* live. Its symbol, after all, was the sword.[3]

When Harry exercises this right the holiness of his cause is confirmed: God *is* for Harry, and Saint George for England! At such a moment Hotspur seems immortal after all; he apparently lives on in King Harry.

Without death, it becomes apparent, Hotspur cannot live. Death is the food of life, and he can never get enough of it. For the moment of survival not only sends a rush of immortality through his veins, it also fills him with sacred power in the form of honor, fame, and glory—so much so that even King Henry, the fount of sacredness, wishes Hotspur were his son. Honor for Hotspur is life, liver, mana, chivalric ambrosia, and he will seek it at the bottom of the sea or in the dust at Shrewsbury, even if it requires taking his ragamuffins where they are peppered.

Which is to say that Hotspur's greediness for honor is as destructively self-absorbing as Falstaff's greediness for money and a life of self-indul-gence. Eating, after all, is a private business; you can feed someone else, but you can't eat for him. So to feed himself Falstaff buys up a quantity of pitiful rascals whose qualification for war is their ability to die; they will "fill a pit as well as better. Tush, man, mortal men, mortal men" (4.3). As mortal indeed as Hotspur's men, sent into the field without reinforcements for fear

Hotspur might have had to share the glory of the victory. All are, as Falstaff says, "food for powder, food for powder." Which brings us back to appetites.

That Hotspur's pursuit of honor is a military version of Falstaff's gluttony is suggested by Prince Hal's burlesquing speech about "the Hotspur of the north, he that kills me some six or seven dozen Scots *at a breakfast*, washes his hands, and says to his wife, 'Fie on this quiet life, I want work!' " (2.4) Hotspur consumes Scots by the dozens like so many eggs at a sitting. In his way he is as voracious and round-bellied as Falstaff, if we transform capons and sack into titles and renown. In fact two quotations from Canetti about primitive beliefs catch the spirit of Falstaff and Hotspur with respect to consumption. The first refers to the so-called champion eater chiefs of some tribes, men who qualify for chiefdom by virtue of their matchless gluttony. Of such a chief, Canetti says "His full belly seems to [his people] a guarantee that they themselves will never go hungry for long. It is as though he had filled it for all of them."[4] Similarly, no one can believe in starvation as long as Falstaff—"that huge bombard of sack, that stuffed cloak-bag of guts, that roasted Manningtree ox with the pudding in his belly"—is King of Misrule in the Boar's Head Tavern. Nor could anyone believe in cowardice when the King of Honor is in the saddle. Hotspur's outsized chivalric spirit is explained by the belief of Australian aborigines about the slayer and the slain, according to which "the spirit of the slain man enters the body of the slayer, who then not only acquires double strength, but actually becomes larger."[5] Hotspur fills himself with glorious life as he consumes warrior after warrior, and his people, confident of sharing his immortality, gladly answer his cry "Die all, die merrily!"

But even the immortal Hotspur goes down in battle, reduced at last as he admits to "dust and food . . ."—"for worms," Hal adds (5.4). Falstaff too is very nearly reduced to food when he more willingly finds a place to fall and, in response to Hal's remark that he will shortly see his "dead" body embowelled, rises up grumbling "Embowelled! If thou embowel me today, I'll give you leave to powder and eat me too tomorrow" (5.4)—an invitation only Polyphemus could accept with any prospect of success.

For all his rough and engaging eccentricity, Hotspur is a literalist of the imagination. For him all the grand words of his times—*courage, honor, espérance*—have an exact and demanding reality; they call him to battle as exigently as words like *God, sin,* and *sacrifice* call saints to the stake. In both cases immortality is in the offing. However, Hotspur seeks immortality not by yielding his life but by absorbing so much life and fame that he becomes too great for death to swallow. Wars eat men, but not Hotspur—until Hal carves him for the emperor worm's table.

2. Falstaff

Falstaff is even more anxious to keep death's appetite unappeased. However, his famous instinct tells him that he is better equipped simply to preserve himself than to make conquests of death. Self-preservation consists mainly in eating and not being eaten, a talent Falstaff labors to perfect. In a world in which the dace, and especially a portly dace, is always fair game for the pike, staying alive is often no more complicated than fleeing. Thus scenes of danger activate his instinct, his discretion, and especially his legs. At Gadshill his instinct warns him that it is wiser to haul one's guts away, even to run and roar a little, than to assail the true Prince; and at Shrewsbury his discretion advises him that playing dead is infinitely preferable to being dead.

Hiding from death at Shrewsbury by becoming deathlike keeps Falstaff alive whereas challenging death with too much life turns Hotspur to dust. While Hotspur is down at Shrewsbury but not yet dust, Falstaff takes advantage of his opportunity to grow great in noncorporeal ways. He feeds on Hotspur's mana, not by following him but by killing him, by wounding him in the thigh and hence stealing his sexual-military potency. Standing with his foot figuratively on the chest of the fallen hero, Falstaff feels that his heroic performance should insinuate him into the ranks of the culturally immortal: "I look to be either earl or duke, I do assure you" (5.4).

Devouring dead heroes is not really Falstaff's preferred modus vivendi. He is more comfortable at table, where his courage is legendary: capons if not knights tremble at the sound of his name. But although he does more than his share of actual eating, his cannibalistic project is conducted symbolically by confiscating other men's money. At Gadshill he relieves the King of his crowns, and in Warwickshire (in Part 2) he sets about making "a philosopher's two stones" of Shallow. But this scramble for capons and coins has the great disadvantage of being a moment by moment affair that lays up nothing against one's declining years, especially when the years have already been declining for some while: "I am old," he murmurs unhappily to Doll Tearsheet, "I am old" (2HIV 2.4).

The words "I am old" shadow the Falstaff of Part 2. Self-preservation without self-transcendence is merely a daily staving off of death, just as in Hotspur's case self-transcendence without the self-preservational instinct is an open invitation to extinction. Falstaff requires some access to the sacredness of a culture from whose most holy concepts he is an apostate. So he hitches his long-range hopes of survival to Prince Hal's solar chariot, and when the chariot pulls up abruptly at Westminster Hall for Hal's coronation, Falstaff tumbles off. "Master Shallow," he says, "I owe you a thousand pound." At Shrewsbury Hal had said "Thou owest God a death," and Falstaff demurred: " 'Tis not due yet; I would be loath to pay him before his day" (*1HIV* 5.1). Now when Hal pays England the debt he never promised, in part by spurning the "feeder of [his] riots," it is Falstaff who pays also, an even stiffer price. To acknowledge his debt to Shallow is to acknowledge his liability to death in a world where, without investments in cultural immortality, even old heroes are held to strict account.

3. Prince Hal

These monetary terms are appropriate inasmuch as *Henry IV* is dominated by such concepts as debt, redemption, counterfeiting, and robbing. For instance, at Shrewsbury while Falstaff is counterfeiting death, the King is counterfeiting himself. In hopes of hiding from death he strews the field with false crowns and kings—"The King hath many marching in his coats" (5.3). Such counterfeiting underscores the fact that Bolingbroke's own crown is illegal tender, minted as it was by might instead of right. His robbery of Richard's royal exchequer is merely an aristocratic version of Falstaff's highway heroics at Gadshill.

With the King of Misrule and the King of England both counterfeiting to deceive death at Shrewsbury, the "true prince" stands forth as England's only authentic currency. A prince who "never promiseth but he means to pay," Hal challenges Hotspur before the battle, "redeems" his lost credit with his father by driving off the murderous Douglas, and "robs" Hotspur of his youth (5.3). Monetary imagery of this sort is the measure of the play. That is, it constitutes a kind of mid-level metaphor between high honor and low appetite. Take, for instance, Hal's reply to his father when he is rebuked for being lax in the chivalric virtues, especially by comparison to Hotspur:

> Percy is but my factor, good my lord,
> To engross up glorious deeds on my behalf;
> And I will call him to so strict account
> That he shall render every glory up,
> Yea, even the slightest worship of his time,
> Or I will tear the reckoning from his heart.
>   (3.2)

The bottom line here is a savage biological reckoning that is sublimated into monetary concepts that serve in turn as metaphors for honor, glory, greatness. Because of this, some rather daring symbolism devolves on Hal throughout the play. For the financial terms associated with his princely enterprise not only metaphorize his cannibalistic project of consuming Percy's treasury of honor but suggest also that he plays a Christ-like role as England's redeemer. What he redeems is both his own lack of credit as a candidate for kingship and, more broadly, England's debt of guilt brought on by his father's usurpation. In this role of redeemer, Hal substitutes for his father's long-postponed pilgrimage to Jerusalem.

Hal's delicate task is to meld the spritually high and the corporeally low in a fashion befitting an ideal king. That means he must consume Falstaff and Hotspur without becoming reductively either Falstaffian or Hotspur-rian. It is a matter of robbery. If Bolingbroke stole Richard's crown, Falstaff steals Bolingbroke's "crowns" at Gadshill, only to be "uncrowned" by Hal, who later does what Falstaff could never bring himself to do, return the money. This yielding of the crowns that do not yet belong to him is paralleled in Part 2 when Hal, suspected of stealing Henry's crown prematurely, returns it with an explanation so gracious that he is declared its true inheritor.

Then at Shrewsbury Hal stands triumphant over the presumably dead bodies of both Hotspur and Falstaff. By this time the danger is not that he will be tempted out of princely paths by Falstaff but by Hotspur. The speech cited earlier, about his making Percy his "factor" to collect honor for him, implies that he has adopted the Hotspur code of value, which he once ridiculed, and that in killing Hotspur he robs him in the way he robbed Falstaff at Gadshill. For Hotspur, like Falstaff, has also sought to rob the crown that Henry IV robbed from Richard. He would force the King to stand and deliver at Shrewsbury. But it is Hal who is master highwayman at Gadshill and master swordsman at Shrewsbury.

The danger to England at this point is that Hal seems to have become simply a more glorious Hotspur, with all the limitations that would entail for an ideal monarch. However, Shakespeare takes pains to point the difference. First, whereas Hotspur's greatest failure is his willingness to pay with the lives of his men for a chance to acquire greater personal glory, Hal challenges Hotspur before the battle in an effort not just to enhance his status but to avoid carnage: "In both your armies there is many a soul / Shall pay full dearly for this encounter" (5.2). Second, despite his speech to his father, he is not naively infatuated as Hotspur is with the cult of honor. When Hotspur comes upon him in the field and says "If I mistake not, thou art Harry Monmouth," Hal replies "Thou speak'st as if I would deny my name. . . . I am the Prince of Wales; and think not, Percy, / To share with me in glory any more" (5.4). Taken straight, this suggests that Hal is indeed a convert to Hotspur's cult. But considering the amount of "glory" the Prince has accumulated at the Boar's Head Tavern and Gadshill, his words become a jest at jousting—a Hotspur-nettling hyperbole accompanied, surely, by a raised-eyebrow glance at the audience. As such it makes him an unbeliever within the temple, or at least a man in whom Hotspur's devotion to honor is tempered with Falstaff's sense of pragmatic reality. (This tempering of the Prince forges a king who is difficult to assess, an amalgam of Hotspur and Falstaff and Henry IV that withstands every test and yet seems deeply flawed. But that matter is more appropriate to a later chapter called "Clothing Mortality.") Finally, Hal transcends both Hotspur's appetite for honor and Falstaff's greed for gain by yielding to Falstaff the credit for killing Hotspur: "If a lie will do thee grace / I'll gild it with the happiest terms I have" (5.4). Falstaff's self-serving lie will be gilded and transformed by Hal's self-effacing lie. Even a lie takes on value when touched up by the true Prince; and although it does not buy Falstaff an earldom and immortality, it does buy him a reputation that helps him stave off death a little longer.

4. Prospero, Macbeth, Hamlet

The squeamish reader will be glad to know that not all eating in Shakespeare is cannibalistic, not even symbolically so. Characters more frequently dine on cooked animal bodies than on raw human ones. In comedies generally, banqueting is a form of social communion. If you are what you eat, and you all eat the same, then you all are the same—a collective social body too large for death to attempt. Moreover, because food has in it the gift of life, it is itself sacred, most explicitly in the sacrament of the Eucharist where it represents the god himself. When Ariel sets a banquet before Prospero's enemies and then makes it disappear, he is denying "three men of sin" access to the island's version of the Communion table (3.3).[6] Their spiritual survival is still in jeopardy. In contrast, Prospero's masque is a pagan Communion table on which Ceres and the others spread before Ferdinand and Miranda a visionary feast:

> Earth's increase, foison plenty,
> Barns and garners never empty,
> Vines with clustering bunches growing,
> Plants with goodly burden bowing.
> (4.1)

Here, as in *The Tempest* generally, with its obsessive interest in the visual, it is not the sharing of food that weds the lovers but the sharing of images:

they partake of the gods (goddesses) through the eyes, and this union of each with the other and of both with the sacred is lent an element of immortality when in the midst of the performance Ferdinand, likening the island to Paradise, cries "Let me live here ever." But Paradise and immortality are snatched from him and Miranda, and from Prospero himself, as rudely as the banquet table was from the sinful Italians. When Prospero suddenly says "I had forgot that foul conspiracy / Of the beast Caliban and his confederates / Against my life," we return abruptly to a world in which every third thought can be of death.

If the comedies make banqueting a celebration of ongoing communal life, so do the tragedies, but with a difference. For the tragic hero is scheduled for death, and one indication of this is his inability to join in communal feasting. For instance Macbeth's famous "If it were done" speech takes on added significance from the fact that he delivers it while standing outside the banquet hall into which *"divers Servants with dishes and service"* have passed. On the inside are the Scots warriors, survivors of a bloody battle in which bodies were unseamed and heads hewn off, and in which Banquo and Macbeth were momentarily thought to "bathe in reeking wounds." Such a banquet not merely celebrates the recent victory but affirms a tribal compact: we who eat together do not kill and eat each other.[7] The soliloquizing Macbeth, rapt in regicidal fantasies, stands outside this compact as well as outside the banquet room. Ambition is his meat, and it can be shared only by his wife. Even at his own coronation banquet he cannot join the others at table, having been unseated and unmanned by the ghost of Banquo. Indeed it seems Macbeth drives feasting out of Scotland, as we might well expect from one who associates with witches whose cauldron cookery is hardly, to mix plays, caviar to the general. At any rate, immediately prior to the cauldron scene, two unhappy Scots express a hope that Macbeth may be overthrown so that "we may again / Give to our tables meat, sleep to our nights, / [and] free from our feasts and banquets bloody knives" (3.6). Just that, presumably, is the promise in Malcolm's final lines of the play about all survivors meeting again at Scone for his crowning—after which, of course, the coronation feast. But among a people so given to violence—after all, Macbeth's head is louring down from a pike while all this amity flows forth—we may take leave to doubt whether feasts and banquets in Scotland will ever be free of bloody knives.

In the tragedies generally, feasts and banquets are precisely where the fasting hero will not be found. Hamlet is especially fastidious about eating and drinking. He prefers to keep a ghostly watch on the castle platform, hearing from afar the noise of carousal below in what is now Claudius's hall—a bitter contrast to his fond memories of former days when Yorick's gambols and songs ignited "flashes of merriment that were wont to set the table on a roar." There are no jesters in Elsinore now—Hamlet himself has proved a poor substitute for Yorick—and no feasting princes either. Puritan that he is, Hamlet is repelled by feeding, which is too gross, too bestial, too much, as D. H. Lawrence would say, like other folks' whoring:

> What is a man,
> If the chief good and market of his time
> Be but to sleep and feed? A beast, no more.
>
> (4.4)

Because Hamlet is virtuous he thinks there should be no more cakes and ale. Not at least for himself. But that is because, like Kafka's hunger artist, Hamlet never found a food he liked. In an Elsinore where the "funeral baked meats / Did coldly furnish forth the marriage tables," to eat would constitute a ceremonial confirmation of his father's death and the new regime. Hence he feeds on "the chameleon's dish; I eat the air, promise-crammed" (3.2). Air is thin gruel for a prince to survive on; but then mere survival, as this prince says, is a form of "bestial oblivion" —that is to say, a beastly oblivious- ness to death for which he, death-obsessed as he is, can only feel contempt.

To gather things together in feasting terms: Hamlet's problem is that to eat and drink in Elsinore is not to absorb life but caponlike to invite death. Thus rather than feast, he fasts as a form of death denial—a typically nega- tive strategy in this most negative of plays. And no solution either. For although to feed in Denmark may be an invitation to death, to fast is inevit- ably a denial of life as well. Still, better to fast than simply to sleep and feed. So Hamlet fasts in a paradoxical attempt "to be and not to be" at once, a conundrum he spends so much time pondering that he cannot get round to killing the King.

What, finally, is Hamlet's remedy? It is not perfectly clear what it is, but we can say with some assurance where it is—in the graveyard. In the graveyard his revulsion for a world of sleepers and feeders subsides when he discovers that all must eat, that Lord Such-a-one and Yorick, the beautiful Ophelia, and even Danish princes must come in the end to a last supper. Like the Communion table whose food binds men spiritually to the god, the grave, where all gather at My Lady Worm's table, binds men in a commu- nity of death. Thus it is at the edge of a grave that Hamlet cries "This is I, / Hamlet, the Dane!" and affirms both his individuality and his communal- ity, and apparently achieves a sense of resigned "readiness" that lets re- venge be thrust upon him. To the end he refuses to drink, but when Ger- trude willfully does so, he is insistent that Claudius do so too, finding a "union" with her in death. Death, after all, is the true union and communion. "O proud Death," Fortinbras says, coming into the body-strewn hall, "What feast is toward in thy eternal cell?" A good share of the answer is, a feast to which the long-fasting Prince has had a standing offer that even he can no longer refuse.

III Disguise, Role-Playing, and Honor

1. Falstaff and Coriolanus

The animal instinct to fight or flee in the presence of danger suggests two general ways of denying death. Fighting is the mode of predators like Hotspur, Macbeth, and Coriolanus, who inflate themselves with symbolic immortality by consuming enemies, or at least by consuming their mana, their crown, the breath they lose as they fall. Nonpredatory animals find it wiser to flee, and wisest of all to flee in the middle of a pack or herd. We can say either that they hide within the pack or that they wear the pack as a disguise. Neither Henry IV nor Falstaff is a herd animal, but Henry tries to imitate one when he populates Shrewsbury Field with pseudo-kings and takes cover among them. Falstaff, on the other hand, makes good use of his feet at the battle of Gadshill; but at Shrewsbury, having no royal coats to dress his ragamuffins in and knowing that he is more likely to be peppered if he is with them than if he is not, he must improvise when pursued by that hot termagent Scot, Douglas. Assuming that Death would never look for him among the dead, he adopts the disguise of deathlikeness and succeeds well enough to fool not only Douglas but Prince Hal. Indeed he plays dead so well that he decides also to play Hotspur, or at least *his* version of Hotspur, in which heroism is manifested by stabbing dead men in the thigh. Yet even this scapegrace act is successful, by grace of the Prince's amused willingness to surrender the honor of dispatching Percy. Now, surely, Falstaff will live forever, or achieve the cultural equivalent by becoming earl or duke. At any rate he can be sure that Death will not be looking for him in the role of Hotspur-killer, or in that of "John Falstaff, knight," as he now calls himself.

In this scene Falstaff discovers that disguise and a prudent disregard for honor will not only keep you alive but can become the means to more abundant life, even to a certain social elevation. If that is so, then the reverse should also be true: to assert your identity, to be yourself, and to worship honor may jeopardize your life. In this section let us consider the death denying virtues of disguise and identity and, in the following section, the perils of honor.

Falstaff's use of disguise as a means of denying death is popular with a lot of Shakespearean characters. In *King Lear*, for instance, Edgar, learning that Gloucester has issued his death warrant, promptly assumes the disguise of Poor Tom, which he later discards for that of the beggar who serves as guide to the blind Gloucester, the "fiend" at the top of the supposed cliff, the gentleman at the bottom, the "most poor man" who aids Gloucester after his meeting with Lear, the thick-spoken peasant who cudgels Oswald to it, and the knight who defeats Edmund. How could Death, turning over shell after disguising shell, expect to find the true Edgar underneath?

Edgar's mythical tutors are Proteus, who shifted shapes to avoid having to tell the truth, and Dionysus, who had a bull, a ram, a stag, and a buckgoat in his repertoire of disguises. The need for such quick change artistry suggests that identity is a curse to be avoided at all costs. And to be sure, it is, because it marks you for what you are, a single and therefore vulnerable creature, like the one mysteriously special impala that catches the cheetah's eye. To be distinguished in this manner, to have an identity, a face, and especially a name, is to leave Death your address. That is why primitives give out false names to strangers and teenagers refuse to identify themselves if the object of their current passion is unable to come to the phone. Indeed merely to possess an upright head can be fatal. Man's evolutionary presumption in standing erect and raising his head above those of the beasts is dangerously augmented by the head-raisings of individual men striving for elevation on the social or political ladder. As a result a good many in Shakespeare's time—Essex, Christopher Blount, and Ralegh most notably—were obliged to leave life some seven or eight inches shorter at the top, a public reminder that if you do not incline your head in the presence of queens and kings you may have to do so in the presence of the executioner.

Little wonder, then, that the exiled Coriolanus makes his way to the house of his enemy Aufidius anonymously, with his body and presumably his head so "muffled" that Aufidius cannot recognize his old enemy and must ask for his name six times before he will answer (4.5). After all, the name "Coriolanus," which was once a medal of honor, a sign betokening the conquest of death by the man who entered the gates of Corioli alone and emerged alive, is hardly a guarantee of safe passage among the Volscians. Now, dishonored among Romans, his cultural immortality lost— "Only that name remains"—he is as mortal as Aufidius chooses.

This unmuffling which exposes Coriolanus to death is particularly significant because it reminds us that he has gone unmuffled most of his life. For despite his repeated conquests of death, he has always been more mortal than other men by virtue of his refusal to hide his nature. "Too noble for the world," as Menenius labels him, he has a temper that makes him "forget he ever / Heard the name of death" (3.1). Death, however, is less forgetful.

It has no difficulty remembering the name of the man whose insistence on his own unique nobility constitutes a defiant "Here I am!" to all comers, even to the gentleman in the gray dustcoat.

Surely that is why there are so few disguisings in tragedy by comparison to comedy. Tragic heroes either cannot or will not hide from death. In this respect Coriolanus is almost a reductio ad absurdum of the tragic hero's commitment to constancy. Othello swears "by yond marble heaven" to sweep as irreversibly as the Pontic Sea to his revenge (3.3), and Lear less eloquently says "By Jupiter, / This [banishment of Kent] shall not be revoked" and "I have sworn [to disinherit Cordelia], I am firm" (1.1). Whether the hero presents the same face always like Coriolanus or steers an unvarying course like Othello, Death knows where to find him. Yet, paradoxically, he has a hard time finding himself. Lacking the perspective on self that comes from adopting disguises or roles, the tragic hero, like Lear, "hath ever but slenderly known himself." For him, self-knowledge or anagnorisis is a hard-bought virtue, taking an entire play to acquire and costing nothing less than a life.

2. Feminine Disguise in Comedy

In the comedies, on the other hand, the flexible self-awareness of female characters like Julia, Portia, Rosalind, Viola, and Imogen is reflected in their ability to disguise themselves as men. The fact that these disguisings often seem inadequately motivated suggests not just the conventional indifference of comedy to causation and probability but perhaps deeper motives. At one level these disguisings enable the women not only to get their men but also, as if by proxy, to transform them for the better.[1] But the ultimate motive, I suggest, arises from the need to deny death: the women escape life-threatening situations by abandoning their vulnerable femininity and arming themselves with masculine powers.

In *The Merchant of Venice*, for instance, Portia begins as the epitome of the suppressed female, condemned by her father's will to yield her life and fortune to one of a variety of unappealing suitors. "I am," she says later, "locked in one of [the caskets]" like a corpse awaiting burial (3.2.), and hence it is not surprising that her first line in the play should be "By my troth, Nerissa, my little body is aweary of this great world" (1.2.). Even though she is released from the casket and resuscitated by Bassanio, her plight as a woman in a masculine society has been graphically emblematized as a quasi-death.

Of course it is trickier than that, for Portia's father, though dead, constitutes a patriarchal canopy under which a daughter is culturally compelled to take shelter. From that standpoint it is by adhering to his "will" that Portia is saved from the more predatory financial adventurers who gather around her. In such a world, where wealthy maids are gobbled up in marriage as greedily as Antonio would be gobbled up by Shylock, a woman's only recourse is to transform herself into a man. After all, that is clearly where the power resides. Thus Portia's transformation into the lawyer Balthazar endows her at the trial with the masculine power over life and death—a power she carries back into womanhood and Belmont where as the possessor of secret knowledge she can rescue Bassanio from dishonor and infidelity and can revivify Antonio with news of his ships: "Sweet lady, you have given me life and living."

A similar pattern occurs in *As You Like It* where Rosalind escapes the death-threatening masculinity of Duke Frederick's court (1.3.43–47) and enters a more benign but still masculine world of the forest by transforming herself into Ganymede. "In my heart," she says, "lie there what hidden woman's fear there will, / We'll have a swashing and a martial outside" (1.3). But swashing and martial outsides are unnecessary in the forest, as Orlando discovers when he pulls his sword to demand a hospitality that comes freely with the asking. Arden is by no means a scene of pastoral bliss; the wind blows, the cold nips, and the stomach growls, but here even adversity has sweet uses. The old and near-dying Adam is restored with kindness, and disappears from the play. But if his part and that of Hymen are doubled by one player, then old age is reborn as love. Death, though always a resident of Arcadia ("*Et in Arcadia ego*"), is far more naturally or conventionally a city-dweller.[2] In the forest Death is transformed into love, which is not of the killing variety: "Men have died from time to time and worms have eaten them, but not for love" (4.1).

Rosalind's ability to shift identities to meet occasions, based as it is on her recognition of the mutability of things, enables her not merely to survive in the forest world but also to be worshipped by the doting Orlando. She acquires powers perhaps even more remarkable than Portia's. As a boy actor playing a woman playing a man playing a woman, she marries both sexes within a single identity, and hence becomes qualified to serve as all things to all people, but especially to assume the role of marriage broker:

[*To Sylvius*] I will help you if I can. [*To Phebe*] I would love you if I could. Tomorrow meet me all together. [*To Phebe*] I will marry you if ever I marry a woman, and I'll be married tomorrow. [*To Orlando*] I will satisfy you if ever I satisfied man, and you shall be married tomorrow. [*To Silvius*] I will content you if what pleases you contents you, and you shall be married tomorrow. (5.2)

Rosalind's ability to marry everyone, to form sexual unions, is the ability to deny death by giving life.

The tendency in the festive comedies for heroines to die as women by assuming a disguised manhood and then to return with life-enhancing powers is the very stuff of which the romances are made. Imogen is a transition character in this respect because in her the symbolic death-by-male-disguise of Julia, Portia, Rosalind, and Viola is combined with her apparent death as the boy Fidele and her subsequent resurrection in the last scene as Imogen. In the later romances female characters will similarly die, not into masculinity but as a result of masculine repressiveness, and be reborn later. In the tragedies the heroines actually do die—Lavinia in *Titus Andronicus*, Juliet, Portia in *Julius Caesar*, Ophelia, Desdemona, Cordelia, and Cleopatra—confirming the notion that women suffer death while men impose it. Granted, men do in one another at a great rate also. But how, I wonder, should we interpret the fact that in none of the plays does a woman kill a man, not even Goneril, Regan, or Lady Macbeth? Does it stem from a genuine belief in a supposed gentler nature, a feminine inability to do violent evil; and if so, is this a pseudochivalrous myth actually fostered by a masculine fear of and therefore suppression of feminine violence? Or is it simply owing to the fact that women did then, as they do now, fewer deeds of violence than men? In any event the task of the comic heroine is to die and come to life again in such a way as to oblige the men to graduate from death-dealing to life-giving, from killing to begetting.

In this connection we might pause to speculate about Shakespeare's frequent use of women in male roles. The question that arises is whether he is reflecting the male chauvinism of his times or transcending it. Is a woman's assumption of a male disguise construed as a mark of weakness or of strength? More broadly we might regard this as a version of the cultural practice in Elizabethan society, and of course up to very recent times, according to which a wife takes her husband's name at marriage. How to view it? Does the husband give or the wife take the family name?

Considered in the abstract, as a practice endorsed in Shakespeare's time by a patriarchal culture, the giving of a man's name to his wife was surely an act of masculine conquest disguised as protective generosity toward the weaker vessel. But could it not also point up a subtle form of feminine conquest—not an aggressive seizure but a mature acceptance of the male name? That is, feminine submissiveness in such cases might derive from feminine self-assurance, since women are able to subsume themselves nominally without fear of losing their personal identity—something men can never do. This is probably owing to the fact that women define themselves in terms of gender simply by *being* themselves, while men define themselves by proving they are not women.[3] For instance women can accept masculine common nouns (e.g., *guy*) and pronouns (e.g., the much-maligned *he, him, his*) or feminized names of men, like Johanna, Caroline, or Michelle, without feeling psychologically threatened by masculinity, whereas the male ego, or lack of ego, cannot reverse the procedure without a loss of face. The male ego is simply more fragile and vulnerable, based as it is on a culturally endorsed repudiation of the female. Thus transvestism today means a male dressing in female clothing, not the reverse, because the adoption of male dress by women has come to seem perfectly natural; and to other males such transvestism is repellent in a way that suggests a deep fear of loss of identity. It can only be endured when dealt with humorously by Three Stooges or Jerry Lewis types.

Needless to say, the only males in feminine clothing in Shakespeare's plays, if we exclude priests, are the boy actors, although Cleopatra reports that she once adorned a drunken Antony with her "tires and mantles" while she paraded about with his sword.[4] However, even dressing boy actors in women's clothing aroused the ire of Puritans like Stephen Gosson and William Prynne, who attacked this theatrical practice as a violation of the Deuteronomic ban: "The woman shall not wear that which pertaineth unto a man, neither shall a man put on a woman's garment: for all that do so are abomination unto the Lord thy God" (22:5).

As Jonas Barish points out, the real fear of fulminating Puritans was the blurring of sexual boundaries, the typical male phobia about effeminancy.[5] For Shakespeare even to associate with the theater, then, implied at least his willingness to flout the more publicly repressive forms of sexual differentiation in his day.

Whatever the psychological implications of all this, Shakespeare's disguised heroines do reveal a maturity of social understanding and a flexibility of behavior that makes them the controlling influence in their plays. By comparison their male lovers often seem naive, fatuous, and uninterestingly one-dimensional.

Before leaving this subject I should mention two of Shakespeare's female characters who do not explicitly adopt masculine disguises but nevertheless take on male characteristics to deal with death—Lady Macbeth and Volumnia. In *Macbeth* feminine vulnerability of the sort we have seen in the comedies is assigned to Lady Macduff, whose life is forfeited to Macbeth's death-bent agents when her husband abandons her for the safety of England. Her opposite, Lady Macbeth, in order to arm herself for regicide calls on spirits to "unsex me here" and on murdering ministers to "Come to my woman's breasts / And take my milk for gall" (1.5). This is the most graphic instance of the annihilation of femininity through a masculinizing of the heroine, though in this case the motive is not to escape death but to assume its lethal powers. It represents an inversion of the comic heroine's adoption of "a swashing and a martial outside," as Rosalind says, to conceal a "hidden woman's fear." With Lady Macbeth the woman is all on the outside, a veneer of femininity, while the murderous male lurks within; and the toll taken by this willed perversion of nature is registered much later when the lady sleepwalks her way to suicide.

Lady Macbeth's example suggests that we do better to regard Volumnia as an instance not of devouring motherhood but of masculinized woman-hood. The devouring aspect of the mythological Great Mother lies in her smothering possessiveness, her refusal to release the male child from her enveloping femininity to find his place in the masculine world. Volumnia, however, is not an enveloper in this sense; she is a masculinized female, a father substitute who drives the son away from the hearth:

> When yet he was but tender-bodied and the only son of my womb, when youth with comeliness plucked all gaze his way, when for a day of kings' entreaties a mother should not sell him an hour from her beholding, I, considering how honor would become such a person, . . . was pleased to let him seek danger where he was like to find fame. To a cruel war I sent him. . . . (1.3)

Like Lady Macbeth with her husband, Volumnia makes a project of creating a man who will serve as the instrument of her own death-dealing desires. Coriolanus is a sword she has been forging since his birth. Forswearing the vulnerable role of woman—the gentle and fearful Virgilia takes that part in the play—Volumnia says with Lady Macbeth "unsex me here" and then casts Coriolanus in the image of her masculinized self. In a fail-safe version of death denial, she lives her life in him, vicariously sharing in his triumphs and survivals—"Methinks I see him stamp thus, and call thus . . ." (1.3)—and yet keeps a life insurance policy in his name that will pay off in honor and "good report" should he die:

> VIRGILIA.   But had he died in the business, madam, how then?
>
> VOLUMNIA.   Then his good report should have been my son; I therein would have found issue.   (1.3)

By investing in Coriolanus's martial prowess and honor Volumnia acquires immortality by proxy. If he triumphs over death, as he does at Corioli, she triumphs with him; if he dies, she survives as mother to his "good report." The only proviso is that he must die honorably; otherwise she dies with him—which helps explain her interminable speech dissuading him from attacking Rome and thereby becoming infamous (5.3). Preserving his honor, the source of her own immortality, is more important to Volumnia than preserving his life, as he somewhat ruefully implies upon capitulating:

> But for your son—believe it, O believe it—
> Most dangerously you have with him prevailed,
> If not most mortal to him.

3. Honor and Honesty

Volumnia's claim that Coriolanus's "good report" would serve as her son should he die is as obvious an example as we shall find of the translation of the corporeal into the spiritual in order to deny death. Hero after hero in the plays clothes his life in the vestments of honor, and if these are stripped away he is exposed as the shivering forked creature he corporeally is. Thus Cassio, disgraced by drunkenness, laments the loss of his "immortal part," reputation, and declares that he is hurt "past surgery" (2.3). Antony on the other hand believes that only surgery can repair him. Thinking Cleopatra dead, he mourns not only for her but for his lost honor— "I have lived with such dishonor that the gods / Detest my baseness"—and asks Eros to kill him, "for with a wound I must be cured" (4.14).[6] However, the immortalizing powers of honor are almost always expressed against a background of skepticism. For every Cassio whose wounded reputation is beyond surgery there is an Iago to reply—

> As I am an honest man, I thought you had received some bodily wound; there is more sense in that than in reputation. Reputation is an idle and most false imposition oft got without merit and lost without deserving. (2.3)

Similarly Falstaff, Thersites, and Enobarbus constitute a gravitational field of skepticism that makes the flight toward glory hard going for Hotspur, Hector, and Antony.

The deflation of honor is most pronounced perhaps in *Troilus and Cressida*, where all swollen values lose air at a great rate. Hector suffers the most, not merely because he proves a veritable Tertullian of absurd faith in the council scene, where his morality and honor part company, but also because he dies ignominiously. Enamored of a suit of "goodly armor," he challenges its owner to combat. When the Greek flees, Hector pursues: "Wilt thou not, beast, abide? / Why, then fly on, I'll hunt thee for thy hide" (5.7). This symbolic bestializing of honor is paralleled by the bestializing of love in the following brief scene when, while Menelaus and Paris fight, Thersites cries "The cuckold and the cuckold-maker are at it. Now, bull! now, dog!" Then Hector is discovered with his new-won armor, from which he has dumped the body of its owner, saying "Most putrefied core, so fair without, / Thy goodly armor thus hast cost thy life" (5.8). But it has cost the covetous Hector his life too, because Achilles and his Myrmidons arrive shortly thereafter and dishonorably attack and kill the unarmed Trojan hero. From being man's immortal part, a means of transcending his corporeality, honor becomes merely a glittering surface over a putrefied core, the self-aggrandizing pursuit of which leads not toward immortality but death. And yet, in this degrading play, what remedy is there? Shakespeare leaves us in the Antigone situation, faced with a damned-if-we-do-damned-if-we-don't choice between Hector and Achilles: a fatuous excess of honor versus a cynical lack of it.

This image of honor as the resplendent clothing of narcissistic impulses was everywhere to be seen in Shakespeare's time. Indeed it was especially relevant to Shakespeare's own generation of aspiring courtiers, as Anthony Esler has shown:

> But at the root of the cult of honor, as of the lust for power, lay, in the last analysis, the hugely inflated ego of the young courtier himself. The code of personal honor, the savage competition for place and power, the extravagant dress and hundreds of liveried retainers, even the majestic strut which Elizabethan courtiers and captains affected—these were the external manifestations of tremendous egotism.

And as Esler says elsewhere, a sense of "baroque religiosity" coupled with this egotism caused "the younger generation [to array] themselves in worldly magnificence to convince themselves that they were indeed men set apart, very gods of this earth."[7]

To be one of the gods of this earth, however, is a hazardous ambition; the means of your deification can be identical with the means of your demise. The sacred is always paradoxically akin to death. Whatever your secular religion—country, king, family, honor, love, children, money—by participating in it you deny death and acquire immortality while living. But at the same time, precisely because it *is* sacred, you will not only kill but die for it. Honor, as Falstaff says, pricks one on; but, unfortunately, it pricks one off too. Cries of *"Pro patria et rege!"* echo through every graveyard. Wars, assassinations, highjackings, mass suicides, political fasts, immolations, all are holy ventures in which the faithful set sail for eternity in the body's leaky boat—and end up, Shakespeare often suggests, where Sir Patrick Spens and the Scots lords keep court.

The polestar of these ventures in Shakespeare is usually honor, whether you are man or maid. For the honor of a woman is "honesty," which is to say chastity—the virginity of a maid, the fidelity of a wife. This kind of honesty is sacred in a patrilinear society because it guarantees the authenticity of inheritance and the continuity of family name—the most practical forms of socioeconomic immortality. It all depends on begetting.

But of course it depends on what the begetting begets, a boy or a girl. In a patriarchal, patrilinear society a girl represents an interruption of the male line and perhaps even the death of the family name. In that case a girl destroys her father's immortality as effectively as the death of young Hamnet destroyed Shakespeare's immortality.

The cause of these barren births is of course the mother, as Henry VIII quickly concluded when Catherine of Aragon and Anne Boleyn criminally failed to produce a surviving male heir. Women simply cannot be counted on at birth—nor, for that matter, at conception either. Paternity is notoriously a source of male insecurity. From a genetic standpoint a woman has no difficulty proving her maternity, inasmuch as she is painfully present at the birth; but since the father is not present, in quite the same sense, he may have cause to wonder where his nightcap was when the child was conceived. For proof of his fatherhood the male is obliged to rely on his wife's honesty in the modern as well as the old-fashioned sense of the word. Falstaff gives point to the problem when he plays the role of Hal's father in the Boar's Head Revels:

> That thou art my son, I have partly thy mother's word, partly my own opinion, but chiefly a villainous trick of thine eye and a foolish hanging of thy nether lip, that doth warrant me. (*1HIV* 2.4)

In the absence of villainous eyes and hanging lips, however, one must rely on feminine honesty. Little wonder it is a sacred virtue and an honest woman a secular saint. But let her lose her honesty and the saint becomes a witch. Even "mere suspicion" of witchery, as Desdemona's case illustrates, is reason enough to be put to death.

In comedy purgative death is figurative, in tragedy quite literal, and never more literal than in *Titus Andronicus* where the deflowered Lavinia suffers not only the loss of hands and tongue but, worse yet, her virginity. Titus, as a good Roman father, endures Lavinia's mutilations bravely enough, but her dishonor is more than he can bear; so in the final scene he mercifully puts himself out of his misery by stabbing her to death.

Titus Andronicus, inasmuch as it reflects a long history of masculine rapacity and seduction, makes it clear that the bottom line of male domination is simply animal strength.[8] As though having established that fact early on, Shakespeare then uses the play as a corporeal model for later plays in which actual rape is supplanted by symbolic rape or accusations of infidelity. Cassio need not actually bed Desdemona to ensure her death, not with Iago around. Once Othello has acquired ocular proof of her infidelity, she is doomed.

Symbolic rape, however, is far more frequent in the comedies, where it is an immediate prelude to symbolic death. Hero in *Much Ado About Nothing* is a classic case. When Claudio rudely challenges her sacred honesty—where else but in church?—she faints and then subsequently suffers death by rumor. Later she is symbolically raped by the villainous Don John, who arranges for her pseudoseduction; but the real cause of her supposed death is Claudio's accusation, which destroys her virgin honesty and good name. Shakespeare's maids are as deeply immersed in a shame culture as his chivalric heroes are; they live by their public reputation and die by it.[9] Not until Hero's honesty is publicly confirmed can her life be restored.

A similar fate awaits Imogen in *Cymbeline*. Her "rape" by Iachimo results in a decree of death by Posthumus, the enactment of which takes displaced form when she swallows the sleeping potion and "dies" beside the dead body of Cloten, who had—just to make the point clear—intended to ravish her. In the final scene she is brought to life as the boy Fidele, but she remains dead as the maid Imogen until Iachimo, unaccountably grown honest himself, proclaims her honesty. In *The Winter's Tale* Hermione undergoes a similar experience, but in *Pericles* Marina inverts the sequence. Instead of an accusation of dishonesty producing a symbolic death, a literal attempt upon her life lands her in that graveyard of virginity, a brothel. For all the outside world knows, she is dead or wanton. Yet so sacred is her honor that when she carries it like a cross through the house of sin its glister sends whore after whore to her repentant knees. Not much time passes, as one would expect, before she and her "peevish chastity," as the brothel-keepers call it, are shipped to an honest household where the appearance and the fact of her virginity can live respectably as one.

If mere accusations of lightness can cause female characters to die of shame (unless of course they have names like Doll Tearsheet or Mistress

Overdone, in which case a bad reputation will make their fortune), they can just as easily succumb to a kind of terminal virginity. Death and virginity are associated as early as *A Midsummer Night's Dream* when Egeus demands the law upon his daughter Hermia if she fails to follow his marital advice. Since the law requires that such a wayward daughter be put to death, either literally or by being made to "live a barren sister all [her] life, / Chanting faint hymns to the cold fruitless moon," it seems a maid must be bedded one way or another. If she does not yield her virginity to a man, then she must to Death. Hence the competition between Death and Romeo to see who will lie with Juliet.

In the problem comedies the denial of death depends not just on a Rosalind-like ability to form marriages but on sexual unions themselves. Normally of course the sexual act is regarded as a source of life. However, it may also be a source of death. The two are abundantly confused in *Measure for Measure*.[10] In puritan Vienna the primrose path of dalliance leads to the gallows—or so it seems for Claudio anyhow, although if his sister were to trip the same path with Angelo it would restore his life. Thus Claudio is somewhat puzzlingly scheduled for death because he has engaged in the sexual act and because Isabella has not. Mariana, on the other hand, like Hero and Imogen and Hermione, perishes because she is thought to have been "light"—"her reputation was disvalued / In levity" (5.1)—and yet recovers her life by means of the "bed trick." Or partly recovers her life, since when she appears in the denouement she is physically alive but socially dead. "What, are you married?" the Duke asks, and she replies that she is not married, not a maid, and not a widow, whereupon he says "Why, you are nothing then." Only the revelation that she has lain with Angelo, hence fulfilling her femininity, can fully restore her (and him) to life and love.

All's Well That Ends Well pursues the same theme, only, like its heroine, more doggedly. Like Mariana, Helena is a wife abandoned and hence not really a wife at all. This *matrimonium interruptus* causes Helena to betake herself as a pilgrim to Saint Jacques le Grand, a get-thee-to-a-nunnery form of sexual death that seems literalized when it is reported that penitential pining has removed her forever from the embraces of the unloveable Bertram. Meanwhile, after the bed trick, Bertram congratulates himself on his efficiency, having in one night, among other things "buried a wife, mourned for her," and bedded "Diana" (4.3). But of course it is this bedding that enables Helena to rise from her grave and in the final scene restore not only her own life but—as a test of the audience's credulity—Bertram's honor as well.

All's Well establishes the source of the redemptive power of the sexual act more explicitly than *Measure for Measure*. For it is not just sexual activity as such that saves Helena and Bertram but that most familiar of immortality projects, the child intended and begotten by it. As Diana says,

> Dead though [Helena] be, she feels her young one kick.
> So there's my riddle: one that's dead is quick:
> And now behold the meaning.   (*All's Well* 5.3)

Thus disguise, role-playing, and the maintenance of an honorable reputation can all be thought of as variations on the theme of hiding from death. The fundamental danger is to possess an identity, because Death, like cheetahs and highway patrolmen, likes to single out individuals and run them down. To escape, you must play dead like Falstaff, play male like the comic heroines, or play Isabella or Diana if you are Mariana or Helena. Such tactics will hardly qualify you for immortality, but they may at least confuse Death and keep you breathing awhile longer.

IV   Death, Sex, and
the Body

In the previous chapter I suggested that feminine honesty is a sacred virtue in Shakespeare's plays in part because it guarantees a man's paternity and hence his immortality. Of course honesty becomes a woman's immortality project also. Her life depends on it as much as his. In Hero, Helena, Imogen, and Hermione we see a dramatization of this fact: the loss of honesty is tantamount to death. The appearance of dishonesty transports these heroines into a liminal state analogous to that of a dead but as yet unburied body.[1] The sexual act therefore can be either a wanton pleasure conducing to death or a procreative virtue conducing to life. In this section I want to point up the death-threatening aspect not merely of wantonness but of all sexuality and suggest how this affects the status of women. To get round to this, however, let me return briefly to the theme of the spiritual and corporeal as it bears on man's relations to animals.

1. Animals and Death

Because the great enemy of immortality is the human body, the suit of flesh that gradually metamorphoses into sackcloth, any denial of death entails a denial of the body and what the body represents, our kinship with animals. In his essay "Of Atheism," Bacon says, "They that do deny a God destroy man's nobility; for certainly man is of kin to the beasts by his body; and, if he be not of kin to God by his spirit, he is a base and ignoble creature." The beast in us must be kept down if evil and death are to be denied. Elizabethan theology went out of its way to reinforce this denial. With God's gift of reason teetering on the highest rung of the ladder of man's tripartite soul, and his animal and vegetable souls relegated to the nether regions, evil can only seep up from below. Not from the vegetable soul surely; the potential for evil of cabbages and ferns seems limited. If evil creeps into man's soul it must come on all fours, or at least slithering as it did into the Edenic soul.

Earlier of course, in Homer, evil could descend on man through the agency of jealous and vindictive gods. But once the gods are defined as good, as in Plato or Christianity, then animals must accept all the blame. For when Reason sleeps, as Plato says,

> the Wild Beast in us, full-fed with meat and drink, becomes rampant and shakes off sleep to go in quest of what will gratify its own instincts. As you know, it will cast off all shame and prudence at such moments and stick at nothing. In phantasy it will not shrink from intercourse with a mother or anyone else, man, god, or brute, or from forbidden food or any deed of blood. It will go to any lengths of shamelessness and folly.[2]

Given Plato's influence on Christianity it comes as no surprise that similar views existed in Shakespeare's time and that again and again he attributes the most characteristically human forms of evil to animals. Though animals are not noted for the "particular fault" of drunkenness, the fact that Danish man *is*, Hamlet complains, causes the national reputation to be soiled by "swinish" allusions from their straighter-laced neighbors. Of which the Italian Cassio is not one, having indeed a fair share of Danish swinishness in his veins, so that when he loses his "immortal part" along with his job, all that remains, he sighs, is his "bestial" and still tipsy body. By a similar token, when Lavinia's uncle, Marcus, comes upon his recently deflowered and still uncoagulated niece he longs to rail upon "the beast" that did it (2.4), although the recorded instances of male animals raping females and lopping off their hands and tongue are relatively few. Macbeth says he dare do all that may become a man but "who dares do more is none" (1.7)—is a beast, that is, and probably a regicidal wolf, because later on when Macbeth marches toward Duncan's chamber, he imagines himself accompanied by "withered Murder" aroused by its sentinel, the wolf (2.1). For Shakespeare wolves are particularly evil. They are not merely the shepherd's bane but the embodiment of a metaphysical ravenousness, so that Ulysses can speak of the ultimate disintegration of civilized life in terms of power converting to will, and will to appetite, and appetite, a "universal wolf," making a "universal prey" and at last eating up itself (1.3). Ulysses' reasoning is a bit wolfish itself, eating up the truth at a ferocious rate. After all, the hierarchical order he extols as the essence of civilized life has produced seven years of intermittent slaughter at Troy. Degree having gobbled up everything in sight, one wonders what remains for the wolfish appetite to feed on.

We need not catalog the dramatic occasions on which wolves, tigers, bears, bulls, dogs, foxes, cats, rats, and the odd dragon are assigned a viciousness, guile, devilishness, or fawning hypocrisy that is in reality peculiar to man. The point is simply that Shakespearean man, like man in general, endows himself with a unique and superior nature by distinguising himself from animals. Whether man's special gift is held to be his reason, his language, his religiousness, his tool-making, his upright stance, his laughter, or, as Aristotle held, his inability to wiggle his ears, it is a gift that animals lack. Yet it is a wonderful lack, because without these incomplete lower creatures to serve as a basis for negative definition, man could not exist through history in the same conceptual form. Man is human because he is more than and different from animals. If God is defined as what man is not—omniscient, omnipotent, omnipresent—then man is defined as what animals are not—sentient, soulful, and stationary of ear. Merely a glance at the terms *beast* and *beastly* in the Shakespeare concordance reveals that pity, reverence, eloquence, love, reason, truthfulness, and temperateness are peculiarly human attributes because their opposites exist in animals—in beasts "that want discourse of reason," that are "devoid of pity," that are "unruly," furious, irreverent, and so forth.[3]

From the standpoint of death denial the most significant feature of animals is simply that their lives are limited, and when they die there is nothing spiritual left over. That is no cause for sorrow, however, since "the life of a beast," a seventeenth-century preacher opined, "[is quite] long enough for a beast-like life." Beasts were born to die; it is what they deserve for being bestial. Moreover, if they were born to die, then it behooves us to help them fulfill their destiny by killing and eating them. After all, to do so is sanctioned by the highest authority when Jehovah gives man dominion over beasts (Gen. 9:2–3):

> The fear of you and the dread of you shall be upon every beast of the earth, and upon every fowl of the air, upon all that moveth upon the earth, and upon all the fishes of the sea; into your hand are they delivered. Every moving thing that liveth shall be meat for you.

At the same time, however, eating animals blurs the border between us and them. If we are what we eat, we may find ourselves disconcertedly wondering how many animal carcasses compose our bodies, how many pigs, chickens, cows, and so on would come tumbling out of our mouths if in our later years we were shaken by the heels. Moreover, eating what we kill, we dine on death and have it inside our own body where it dines on us: we are consumed by what we eat. Shakespeare's repeated condemnation of appetite as wolfish points unwittingly, metaphorically, to the literal merger of man and animal that occurs when the human appetite is satisfied carnivorously—or of course when the animal appetite is satisfied anthropophagously.

As the case of eating suggests, anything that blurs the borders between man and beast fills us with anxiety. In medieval times mothers frightened their children into staying close to home by invoking images of the Wild Man, that mythical beast-man that romped and raged in the woods outside villages, just waiting for little boys and girls and nubile maidens.[4] Along the borders of Elizabethan maps, beyond the edge of the known world, were all kinds of monstrous creatures; and within the known world, or at least within the heard-of world, existed Anthropophagi and men whose heads do grow between their shoulders, as though the monstrous animals on the borders of the maps were marching toward England and becoming more human all the time, or as though the further you got from England the more monstrous you were liable to become.[5]

2. Masculine Identity

In the sixteenth and seventeenth centuries uncleanliness, naked-ness, long hair, working at night (when beasts are seeking their prey), even swimming (appropriate only to fish) threatened the dividing line between man and animals the way a monstrous birth did. But more frightening and repulsive than anything else was the crime of "bestiality." As Keith Thomas says,

> Bestiality, accordingly, was the worst of sexual crimes because, as one Stuart moralist put it, "it turns man into a very beast, makes a man a member of a brute creature." The sin was the sin of confusion; it was immoral to mix the categories. Injunctions against "buggery with beasts" were standard in seventeenth-century moral literature, though occasion-ally the topic was passed over, "the fact being more filthy than to be spoken of." Bestiality became a capital offence in 1534 and, with one brief interval, remained so until 1861. Incest, by contrast, was not a secular crime at all until the twentieth century.[6]

Bestiality in this sense constitutes a kind of unmentionable missing link between the revolting sexuality of animals and that of humans. Even when dignified by marriage or purified by procreative intent, the human sexual act is never quite untinged with the shame of its animalistic associations. As Kant said in his *Lectures on Ethics*, "Sexuality exposes man to the danger of equality with the beasts."[7] And Sir Thomas Browne expatiates on the degrading aspects of the sexual act:

> I could be content that we might procreate like trees, without conjunc-tion, or that there were any way to perpetuate the World without this

> trivial and vulgar way of union: it is the foolishest act a wise man commits
> in all his life; nor is there any thing that will more deject his cooled
> imagination, when he shall consider what an odd and unworthy piece
> of folly he hath committed.[8]

This from a man who contributed ten children to the perpetuation of the
World—presumably by pollination.

This helps explain why Shakespeare associates sexuality not only with
immortality but also with death. For if sex threatens to equate man with
beasts, it is because erotic impulses arise not from immortal souls but from
mortal bodies, from creatures made in the image of apes, not God. To
"[make] the beast with two backs," as Iago repellently describes it, is to
metamorphose from human into monster and hence to make love to death.[9]
Only a professional degrader like Iago or a morbidly disillusioned prince
like Hamlet will want to keep such images before him. For ordinary men
animalistic sex and its mortal corollary must be vigorously repressed. Just
how vigorously is suggested by Claudio in *Much Ado*. The very viciousness
of his attack on Hero—

> But you are more intemperate in your blood
> Than Venus, or those pampered animals
> That rage in savage sensuality   (4.1)

—and his indifference to her supposed death imply that at some level of
consciousness he regards her "savage sensuality" as a threat to his ideological life-support system: to the sacredness of feminine honesty and masculine honor, both of which affirm man's spiritual ascendancy over beasts.
Claudio reacts to Hero's supposed lechery as though he had removed her
slipper and found a cloven hoof inside.[10]

Lear takes the same line: "Down from the waist they are Centaurs, /
Though women all above" (4.6). The phrase catches the ambivalence of the
Elizabethan male toward women. In her equine aspect woman is bestial
and inhuman and therefore mortal—perhaps even so wholly mortal as to
lack a soul. This surprising notion had a good deal of currency in Shakespeare's time. Among his "Paradoxes and Problems" Donne wrote a short
essay entitled "Why Hath the Common Opinion Afforded Women Soules?"
the tone of which is an uneasy combination of humorous irony, misogynous
malice, and genuine puzzlement. The fact is that the "common opinion"
sometimes did not afford women souls. As Thomas summarizes:

> At Witley in Surrey in 1570, one Nicholas Woodies allegedly asserted that
> women had no souls; at Earls Colne, Essex, in 1588 the minister himself

said the same; and in the diocese of Peterborough in 1614 a local wit was reported for "avowing and obstinately defending that women have no souls, but their shoe soles."[11]

Lear does not literally charge that women are devoid of souls, not even Goneril and Regan, except "down from the waist." Because of the centaurian nature of women, what occurs down from the waist must be bestial—not only the act of sex but that of childbirth as well. It is peculiarly galling that men cannot make an entrance onto this great stage of fools except through a woman's body. Why should this be so harrowing a matter, especially since women make a similar exit/entrance, and it seems not to bother them? But of course the reason a woman can accept this with equanimity is simply because her identity is entirely consistent with having been carried and birthed by a woman, whereas that of a male is not. A woman's sexual identity is given, but a man's must be proven; and a timeless way of proving it is by cultivating antifeminine attitudes and behavior. As Walter Ong says of boys,

> They must cut girls out of their lives, scorn feminine sources of comfort and safety, do things that they hope their mothers and sisters cannot do. They have to fight "it"—"it" being anything that seems easy. They must discover or invent risks. Accusations of "effeminacy" normally strike the male heart with terror: you have not had the strength to become yourself.[12]

From this point of view males become masculine by protesting too much that they are not feminine. Baptism may have been the first effort of patriarchal societies to deny the potential femininity of males. Baptizing babies shortly after birth, that is, implies among other things that the passage through a feminine body is contaminating. The woman must be washed away to guarantee masculine purity.

Let me pause at this point for a Shakespearean illustration of these notions.

3. Adonis and Bertram

Venus and Adonis and *All's Well That Ends Well* both feature heroes who try to find their masculine identity by exorcising the female in themselves. Adonis flees the embracements of Venus to hunt the boar of Death, and Bertram flees the amorous Helena for the suggestively boarlike Tuscan wars. Adonis dies symbolically not so much from the boar's tusks as from a lack of self-knowledge: "Before I know myself," he tells Venus, "seek not to know me" (525). To know himself would mean, I assume, conquering the boar—that is, transcending death by integrating it into the personality. It is the age-old masculine strategy of defining oneself by contesting with death: the boar is to Adonis as a lion is to a Dinka warrior. In Adonis's case the bellicose project is given sexual overtones. He runs on the boar "with his sharp spear," only to find himself amorously conquered: "And nuzzling in his flank, the loving swine / Sheathed unaware the tusk in his soft groin" (1115–16). This surprising turn—Adonis assuming a feminine role as he dies—suggests a metonymic equation of death and masculinity. If you become a man by inflicting death, then Death is male, as of course the Grim Reaper and his confederate, Father Time were portrayed as being. Symbolically at any rate men meet Death on the battlefield, not in the boudoir; and if they kill, then they acquire Death's power and are the more masculine for it. But if they are killed, then their killer is endowed with Death's masculine mana, and they are rendered feminine or incompletely male. Achieving a fully masculine identity was a special problem for Adonis because he was raised in a nonmasculine world by nymphs; but even the indisputably masculine Hotspur, once dead, is gored in the thigh like Adonis by the porcine Falstaff.

Bertram, though he turns his sharp sword Adonis-like against the Tuscans, does not die. He suffers a worse fate, the bed trick. He has already had the feminine imposed upon him by the King, who, when Bertram protests, says "Thou knowest she has raised me from my sickly bed." Bertram answers "But follows it, my lord, to bring me down / Must answer for your raising? I know her well." Bertram's bawdy puns here equate the highs and lows of social class—about which he the aristocrat is so sensitive—with the phallic ups and downs of the sexual act. His failure to know Helena's virtues forecasts his refusal to know her sexually, and both derive from his failure first of all to know himself.

To know himself—to acquire a fully masculine identity—Bertram goes to war where he not only keeps his flank unnuzzled by the Tuscans but even captures the enemy's "greatest commander" and slays the Duke's brother (3.5). However, when he seeks to extend his conquests to the fair Diana, he is himself conquered by his wife, who "gets the ring upon [his] finger that never will come off" (3.2). The bed trick represents his sexual mortification. In the darkness, naked, Helena loses the social and personal insignia he prizes and becomes merely a female body, an object of lust. His ring of family honor disgracefully given away, his wife bedded but unknown, Bertram from this point on becomes even more despicable than before. His newly won manhood is not sufficient. He can be redeemed only by acquiring a self-knowledge that entails an acceptance of the feminine. To know himself, he must come to know that he has known Helena. The proof is in Helena's possession—the ring and the child—but whether Bertram can be made to know much of anything is dubious. Yet it seems clear that in Bertram, Shakespeare is giving us an example of the need for the male to be liberated from his bondage to pure masculinity by incorporating an element of the feminine.

4. Sex and Death

From the standpoint of death denial, a man's fear of femininity is grounded not merely in anxieties about his identity but also in his association of femininity and death. The male invests his immortality in his maleness and must drive the woman from himself, just as humans in general invest their immortality in their humanity and must exorcise the beast within. That is one reason why Elizabethan women are often thought of as bestial. If man is defined most fundamentally by his difference from beasts, then whatever else he wants not-to-be can be rendered "naturally" alien to him by supposing it to be bestial. In Shakespeare's time this meant not only women but the Irish, the Indians, the Africans, the Jews, the poor, the mad, and even the child, all of whom were, like animals, incompletely human.[13]

Another reason why woman is repellent to man is that, apart from her animality, her presence is a constant reminder of his mortality. Without Eve, Adam would have been self-sufficient and hence immortal. With her he is a creature that is born and therefore dies. Tertullian railed on the subject: "Do you not know that you are Eve? . . . You are the devil's gateway. . . . How easily you destroyed man, the image of God. Because of the death which you brought upon us, even the Son of God had to die."[14] Odilon of Cluny is of the same opinion. When he says "Consider that which is hidden in the nostrils, in the throat, in the bowels, filth everywhere," you would think he used such language, as Donne did, to put us in mind of our deterioration toward death. But his point, rather, is to dissuade us from intercourse, for "we, who would be loath to touch vomit or dung even with our fingertip—how can we desire to clasp in our arms the bag of excrement itself?"[15] And although he says filth is endemic in bodies and uses the inclusive "we," we can be pretty sure which gender of body he really associates with excrement.

This church-sanctioned avoidance of intercourse derives ultimately from Eve's weakness in the Garden, but the biblical depiction of her weakness may have arisen from an even more basic masculine fear of feminine corruption. It goes without saying that from Eve and Pandora on down through Delilah, Cressida, Dido, and Duessa, women have released evil into the male world or tempted men away from their heroic destinies. In the immortal lines of Parolles,

> To the wars, my boy, to the wars!
> He wears his honor in a box unseen
> Who hugs his kicky-wicky here at home,
> Spending his manly marrow in her arms,
> Which should sustain the bound and high curvet
> Of Mars's fiery steed.   (*All's Well* 2.3)

In his phrase about man's spending his manly marrow in woman's arms, Parolles expresses the ancient masculine fear that the sexual act entails a sapping of powers. Physical contact with women despiritualizes, dispirits, vitiates—in short, feminizes men. Boxers who remain celibate prior to their fights take a lesson from Adam and Aeneas; and Freud translated that lesson into psychological and civilizational terms with his theory of libidinal sublimation.

From this standpoint women and sex drain off a man's masculine powers and leave him vulnerable to death. Thus Hotspur, tugged homeward by Kate, would seem at a disadvantage at Shrewsbury when he meets Prince Hal, who is, though not perhaps celibate, at least single. And Hal in his turn is all-conquering until he marries his own Kate and shortly after dies. Although women seem an alternative to death—you must choose either Venus or the boar—they and death are similarly emasculating. The little death may not kill, but it points the way to the grave.

Death and sex are bound together biologically as well as symbolically. We can say either that because animals die they must reproduce themselves, which accounts for their being here at all, or that because they reproduce themselves they must die, which accounts for their not having overrun the earth. In either case the mere presence of women reminds a man that despite his symbolic self-aggrandizements he is corporeally no different from other dying animals. Of course the reverse is equally true, that the presence of men reminds women of death; but men like Tertullian and Aquinas made that thought impossible to think for a very long time. In any event, to acknowledge sex is to acnowledge death, insofar as the procreative act that aims to nullify the death of the individual inevitably declares the mortality of both parties.

The point is that sex and death are the two great sources of human behavior, and yet, seated as they are in the body, they undermine the whole cultural project of transcending nature. Because of them we cannot clearly distinguish ourselves from lower creatures who likewise couple and die. To put it that way, as a coupling and dying, is to say dully what Shakespeare says wittily in Jacques' lines "and so from hour to hour we ripe and ripe, / And then from hour to hour we rot and rot; / And thereby hangs a tale." Here the so-called little death of love is generalized so that man's phallic declination from whore to whore epitomizes his descent toward the grave. Sex is life but also death.

This merger of woman with death and animality is particularly repellent in the tragedies. Hamlet likens conception in Ophelia to the sun breeding maggots in a dead dog (2.2) and graphically imagines his mother betraying his crafty madness to Claudius during the flesh-paddling act of copulation (3.4). Edgar finds a peculiar justice in the notion that "the dark and vicious place" where Edmund was begot cost Gloucester his eyes (5.3), and Lear madly associates his daughters' betrayal of him with rampant sexuality. Wrens and gilded flies go to it, and "yond simpering dame" has as riotous an appetite as the fitchew and the soiled horse. One wonders who the simpering dame goes to it *with*, since sex seems so exclusively feminine and in its femininity so peculiarly disgusting:

> But to the girdle do the gods inherit,
> Beneath is all the fiends'.
> There's hell, there's darkness, there is the sulphurous pit,
> Burning, scalding, stench, consumption. Fie, fie, fie!

In his association of the womb with hell Lear makes explicit the metaphor begun by Ophelia with man treading the "primrose path of dalliance" (1.3) and concluded by the Porter in *Macbeth* as the "primrose way to the everlasting bonfire" (2.3)—with an assist from the Clown in *All's Well* speaking of "the flowery way that leads to the broad gate and the great fire" (4.5). Woman, as Tertullian declared, is the gateway to hell. To enter the womb is to embark on a journey that leads through death to devilish regions below. If the male traveler does not get quite that far, still he may suffer the Neopolitan bone-ache and fleshly rot that mark him as a creature meant for death. In the scabrous language of Thersites and Timon, for instance, woman is merely a breeding-ground of disease (see chap. 1). And if that is so, then what is birth if not an emergence from a chamber of disease, hell, and death? No wonder men "come crying hither." Coming or going, they are doomed.

Only Macduff seems to escape this fate by virtue of being ripped untimely from his mother's womb, a virginal birth that endows him with the kind of *virtù* that betokens death to Macbeth.

Only the tragedies bring such matters to the surface of consciousness, and the vileness of their depiction there suggests the force of their repression. On the one hand men need this image of animalistic, death-associated woman as a daily reminder of their own superiority. In social terms it justifies the exclusion of women from education, politics, law, church, and other forms of power that both reflect man's status as a superior being and of course create and perpetuate it. Altogether it is a kind of cultural killing off of women so that men can experience a symbolic survival of death.

On the other hand, men need women not only for death-denying but also for life-preserving purposes—marriage and procreation. Picturing your fiancée, your wife, or the mother of your children as centaurian does not conduce to peopling the planet. Only repression and sublimation of the sort mentioned in the previous section can get the male out of this impasse. Woman must be transformed from a breeder of death into a source of life, her honesty a guarantee of her husband's immortality. Or else she can be desexualized into an image of virginal purity—although Shakespeare never fully endorses this kind of cold and unused virtue, as the example of Beatrice in *Measure for Measure* suggests. Or she can be made the object of religious adoration in the comedies, a Julia or Rosalind or even a tragic Juliet, though Juliet herself prefers to be a lady of flesh and bone instead of a Petrarchan divinity for Romeo to waft vows at (2.2.). Still again, as Laurie A. Finke argues, "the male poet of the Renaissance [may attempt] to deny mortality and neutralize the threat posed by woman's carnality by transforming her, through his lyric, through art, into an ideal, eternally changeless because essentially lifeless."[16] As this suggests, Renaissance poets, like Renaissance men, are altogether willing to sacrifice women of flesh and blood on the altar of idealization, to paint the skull of feminine death an inch thick if need be—and the need does seem to be.

However, as I suggested at the beginning, Shakespeare almost always stands where he has a good view of the corporeal slope of man's or woman's spiritual being. He takes a detour around Petrarch's shrine to court a mistress whose eyes can be looked on without dark glasses and whose breath does not bear discussion (Sonnet 130), whose vows of truth are engaging lies (Sonnet 138), and whose charms lie less in her constancy than, like Cleopatra's, in her infinite variety. He never forgets that the word "nunnery" harbors the meaning of whore house; that the innocent Ophelia, gone mad, can sing bawdy songs with the best of them; or that even the most idealized of his female characters are dependent on the squeakings of the child actors who boy their parts.

To speak of man's willingness to sacrifice the corporeal woman to an idealized image of her as the Petrarchan beloved, the sacred vessel of honesty, or a work of painted art is to suggest that in Shakespeare's time, among others, woman is twice-killed. The reason she is transformed into a lifeless ideal is that she has already been deprived of immortality by being sexually associated with animality and death. Her bestialization necessitates her idealization, yet in neither state is she fully alive—just as Lear's centaur deprives the human of life below the waist and the horse of life above it. This symbolic killing off of woman should remind us of the role played by sacrifice in the denial of death, an issue that deserves a longer look in the following chapter.

V Sacrifice

Sacrifice plays a central role in any Christian society, of course, but it had a special place in Elizabethan consciousness because the Reformation called in question the nature and meaning of the sacrament of the Eucharist. Was Christ physically present in the bread and wine as Catholics maintained, or not so as Wyclif and Hus declared, or only symbolically present as Zwingli held, or as Luther and Calvin argued present both physically and spiritually because the two are not antithetical and because God is omnipresent in all things? And what did the various answers to this question imply about sacrifice? Luther said no sacrifice takes place during the Mass because man has nothing to offer God; he can only receive and give thanks. On the other hand in the quarrel between Thomas Harding, an apostate of Protestantism, and John Jewel, the Bishop of Salisbury, Harding maintained that Christ was offered up symbolically, physically, and mystically, while the Bishop held that the Mass is "unbloody" because after Christ's sacrifice on the cross no more blood sacrifices of the pagan sort were necessary.[1] Whatever the truth of the matter (or spirit), the disputes inevitably focused public attention not only on the Mass but on the nature of sacrifice itself.

Almost as ritualized as the Mass were the sacrifices that occurred so often and on such a sadistic scale at Tyburn when Catholic traitor priests like Edmund Campion, after being racked by the infamous Mr. Norton, were hanged, disembowelled, beheaded, quartered, and hung up for the crowds to contemplate. Such occasions were doubly sacrificial. From the standpoint of the authorities the spectacles were designed as purgative occasions, publicly staged to bind Anglicans together in revulsion at the fate of the dissenters and in relief at being on the side of the elect. What they saw presumably was not a triumph of faith over suffering but the degradation of spiritual presumption to a slaughtered carcass.

From the Catholic standpoint, however, the tortured priest emulated Christ and the martyrs by offering his body to God. In fact, the Campion, Sherwin, Bryant executions in 1581 aided the Catholic cause far more than the three Jesuits had done with all their sermons, pamphlets, and Masses. Their heroism—especially that of the visionary Bryant, who "in the extremity of agony," as an eyewitness wrote, "raised his mangled body and stood upright on his feet to the great astonishment of all beholders"[2]—inspired Catholics and non-Catholics alike and begot a host of broadsheets and libels denouncing the merciless Queen. Something of the sort occurred also in the spectacular public beheadings of heretics like Essex and Ralegh.

These rituals rely on the life-enhancing aspect of death emphasized by Elias Canetti, the tendency for the death of the individual to strengthen those who survive it. At the most elemental level of death and survival, the veins of the victor drink the blood of his fallen foe. Otto Rank gives the same idea a psychological turn: "The death fear of the ego is lessened by the killing, the sacrifice, of the other; through the death of the other, one buys oneself free from the penalty of dying, of being killed."[3]

The natural place to buy oneself free from death is the battlefield. War, as Canetti says, is a "death conductor."[4] Humans are always threatened by death; we are like trees in a continuous lightning storm. None of us wants to die alone, knowing life will go on its way outrageously indifferent. Thus suicides, rather like the pharaohs of old, often kill their entire family first, even their pets; they want to take the world with them and make a greater wound in the cosmos. As Anna Livia Plurabelle says "If I go all goes." Or as Hotspur says "Die all, die merrily!" And what better way to multiply merriment than war? Even if it conducts us to unmerry deaths, at least we do not die alone.

But of course we may not die at all. War itself may save us by deflecting death away from us and onto the enemy. Something primitive in our minds likes to think Death has only so much energy; if he wears himself out on our enemy he may not have enough left to kill us. And, to be sure, if he wears himself out on my comrades in arms he may not have enough left to kill me. Above all, let it be me who survives, no matter whose body I must stand on. When Estragon cries "God have pity on me!" Vladimir asks "And me?" and Estragon simply cries with redoubled vigor "On me! On me! Pity! On me!"[5] When Death is in the field we all chorus Estragon's cry. And if I am pitied, and do survive, surely it is because Zeus or Allah has warded off the spears. The gods love me. I never doubted it.

1. Henry VI

If I am very much loved by the gods—that is, if I am a very great conqueror like Alexander or Caesar—then I bestride the battlefield earth like a colossus:

> His brandished sword did blind men with his beams;
> His arms spread wider than a dragon's wings;

> His sparkling eyes, replete with wrathful fire,
> More dazzled and drove back his enemies
> Than midday sun fierce bent against their faces.
> What should I say? His deeds exceed all speech.
> He ne'er lift up his hand but conquered.

That sounds like Plutarch describing Alexander, but it is the Duke of Gloucester in *1 Henry IV* eulogizing Henry V (1.1). Eulogizing—for, alas, when the gods make heroes into colossi they stand higher than the rest of us and sometimes take the lightning first. As Bedford says, Henry was simply "too famous to live long." Gods make the famous godlike and then remind them of the essential difference between gods and the merely godlike.

After the fall of the mighty, when the aftershocks have ceased registering, we enter a diminished world; the cleverness is gone, as Riddley Walker would say. In the England that survives Henry V, battles are won not by men whose eyes dazzle and drive back their enemies with solar ferocity but by men like Talbot, not "some Hercules, a second Hector," the Countess of Auvergne marvels, but "a weak and writhled shrimp" (*1HVI* 2.3). However, this weak and writhled shrimp is prudently reinforced with pikes, enough to make even the skeptical Countess concede his collective greatness.

The Talbot who wins by teamwork; however, is no more immortal than the Henry who won by force of charismatic nature. When Talbot loses at Bordeaux it is because Somerset and York, transfixed in pride and enmity, fail to bring up their supporting armies. And so "Two Talbots," as one of them proclaims, "winged through the lither sky, / In [Death's] despite shall scape mortality" (*1HVI* 4.7). Winging with them, unfortunately, are the last vestiges of selfless English patriotism. What they leave behind is not merely their gory bodies but an England dedicated to goring itself.

At this point England enters the phase of "sacrificial crisis," as René Girard calls it, a period of multiplying violence in which the squaring off of enemies—the forces of Gloucester and Winchester, and of Somerset and York—produces a symmetry of undifferentiation that can be terminated only through the offices of "good violence," the sacrifice of a *pharmakos*. Death will kill death, and death once dead there's no more dying then. Or as Girard puts it, "Death, then, contains the germ of life. There is no life on the communal level that does not originate in death."[6] During the period of sacrificial crisis, however, the virtues of sacrifice are suspended. The Talbots might have served as *pharmakoi* whose deaths would carry off the evils of English dissension, shaming their survivors into a militant unity that would bode ill to France. That possibility is raised when Sir William Lucy stands over the bodies of the Talbots and says "I'll bear them hence; but from their ashes shall be reared / A phoenix that shall make all France afeard" (4.7). And for a time the death of the Talbots seems to have done just that. The divided English join into one force at Angiers, defeat the French, and capture Joan. But then ensue an "effeminate peace" with France and an ominous marriage between Henry and Margaret of Anjou, with the Earl of Suffolk gloating behind the political arras.

From this time on England is simply a battlefield of competing egos. Death is deflected not onto the French but onto England herself, who eats her own farrow — Talbot, Gloucester, York, Henry himself — as relentlessly as Joyce's Ireland. As violence reaches a state of maximum entropy, all societal distinctions dissolve. With a king more ruled than ruling, the monarchy is up for grabs. Gloucester's wife, Eleanor, aspires to the crown, and both the Duke of York and Jack Cade the clothier declare themselves legitimate heirs. The Earl of Sussex is killed by commoners; Cade's irregulars spill across social boundaries to threaten all civilized values; and ultimately even fathers and sons, indistinguishable in the general rain of blood, kill one another. In a world given over to indiscriminate violence, only King Henry sits alone and apart on his molehill, a pathetic king with none of the heroic kingly attributes, cursed by the fact that he does not drink blood or call for heads to be piled up in testimony of his greatness. A heretic to the religion of violence, he represents a rebuke to those who derive their symbolic immortality from inflicting death. Thus he is the true enemy. Beneath all the overt enmities, the secret hatred of the English is for their King, not merely because they want his crown but because his nonviolence threatens their lives. Innocent of the lust for blood, he must be killed by the bloodiest of them all, Richard Crookback.

Henry is the perfect *pharmakos* because he is central to the violence and yet innocent of it. In contrast to all earlier murders, his will produce no revengers to perpetuate the violence, and scarcely any mourners. With Richard Crookback around, however, Henry's sacrifical role inevitably fails and violence is perpetuated, not through revenge, but simply because it is Richard's natural medium. In him, despite his insistence on his uniqueness, all the evils of his fellow English conglomerate to form both a "wretched, bloody, usurping boar" and a good candidate for the role of *pharmakos*. Thus when Richmond kills him ("the bloody dog is dead" [5.5]) he can figuratively stand with his foot on the beast's carcass and proclaim to the survivors "Peace lives again." The Tudor dynasty has survived just in time to prevent England from sacrificing itself into extinction.

2. Henry V

An even more classic example of sacrificial death begetting life is the career of Henry V because in his case we see victimage graduate from the individual to the nation as Hal's causes grow more holy. His first cause, to attain the crown, is achieved through the sacrifice of Hotspur, Henry IV, and Falstaff. Killing Hotspur in battle, he acquires his proud titles and grows somewhat glorious, although some of his luster is eclipsed by Falstaff's usurpation of his accomplishment. But he in turn unseats the great knight at Westminster with a lance of royal aloofness. With the death of his father, the churchmen say, the new king's "wildness [i.e., Falstaff] mortified in him"; and his body, purged of all those calories, became as if by miracle a "paradise / To envelop and contain celestial spirits."

This celestializing of the King is good news to England but also something of a bad omen. After all, a return to paradise is a return to the place where the prospect of being as the gods, proposed with a hiss, brought on death and a dolorous cortege of ills. Before the English applauded Harry's celestialization, they should have read Pascal: "When men seek to become angels," he said, "they become beasts."[7] They do so particularly when they suspect they may be a little beastly already, because then they must purge themselves of guilt; and the way to kill the beast in yourself is to make beasts of others and kill them first. Thus although Harry seems to have purified himself, his paradise is tainted by his continuing fear that he has inherited the guilt that dogged his father throughout his reign, what Henry IV himself called "the soil of [his] achievement [of the crown]." Because the soil of this achievement must be washed away, Harry's first angelic act is to declare war against France. For the French are always soiled with guilt; they are, after all, French.

Thus Harry's military quest in France is a sanctified substitute for his father's oft-promised but unperformed pilgrimage to Jerusalem, the purpose of which was to atone for the murder of Richard and to keep men from looking "too near unto [Henry's] state" (2HIV 4.5). If the expiation of guilt cannot be attained in the Holy Land, then it must be sought in a holy war. And never was a war more holy. The opening scene of *Henry V* is little more than a baptismal rite in which Harry and his politics are dipped in the font of the Church. "The sin upon my head," the Archbishop declares (1.2).

Harry is an expert at crowning other heads with sin and his own with innocence. The Archbishop is not the last of the King's scapegoats; behind him follow as if in a sacrificial queue the English traitors, the citizens of Harfleur, Bardolph of the flaming nose, and finally the French prisoners.

As each victim falls, Harry proclaims their guilt and affirms his own purity. If he kills them, it is only at their own invitation. The traitors condemn themselves to death, the citizens of Harfleur are "guilty in defence," and Bardolph was caught stealing a "pax" in church—a very small theft compared to Harry's theft of the peace between England and France.[8]

This sustained ritual of sacrifice purifies Harry almost beyond human recognition. Old friends from court and tavern alike go to it, but their deaths come not near him. And rightly so. After all, he is God's martial vicar—remote, unalterable, a polestar by which his army takes its bearings. Yet all this changes the night before Agincourt when he reveals his doubts about the legitimacy of his reign.

At this point we realize that for Harry the war has a dual purpose. We have already known one of these—that it is designed as a secular atonement for his father's usurpation of the crown, a way to busy "giddy minds" and unite the nation. In this respect the war is marvelously successful. As Harry crosses France, the giddy minds of the Scots, Irish, and Welsh are focused into a British arrow pointing at the French. And at Agincourt sacred slaughter welds the bands of brotherhood. As Hugh Duncan says of the binding powers of violence, "as we wound and kill our enemy in the field and slaughter his women and children in their homes, our love for each other deepens. We become comrades in arms; our hatred of each other is being purged in the sufferings of our enemy."[9] The promise of victory is nothing less than the promise of immortality, of being bound together everlastingly by the deaths of others. As Harry points out to his men, the battle takes place most appropriately on Saint Crispin's Day,

> And Crispin Crispian shall ne'er go by,
> From this day to the ending of the world,
> But we in it shall be remembered,
> We few, we happy few, we band of brothers.
>
> (4.3)

Yet Harry's uncertainties on the eve of battle suggest that the war is also a personal test of divine favor, as war usually is.[10] And a risky test at that, for despite Harry's God's-on-my-side rhetoric en route to Agincourt there is no guarantee that God regards him as anything more than the son of a usurper and regicide. "Not today, O Lord," he prays,

> O, not today, think not upon the fault
> My father made in compassing the crown!
> I Richard's body have interred new,

> And on it have bestowed more contrite tears,
> Than from it issued forced drops of blood,
> Five hundred poor I have in yearly pay,
> Who twice a day their withered hands hold up
> Toward heaven, to pardon blood; and I have built
> Two chantries, where the sad and solemn priests
> Still sing for Richard's soul. (4.1)

Clearly, however, it is less Richard's soul than his own that Harry is most anxious to indemnify, particularly because the footsoldier Williams, anxious about his own soul, has just suggested that if the King's cause be wrong his followers' obedience "wipes the crime of it out of [them]" and lays the guilt at Harry's feet. The great scapegoater suddenly risks being scapegoated himself. Harry's plight is not unlike that of Falstaff, exposed as a coward and liar in the Boar's Head Inn. And his verbose exoneration of himself— which is summed up in the line "Every subject's duty is the King's, but every subject's soul is his own"—is suspiciously reminiscent of Falstaff's "By the Lord, I knew ye as well as him that made ye!"

Still if Harry is quick to deny guilt, he is equally quick to deny credit. Very much as at Shrewsbury he surrendered to Falstaff his stake in the killing of Hotspur, so at Agincourt he yields to God the laurels of a greater killing: "Take it, God, / For it is none but thine!" (4.8) Needless to say, it is not easy to know what to make of this declaration. If, as seems likely, we are to regard it as the generous act of England's greatest king, we can hardly help thinking also that God has succeeded the Archbishop in being forced to say "The sin upon my head, dread sovereign!" A field piled with legs and arms and heads, as Williams said, the widowed poor and the children rawly left, even perhaps the French prisoners with slit throats gaping: all these are not merely sacrificial offerings to God but God's personal responsibility, "none but thine." God is the ultimate scapegoat; and Harry has run with as much quick dexterity from the guilt of Agincourt as ever Falstaff did from the men in buckram at Gadshill.

3. A Midsummer Night's Dream

An examination of Shakespearean sacrifice would include, most obviously, *Julius Caesar*, with Brutus's efforts to prevent a ritual murder from degenerating into a butchery, and *Coriolanus* where, as suggested above, the grain god must be torn apart and fed to a hungering populace, and various other actual killings that serve a sacrificial function. All tragic heroes are in large part sacrifices whose lives trouble their world and whose deaths bond together their survivors. Their counterparts in comedy are the characters whose anticomic attitudes threaten this societal bonding. Death must be, in Sir James Frazer's words, "carried off"; and hence we have a series of comic death substitutes—Holofernes and Don Armado in *Love's Labour's Lost*, Falstaff in *The Merry Wives*, Jacques in *As You Like It*, Malvolio in *Twelfth Night*, Parolles in *All's Well*, Caliban in *The Tempest*—who must undergo humiliation and banishment, though Shakespeare always tempers the viciousness of our laughter.

So Shakespeare lays out on his dramatic altar lots of sacrifices, actual and symbolic, for the critic to mutilate even further. However, let me discuss instead a play in which sacrifice is remote from actual killing and not very apparent even symbolically, *A Midsummer Night's Dream*.

In some respects *A Midsummer Night's Dream* seems a dramatization of Plato's statement about the Beast Within quoted in the last chapter—that when Reason sleeps the Wild Beast rouses itself and "in phantasy it will not shrink from intercourse with a mother or anyone else, man, god, or brute." The consummation of Bottom's assish courtship of the faery queen Titania is a fair representation of the wild beast fantasy: intercourse involving man, god[dess], and brute simultaneously.[11] In view of the horror aroused by the crime of bestiality discussed earlier, this monstrous union should have released in Shakespeare's Elizabethan audience feelings of alarm and titillation. But it would take a sensitive soul indeed to run in fear from Bottom and Titania. Even so, the bestializing of sex in Bottom serves as a paradigm for the forest experience of the young lovers; he literalizes what is for them metaphoric. That is to say, once the lovers enter the forest they are repeatedly characterized by animal imagery that reflects and culminates in the Bottom-Titania episode.[12] Helena pursues Demetrius like a "spaniel," a "dove," and a "hind," while he flees like "griffin" and a "tiger" (2.1); and she later becomes "ugly as a bear," a "monster" he runs from (2.2). Lysander shifts his affections from the "raven" Hermia to the "dove" Helena (2.2), later calling Hermia a "cat" and a "serpent" he will shake himself free of (3.2). No wonder Hermia awakens from a dream in which a "crawling serpent" was eating her heart away (2.2)—at which point she cries "Either death or [Lysander] I'll find immediately."

This animalizing of the lovers' experience seems a direct result of Oberon's humiliation of Titania:

> What thou seest when thou dost wake,
> Do it for thy true-love take,
> Love and languish for his sake.

> Be it ounce or cat or bear,
> Pard or boar with bristled hair,
> In thy eye that shall appear
> When thou wak'st, it is thy dear.
> Wake when some vile thing is near.
>
> (2.2)

Then *Enter Lysander and Hermia* talking in Petrarchan accents and lying, not with one another, but chastely apart. Nevertheless, their experience is shadowed by that of Titania and Bottom. The lovers' comings and goings in various animalistic forms are the surface sublimations of the bestial intercourse between the faery queen and her liminal lover. While reason sleeps in Athens, Plato's Wild Beast wakes in the forest, with monstrous appetites.

In what sense is this a denial of death? In no sense: in fact it is just the reverse, a comic movement toward a loss of identity in the forests of death. The descent to animalism is merely one rung short of the descent to death. As such, the lovers' arboreal experience bears out Lysander's early remarks about the affinities of love and death. Love, he said, is always subject to "war, death, and sickness," always one blithe step away from devouring "jaws of darkness" and the "confusion [into which] quick bright things come" (1.1).

From this standpoint we might argue that the confusions of the forest are a comic version of Lear's storm: both represent all that reason and the court world repress. So, for that matter, does the play of Pyramus and Thisbe. What it depicts is the course of true love, which leads the unhappy pair to a bestial and ferocious Lion and thence through confusion to death: "Tongue, lose thy light; / Moon, take thy flight. / Now die, die, die, die, die," (5.1). There but for the grace of genre goes Lear's "Kill, kill, kill, kill, kill, kill" (4.6).

But of course no one will confuse this play with *King Lear* or take Snug the joiner's Lion for Richard III's wild boar. That is precisely the point. The repressed Beast Within, rapacious and murderous, the embodiment of all that deprives man of angelic status, emerges in this delightful comedy as a Bottom marvelous hairy about the face, and a Lion very gentle, of good conscience, and most anxious not to frighten the ladies. The Beast Within is allowed only a small roar and a little rage, and in the end must be sacrificed altogether. Thus it is almost allegorically appropriate that Theseus should come upon the lovers while hunting with Spartan hounds like those that once "bayed the bear" in Crete (4.1).[13] Theseus's hounds bay the bear of ungoverned impulse in the lovers, their harmonious cries reflecting the harmony of love finally fashioned out of the cacophony of "derision":

"When they next wake, all this derision / Shall seem a dream and fruitless vision" (3.2).

Thus as if by a wave of Plato's wand, the bearish beast fades into dream at the moment the lovers waken into the world of Theseus's reason. Only by repressing the beast of the forest can the lovers aspire to marriage in the palace. But only by unshackling and confronting the beast in the first place — by escaping from the harsh rational law of Athens and from the milder decorum of courtship — can the lovers come to recognize the rough impulses that underlie and influence mature love. Or as we would say now, the Ego must confront the Freudian Id or the Jungian shadow for the psyche to be maturely married.[14] The price of this marriage, however, is a sacrificial repression of animalism and death, the banishment of the forest experience into a mere "dream past the wit of [either lovers or Bottom] to say what dream it was." But repression is not extinction; the realignments of love that took place in the forest are sustained and ratified in Athens. Moreover, as part of a sacrificial quid pro quo between reason and impulse, if the beast that represents impulse at its worst is suppressed, so is the harsh Athenian law that represents reason at its worst. Through such sacrificial negotiations humans may sometimes find their way to the rational life without entirely forfeiting the liberating virtues of the imaginative vision.

VI   Clothing Mortality

1. Custom and Costume

In his essay "Of the custom of wearing clothes" Montaigne anticipates Lear's remarks about unaccommodated man owing nothing to nature:

> Now, since [every other animal] is furnished with the exact amount of
> thread and needles required to maintain its being, it is in truth incredible
> that we alone should be brought into the world in a defective and indigent
> state, in a state such that we cannot maintain ourselves without external
> aid.[1]

Indeed so incredible is this state of bodily affairs that Montaigne denies its
existence. The human body, he says, is hardier than we think; without our
foolish sartorial customs we could compete quite favorably with furrier
beasts in withstanding the cold. This of course implies a kinship between
us and "lower" creatures, a kinship not in the least disconcerting to Montaigne, who took every opportunity to compare civilized man unfavorably
to the cannibalistic primitives and animals he admired. Primitives themselves, however, have never appreciated Montaigne's view. For them the
primary purpose of clothing and body decoration is not to keep out wind
and weather but to distinguish *us* from *them*, especially when "them" means
other animals.

To be sure, even Montaigne admits in the "Apology for Raymond
Sebonde" that there is good cause for us to clothe ourselves, despite our
hardihood. It is because we are ugly. Some animals are ugly too, he admits,
but that is small consolation inasmuch as their ugliness derives from their
resemblances to us. Apes and pigs are the ugliest of the lower creatures,
and that explains why our own faces are simian and our insides porcine.[2]
No wonder we hide ourselves in clothing.

The Bafia people of Cameroon were as quick as Montaigne to see the
virtue of adorning themselves distinctively, especially in the company of
apes and pigs:

> [They] say that without their scarifications they would be indistinguish-
> able from pigs and chimpanzees. The Maori woman of New Zealand

claims that if she neglected to tatoo her lips and gums she would resemble a dog with her white teeth and red mouth. The Nuba of the Sudan perceive that the crucial difference between men and animals lies in men's ability to shave their heads and bodies to make their skins smooth. This capacity distinguishes them from every other species: even language was once shared between men and monkeys.[3]

Thus when asked why his people paint their bodies and wear feathers, Aeroe, the Tuaremi Indian in Peter Matthiesson's *At Play in the Fields of the Lord*, replies, "We are naked and have nothing! Therefore we must decorate ourselves, for if we did not, how are we to be told from animals?"[4]

Obliquely, then, Montaigne's association of culture (custom) and clothes is wonderfully apt; for clothing makes obvious the intent of culture to super-naturalize man. We adorn ourselves with culture to conceal our pathetic bodily plight, our animal kinships, and what we owe to both—death. That Montaigne should want to unclothe us is in keeping with his more general project to "unculture" humankind: to devalue reason and education in the interests of reducing us, in Lévi-Strauss's terms, from a cooked to a raw state.[5] This grand divestiture is in keeping with Montaigne's conviction that men must live with, and indeed found their lives upon, the foreknowledge of death.[6] Only someone like him, priding himself on having seen the skull beneath the skin, would so willingly strip off man's cultural apparel and announce to the Raymond Sebondes of his day *"Ecce homo!"*

This cry also resounded in the England of Shakespeare's time, often with amplification. Young Jack Donne the poet might liken his mistress's naked body to "America! my newfound-land" and exhibit a lusty longing to abandon poetry for geographical exploration, but years later, propped in his pulpit at St. Paul's, long of tooth and lean of desire, the dour Dean charted less appealing corporeal terrain for his congregation: "Between the excrementall jelly that thy body is made of at first, and that jelly which thy body dissolves to at last; there is not so noysome, so putrid a thing in nature" (Sermon 14). The only amorously "roving hands" this body will attract are Death's.

Hamlet takes a similar view when he directs Yorick's skull to inform "my lady" that though she "paint an inch thick, to this favor she must come." He and Donne had little patience with ladies who thought they could paint over the face they owed God and the skull they owed Death. But the Prince and the Dean were by no means alone in exposing the noxious corporeality of death. Hamlet merely studies Yorick's skull, but Erichtho in Marston's *Sophonsiba* (4.1) is positively necrophiliac, and characters in Webster, Dekker, and Tourneur often dilate with grim relish on Death's foul erosions of human bodies (e.g., Bosola in *The Duchess of Malfi*, Hippolito in *The Honest Whore* [I, 4.1] and Vindici in *The Revenger's Tragedy* [3.5]). When even heavy-gauge skin cannot hold all this rotting flesh and bone together, sumptuous clothes and inch-thick paintings will prove of little avail.

But these gruesome discoveries were made in the theater or pulpit, not in the courts of Elizabeth or James. After all, what playwright or courtier would volunteer to speak of the vanities of fabric to a king who, as Lawrence Stone records, "over a period of five years from 1608 to 1613 bought a new cloak every month, a new waistcoat every three weeks, a new suit every ten days, a new pair of stockings, boots, and garters every four or five days, and a new pair of gloves every day."[7] And who would lecture a queen who, despite her notorious parsimony, boasted "I am, as it were, half-Italian," and proved it by steeping herself in a sea of cloth and jewels so rich that at her death the Keeper of the Great Wardrobe pocketed £60,000 by selling the clothes alone?[8]

Beneath this sumptuousness, however, the human body made its presence known, in part because the bodies of the Queen, the King, and their attendant lords and ladies were rarely scrubbed, but also because Hampton Court reflected the plight of the human body. That is, castles, palaces, and the like are themselves, like clothing, intended not merely to protect our bodies but to deny death by creating an air of sumptuous permanence. Every castle is part pyramid.

Unfortunately death and the body will not be put off so easily. Without a sewage system, Hampton Court assaulted the nostrils with the odors of discarded garbage, soured wine, animal droppings, and the stench from servants' privies and the "close stools" of the gentlefolk.[9] Since of all sensory organs, the nose seems most fastidious about death and its foretokens, Elizabeth and her courtiers protected themselves against the smell of bodily refuse by sniffing aromatic pomanders even in the Queen's privy chamber, where the close stools were inventively but ineffectively disguised "in sugared cases of satin and velvet."[10] Although Montaigne would hardly approve of devout courtiers jetting about with beards dyed purple or green to match their cloaks and with perfumed handkerchiefs at the ready, he would surely regard these customs and costumes as symptomatic of the vain desire of *le beaux monde* to keep its ape-and piglike aspects under wraps.

2. Styles of Clothing

Clothing, then, especially the grand clothing of Shakespeare's day, is admirably suited to suggest that culture is a vast immortality project, a form of conspicuous consumption designed to keep mortal consumption inconspicuous. Shakespeare's characters repeatedly employ fine clothing to acquire an identity superior to their forlorn natural status. Even rough clothing will sometimes suffice, as it does in *King John* when the Bastard Faulconbridge, backdoor son of Richard the Lion Hearted, encounters the fatuous Austria, who is somehow possessed of the dead Richard's famous lion skin. To confirm that he has come one way of the Plantagenets, the Bastard must of course kill Austria and confiscate the lion skin, and he does so in short order. This action defrocks not only the mock-warrior Austria, who has stolen Richard's leonine cloak, but also by implication the mock-king King John as well, who has stolen Richard's (and now Arthur's) crown. Only the Bastard is legitimate at this point, the natural son proving super-natural by assuming his dead father's garb.

In *The Winter's Tale* Perdita experiences a similar exaltation when she dons the robe that makes her queen of the sheep-shearing festival (4.4). "Sure this robe of mine," she says, "does change my disposition." In fact, of course, it only confirms her natural status as a princess by concealing her seemingly natural status as a peasant. This enhancement of nature is famil-iarly glossed by Polixenes when he explains that gillyflowers are not made "bastards" through grafting, as Perdita says, but are improved by an art that "does mend Nature, change it rather, but / The art itself is Nature." When she acknowledges this, Polixenes says "Then make your garden rich in gillyflowers, / And do not call them bastards." The Bastard in *King John*, himself the product of a sexual grafting between his plain gillyflower mother and his royal father, would surely approve.

In these cases clothing is a kind of cultural second nature that confirms the natural status of the wearer. The trick, of course, is that the clothing must fit, which means that it must be tailored not just to the outward anatomy but to the inward parts as well. With the Bastard and Perdita it is. With Macbeth it is not. Macbeth "cannot buckle his distempered cause / Within the belt of rule," and as the English forces approach, he feels "his title / Hang loose about him, like a giant's robe / Upon a dwarfish thief" (5.2). Much earlier, just after the murder of Duncan is discovered, Macbeth cries to his fellow Scots "Let's briefly put on manly readiness, / And meet in the hall together" (2.4). Later, however, as Birnam Wood commences its march, Macbeth again puts on his armor, his "manly readiness," but be-cause he lacks the inward readiness to go with it, he takes it off again, and then finally puts it back on and takes to the field plagued with what his wife would regard as unmanly misgivings.

What fits Macbeth best is the blood of other men. In this sanguine attire he makes his ascent from Glamis to Cawdor to King of Scotland. After so close-fitting a garment, however, even the ermine of kingship must prove unsuitable. Thus we can chart Macbeth's career sartorially, as a passage from battlefield blood to loose-fitting gown of royalty and back to blood again. Garbed in the blood of other men, he conquers death and acquires the robe of greatness that gradually slips from him until at the end he is clothed in his own blood, not like Macduff at birth but at death. No one's blood fits Macbeth quite so well as his own.

The battlefield at Troy is as bloody as those in Scotland, but there is a greater gap there between armor and flesh, as Hector unhappily discovers. His pursuit, conquest, and stripping of the sumptuously armored knight outside the walls constitute a graphic exposé of the futility of masking man's "putrified core" either in armor or in honor (5.8). For the glittering armor is as hollow as Hector's irrational code of honor, and as meaninglessly superficial as the fame accruing to Achilles' dishonorable conquest of the unarmed Hector himself a few moments later.

Hector's putrefied knight in fine armor is a precursor of Cloten, who in *Cymbeline* dons the clothing of Posthumus in order to fit his revenge to Imogen's offense—"that she held the very garment of Posthumus in more respect than my noble and natural person" (3.6). Since Posthumus's clothes fit well, why should Imogen, "who was made by him that made the tailor, not be fit too?"—not be fit, that is, for his sexual wear (4.1). But Cloten places too much confidence in the outward fit of things. When he encounters the royal Guiderius he bridles at the lack of deference shown him by this ill-clothed rustic. "Know'st me not by my clothes?" demands the Queen's son, and receives the sort of reply Kent gave Oswald in *Lear*:

> No, nor thy tailor, rascal,
> Who is thy grandfather. He made those clothes,
> Which, as it seems, make thee.   (4.2)

At this insult Cloten and his clothes take on a manly readiness; but in the skirmish that follows he finds that in the apparel of Posthumus he is less likely to be Posthumus than to become posthumous. Thus in a very short while Guiderius is discovered wearing Cloten's head neatly tucked under his arm. A head is all Cloten has to offer: "This Cloten," Guiderius says, "was a fool, an empty purse; / There was no money in it." So the purselike Cloten joins Hector's armored knight to represent the ultimate in this kind. They not only do not fill out their clothes but have shrunk inside them to become merely an encased emptiness.

The armor that entices Hector appears to come from the same shop as the "trumpery" and "glistering apparel" hung up before Prospero's cave.

Clothing in this case may not represent a denial of death, but it is a means to prevent it, because it has been set out to distract Caliban and company from knocking a nail through Prospero's head and taking command of the island (4.1). It is significant in terms of Montaigne's separation of nature and custom (costume) that the clothing causes Caliban to part company with his god-king confederates. When Stephano and Trinculo quarrel like fishwives at a bargain counter over the possession of a gown, Caliban the natural man remains as insensible to the cultural enhancements of clothing as he is to those of language: "Let it alone, thou fool! It is but trash."

Trash indeed! Tell that to Leicester or Essex or Ralegh or a host of lesser lights who dressed themselves against a deeper chill than even the English climate afforded. At court, the center of symbolic immortality, they puffed up in taffeta and silks into something more than merely human. Caught up in this mad competition of cloth, they could hardly believe they possessed bodies as mortal and gross as Caliban's. Even the royal Stephano realizes you cannot be a proper king without dressing for the part. But to Caliban all this is meaningless. Perhaps like the savages in Montaigne's essay "Of Cannibals" he has a hide impervious to weather, to go with a mind impervious to the symbolic costumings of culture. At any rate, in denouncing his gods he strikes a blow for nature that Montaigne might have applauded.

3. Thrice-Gorgeous Ceremony

The Greek knight's sumptuous armor, Posthumus's clothes, Prospero's fetching island fashions—each is putrid or empty or trash. We may begin to wonder if there is no fine clothing that fits except at sheep-shearing festivals in Bohemia. Well, even more glittering and grand than the garb of Bohemian royalty is the crown of England; and in his history plays Shakespeare brings forth one customer after another to try its look and fit in hopes of purchasing a share of immortality with this golden headgear. However, the crown is too drab and worldly for Henry VI, who is more interested in shopping for halos; too confining for Hotspur, for whom a kingdom is too small a bound; too shiny for Richard Crookback, whose nature is suited only for black; too large for Richard II, who thinks it *is* a halo; and too soiled for his usurping successor Bolingbroke, who spends his entire reign scrubbing and polishing it for his son.

Which leaves us with his son, Henry V, whom even he considers at first glance a more likely candidate for prison garb than for balm and crown imperial. But ultimately the crown settles comfortably albeit briefly on

Harry's brow. The reason is that he earns it, in part by catering to his subjects' need for mystification. No sooner did his father die than the magic of the crown killed off his own "wildness" and left "his body as a paradise / To envelop and contain celestial spirits" (1.1), or so the churchmen claim, though their description of Hal's amazing grace sounds a bit like Richard Crookback strategically praying between two bishops as the Londoners weigh his qualifications for kingship. At any rate Hal is no more deceived by the trappings of monarchy than Richard, and he is just as adept at staging his royalty. It is a bit disconcerting to find England's best king sharing with her worst an ability to don the robes of what he calls Ceremony and to remove them at will.[11] But of course no attentive young prince could listen to Falstaff's debunkings of piety, sobriety, and honor without casting a somewhat dubious glance at the grandeurs of royalty, especially with a father who admits he came to the crown by indirect and crooked ways. If Falstaff will have nothing to do with honor because it cannot "set to" a leg or an arm "or take away the grief of a wound," because it "hath no skill in surgery" (*1HIV* 5.1), neither will King Harry be taken in by Ceremony, which cannot "give [kings] cure" when they fall sick (4.1).

Ceremony, Hal realizes, does not cure the body's mortal infirmities; it merely conceals them inside glittering raiment. By so doing it ministers to the souls of timid subjects, serving as an idol or pseudogod whose sacredness takes visible form in

> the balm, the sceptre, and the ball,
> The sword, the mace, the crown imperial,
> The intertissued robe of gold and pearl,
> The farced title running 'fore the King,
> The throne he sits on, [and] the tide of pomp
> That beats upon the high shore of this world.
>
> (4.1)

In the religion of politics "thrice-gorgeous Ceremony" is designed to create "awe and fear in other men" — and of course to persuade kings like Richard II that they differ not merely in degree but in kind from lesser mortals.

This "thrice-gorgeous Ceremony," the centerpiece of King Harry's religion of royalty, interestingly reflects the practice of the Tudor monarchs, who, as Stephen Orgel has shown,[12] were short on legitimacy and consequently long on Ceremony. Henry VII, who was even more lacking in royal credentials than Bolingbroke, shrewdly put on the trappings of medieval chivalry to create an image of a kingship sanctioned by the past and instinct with dignity and tradition. Not only did he foster the Tudor myth, whereby he and his heirs were Arthur reincarnate, but he consciously "imported Burgundian chivalric models to project the image of a noble and honorable court."[13] Henry VIII—like Shakespeare's King Harry the son of a monarch with doubtful if not nonexistent title—continued the Tudor stress of pomp with such splendors as the Field of the Cloth of Gold. Elizabeth, legally illegitimate yet included by Henry in the line of succession, had similar need of ceremonial fictions. From about 1572 onward Accession Day tilts combined with royal progresses and court entertainments—some of which were of course theatrical—to stage the greatness and reinforce the authority of the Virgin Queen. In short, if all the world is not a stage, at least England can be made into one if the political need is great, as it certainly was for the Tudors and for Shakespeare's King Harry.

That Ceremony is substanceless pomp and show, Harry knows well enough. After all, he was schooled by Falstaff to recognize lies, and it is to his credit that he discerns his own as well as those of other men. "I think the King," he says to his soldiers, "is but a man, as I am, [for] his ceremonies laid by, in his nakedness he appears but a man."

At this point, on the eve of Agincourt, Harry dons Erpingham's cloak, concealing his royalty, and goes among his soldiers unrecognized. His disguising of himself in this manner is also an undisguising, a "laying by" of the "intertissued robe" of Ceremony and of the comforting illusions of greatness. Thus he takes precisely the opposite approach to death from his father at Shrewsbury. For there Henry IV hid from death by distributing his royal wardrobe about the field: many, Hotspur remarked, went "marching in his coats" (5.3). In effect Henry denies his kingship in order to deny death. But Harry assumes his disguise not to escape from death but to acknowledge his own mortality, putting his royal title and his mortal body in jeopardy.

Thus whereas Richard II took cover behind Divine Right to avoid playing a part in one more sad story of the death of kings, and whereas Henry IV relied on an extensive wardrobe to preserve himself at Shrewsbury, Henry V goes forth at Agincourt with no illusions about Divine Right and Ceremony and with no one in the King's coat but the King himself. Forswearing ransom from the French, he says "Bid them achieve me and then sell my bones" (4.3). Such a line might have come from Hotspur, inflated with a sense of deathlessness by his grand emprise; but it comes instead from a king who does not feel deathless in the least. Harry knows he can be "achieved" and his bones sold, but he also knows he must conduct himself as if he didn't.

Harry is as ruthless with himself as he is with Falstaff, the English traitors, the fiery-nosed Bardolph, and the French prisoners. His war against the

French is a holy war designed to unify Britain and to legitimize his own kingship, and he conducts it as such, as though he were God's vicar and Hotspur's reincarnation. Before Harfleur he is all Hotspur as he calls on his men to "imitate the action of the tiger" by stiffening the sinews, summoning the blood, lending the eye a terrible aspect, setting the teeth, flaring the nostril, and so forth (3.1). This bestialization of his men is perfectly consistent, he apparently feels, with their being the "noblest English" pursuing a sacred cause: "God for Harry! England and Saint George!"

Harry keeps up the pretense of being God's soldier until the eve of Agincourt when he reveals his personal doubts about the sanctity of Ceremony and indeed of the legitimacy of his kingship. In doing so he distinguished himself from the naive Hotspurrian hero who rides joyfully to death spurred by a conviction of his own immortality, and from the wise Falstaffian who sends his ragamuffins to be peppered while he himself honors the instinct for self-preservation. Patriotism to be sure has fallen on hard times of late, but there it is: Hal is patriotic, *Henry V* is patriotic. By the conventions of the history play, God is English and England is God; and when this is so, chauvinism will convey the true believer to Arthur's immortal bosom as readily as piety. For Harry so holy a cause justifies some cunning, much ruthlessness, and a great deal of death—even his own if need be. Thus by stripping himself of the symbolic immortality of Ceremony he earns title to a crown that makes him a most suitable subject to be immortalized in a play like *Henry V.*

VII   Mortal Clothing in *Hamlet*

In the previous chapter I discussed how silks and satins can disguise the human body and endow us with a sense of greatness verging on immortality. But of course it is the clothing itself that is comparatively immortal. For though it may be of penetrable stuff, its wounds, like those of Milton's angels, close quickly. Not so the wounds within. No one was more conscious of this than Shakespeare, no one except Hamlet. So let me now make a sartorial study of the unhappy Dane with an eye to the way in which his apparel, inward as well as outward, proclaims the man in the approved Polonius fashion.

1. Readiness

Hamlet's terse expression "The readiness is all," uttered as he moves ill at heart toward the swordplay that will prove his death, has attracted less attention than Edgar's somewhat similar remark to Gloucester, "Ripeness is all," uttered as the blind old man moves ill at heart back into a life he does not care to live. Probably that is because *readiness* is not as semantically fruitful as *ripeness*. It has none of nature's richness and cyclicism about it, no sense of a plenitude poised for a corruptive fall. Its primary meaning is simply "a condition of preparedness," which is how Shakespeare employs it in at least twelve of its fifteen appearances in his works.

Ripeness is a condition at which fruits and flowers arrive by nature, but readiness is an achievement; one happens, the other is earned. Even the man who is ripe in wisdom seems simply by some inward principle of development to have grown wise. But you cannot be ready without having readied yourself, and in a significant sense Hamlet spends the entire play readying himself. But for what? The answer is by no means explicit in his speech on readiness. Having accepted the King's invitation to fence with Laertes, Hamlet awaits the match with "a kind of gaingiving" that prompts Horatio to say "I will forestall their repair hither, and say you are not fit." Hamlet, however, chooses to defy augury:

> There's a special providence in the fall of a sparrow. If it be now, 'tis not
> to come; if it be not to come, it will be now; if it be not now, yet it will

come. The readiness is all. Since no man has aught of what he leaves, what is it to leave betimes? Let be.

Hamlet's iterative style here, with its seven *its*, rivals that of Macbeth in his famous line "If it were done when 'tis done, then 'twere well / It were done quickly" (1.7). The indefiniteness of Macbeth's *it* conceals a frightful referent, an act of regicide that he will bring himself to commit but cannot at this point bear to name. Hamlet's *it*, on the other hand, might seem at first glance simply to refer to the fencing match with Laertes, the scheduling of which has been uncertain, and then perhaps to a more abstract kind of duel he cannot avoid. But finally his clauses thrust home their meaning, and both fencing match and duel turn into, what they will turn into, death.

In the monosyllabic context of this speech even *readiness* stands out, a word not naturally rich in meaning perhaps but clothed here with special significance by contrast to the plain, even denuded terms around it.

I call on these clothing metaphors because one meaning of readiness that easily escapes us is that of being properly attired. When the inhabitants of Macbeth's castle have been rousted from bed by the discovery of Duncan's body, it is in that sense that Macbeth says "Let's briefly put on manly readiness, / And meet in the hall together" (2.4). To put on manly readiness is not merely to don men's clothing or even armor but to assume as well a hardy warlike temper, some of that heartless inexorability which the Macbeths confuse with manliness throughout the play. Thus *readiness* is a term whose meanings can play between an outward clothing and an inward arming. Let us trace these meanings in *Hamlet*—first the outward, then the inward—to see how Shakespeare provides a dramatic context that amplifies the speech on readiness.

2. Outward Apparel

Clothing is a matter of some moment in *Hamlet*.[1] Much is made for instance of the fact that the Ghost comes in full armor, "so like the King / That was and is the question of these wars" (1.1.). The Ghost's militant appearance creates a link between it and young Fortinbras, who initiated "these wars" and who makes a martial entrance at the end of the play reminiscent of the Ghost's at the beginning.[2] There are of course many other random mentionings of clothes. Rosencrantz and Guildenstern admit that they are not "the very button [on] Fortune's cap" or on the other hand "the soles of her shoe." Perhaps "they live about her waist," Hamlet suggests (2.2). But if in courting Dame Fortune's favors they seek to unclothe her, she in turn undoes them, aided by Hamelt's rewritten death warrant and a headsman's axe.

Again, Polonius, divining that Hamlet's vows of love to Ophelia are "not of that dye which their investments show, / But mere implorators of unholy suits" (1.3.), forbids his daughter to speak to the Prince, and in doing so begins a process of estrangement that eventually ends when, as Gertrude reports, her

> garments, heavy with their drink,
> Pulled the poor wretch from her melodious lay
> To muddy death.   (4.7)

Unholy suits of words and thirsty clothing combine to pull the poor mad lady to her death. There is something more to this clothing than meets the eye.

So it seems in the Closet Scene when Hamlet exhorts his mother to "assume a virtue if [she] has it not."

> That monster *custom*, who all sense doth eat,
> Of *habits* devil, is angel yet in this,
> That to the use of actions fair and good
> He likewise gives a *frock* or *livery*
> That aptly is *put on*.   (3.4)

In this sartorial context, both *custom* (with a hint in it of the meaning that was later to become *costume*) and *habits* suggest that even behavior as superficially external as clothing can become ingrained through repetition: you can be how you dress. The trick is to observe a kind of moral decorum in which "actions fair and good" are habitually donned, rather like the decorum of acting which, as Hamlet explains to the players, dictates that they "suit the action to the word, the word to the action" without o'erstepping "the modesty of nature" (3.2). Actions suited to words, and both suited mimetically to nature, produce good plays and players; and in Gertrude's unlikely case, actions suited to virtues, even if only an "act," may with proper wear produce virtue itself. An outward readying may generate an inward readiness.

But it is Hamlet's readiness, not Gertrude's, that concerns us here. In the Nunnery Scene, Ophelia says that Hamlet was once "the glass of fashion and the mold of form, / The observed of all observers" (3.1). Indeed as this scene indicates—with Hamlet and Ophelia observing one another, and Polonius and Claudius observing both, and we as audience observing all— Hamlet is still the observed of all observers. However, his apparel has taken a turn for the worse since those happier times Ophelia speaks of. When we first see him in the Council Scene his "inky cloak" sets him off from the courtiers of Claudius, whose dress reflects the recent o'erhasty wedding more than it does the almost equally recent funeral. Hamlet further sets himself apart from them and especially Claudius by rejecting "seems," which is the prevailing mode of appearance at court. For himself he knows not "seems," though he knows it well enough in others. His own principle of conduct and dress—the two, we begin to see, are obverse and reverse of the same coin—is decorum, whereby "customary suits of solemn black" are in keeping with the blackness of genuine grief, even though Hamlet still has "that within which passeth show."

Meanwhile Polonius echoes Hamlet in sensibly advising the departing Laertes not to o'erstep either the modesty of nature or the capacity of his purse in choosing his wardrobe, "For the apparel oft proclaims the man" (1.3). Believing this to be so, Polonius thus readies himself to be taken in when Hamlet, thinking it meet "to put an antic disposition on" (2.5), puts it on first by appearing to Ophelia

> with his doublet all unbraced,
> No hat upon his head, his stockings fouled,
> Ungartered, and down-gyved to his ankle,
> Pale as his shirt. . . .   (2.1)

From this time forth Hamlet is clearly meant to dress, if not so wildly as this Malvolio-like apparition, at least in a manner indicative of madness—probably wearing a long and distinctive shirt of some sort, as a minor poet of the time reported.[3]

The next major mention of Hamlet's clothing is of his unclothing. Returning from his sea voyage he conveys to the King a cryptic letter in which he says "You shall know I am set naked on your kingdom" (4.7). "Naked!" Claudius exclaims in puzzlement. "Can you devise me?" But Laertes cannot: "I am lost in it, my lord." They might well think *naked* means, as it can mean, unaccompanied, destitute, and unarmed. But even these meanings point toward the word's common meaning, with its suggestion of that poor, bare, forked state of animal vulnerability of which Lear speaks. From this perspective Hamlet's experience at sea, which reduces him to nakedness, is an attenuated version of Lear's frantic divestitures on the heath. For antic prince as well as mad king, the reduction to nakedness is instinct with death and rebirth symbolism. And like Lear, who wanders about clad in nature's "weeds" until he falls asleep, and then awakes wearing "fresh garments" (4.4), Hamlet next appears in the graveyard dressed differently from when we last saw him. Probably he now wears the "sea-gown" of his ocean voyage, as William Poel and Harley Granville-Barker claimed.[4] If so, then as Maurice Charney says, "There is a new resoluteness and informality about this costume that makes a visual link with the dress of the pirate sailors in Act IV, Scene vi" — the scene in which the sailors bring to Horatio Hamlet's account of his boarding the pirate ship and subsequent capture.[5]

The point of Hamlet's wearing his sea-gown during the Graveyard Scene, or some other gear suited to sailing, is presumably to keep before the audience an image of the adventurous hero who risked his life in combat, in contrast to the irresolute self-doubter who earlier in the play was preoccupied with his own consciousness.[6] Anyhow, no longer cloaked in grief for a lost father or shirted in a "madness" that leads not to revenge but rather by indirections to further indirections, Hamlet appears in the apparel of action, a sartorial equivalent to the "manly readiness" put on by Macbeth and his fellow Scots. In outward appearance, at any rate, Hamlet seems ready for the climactic action of the play.

3. Inward Clothing

"Outward appearance," however, reminds us of Hamlet's speech in the Council Scene in which he inveighed against *seems* and *show* and concluded "But I have that within which passeth show; / These but the trappings and the suits of woe" (1.2). At this point neither clothing nor any other "shape of grief" can denote him truly or, by implication, can denote anyone else truly, especially Claudius and Gertrude, whose shows/shoes of mourning wore out before a month was up. Amid the outward play of signifiers in Claudian Denmark, true signifieds like regicide and incest are well hidden, not least in Hamlet himself, who can hide *son* within *sun* and whole soliloquies beneath the surface of Danish consciousness and his own antic disposition.

Hamlet's inward readiness and unreadiness are best measured verbally. Consider Osric. However Hamlet may be dressed in the final act, we can be sure it is not in the fashion of Osric, whose flourishes with his bonnet suggest that his body is as ostentatiously arrayed as his speech. The flamboyant coincidence of Osric's verbal and sartorial modes reflects the familiar Elizabethan metaphors about the "garment of style" and the "dress of speech." For instance when Puttenham starts to write about "Ornament" he unrolls an almost interminable epic simile to the effect that as grand ladies must not appear in court without their finery so "cannot our vulgar Poesie shew it selfe either gallant or gorgious, if any lymmes by left naked and bare and not clad in his kindly clothes and colours"—clad, that is, like Puttenham's own lines, in the appropriate figures of speech.[7]

In this connection we may recall that Hamlet's antic disposition is something he chose to "put on." This donning of the garb of madness is both visual and verbal. After his encounter with the Ghost, he doffs his "suits of solemn black" in favor of an antic dress, and at the same time (except in soliloquy when he is not "mad") he doffs the blank verse apparel of sanity in favor of an antic prose that is both arrayed in and disarrayed by puns, equivocations, metaphors, ironies, paradoxes, quibbles—all the "clothes and colours" seemingly natural to his unnatural state. However, on returning from his sea voyage he abandons this style of dress and speech as no longer suited to his purposes. Both his clothes and his language are readied for action, and for the death that will attend action.

This readying for death began with Hamlet's mention of self-slaughter in his first soliloquy and continued with his action-losing analysis of what it means "to be or not to be," his shipboard perusal of his death warrant, his graveyard meditations on pocky corses and skulls and the unroyal progresses of Alexander and Caesar through instead of over the earth. From death in the abstract ("not to be"), he has come to experience death in the concrete ("Here hung those lips that I have kissed"), from death as the entrance to an undiscovered country to death as the grave that gapes for Ophelia's body today and for his own tomorrow. In the graveyard, death takes on an earthy, even a wormy corporeal reality for Hamlet. Thus his *it* in the readiness speech, unlike Macbeth's, is not the shying away of a mind yet green in evil, an escape from daggers and spades into indefinition. His *it* is the verbal equivalent of Yorick's yellowed skull: the stark thing itself, all that remains when death has been stripped of its cosmetic vanities and its romantic horror. "Tell her, let her paint an inch thick." In its bleak irreducibility Hamlet's *it* resembles the word he uses when the Gravemaker holds aloft a skull and says "This same skull, sir, was Yorick's skull, the King's jester." Hamlet's reply is no more than a stunned "This?"—but of course everything is in that word from which everything has been removed. It seems altogether fitting that Hamlet's language should have a lean look to it in the graveyard where men themselves are stripped not merely of life but, under the ministration of My Lady Worm and that sore decayer water, of their fleshly apparel as well.[8]

The last words of Hamlet's readiness speech are "Let be," which of course mean more than "Do not interfere." Insofar as they represent an acquiescence to death, his words record his acceptance of *custom*, a word repeatedly associated in the play with *costume* and with death. Thus in the Council

Scene where he first uses the term—"Nor customary suits of solemn black"—his words emphasize the fact that, at least in Claudius's court, the costume that memorializes death is prescribed by mere custom and hence may be ill fitting indeed, a matter of "seems." Later, however, in the Closet Scene he admits that custom/costume may be more than superficial, not merely a matter of seems (seams?) but a molder of the body of behavior it covers, a proper frock and livery for actions good and fair. Finally, in the graveyard he discovers that the Gravemaker can sing at his work because, Horatio says, "custom hath made it a property of easiness in him."

Some of this property of easiness is conveyed to Hamlet during this scene. Ever since his mother asked "Why seems it so particular to thee?" he has made death increasingly particular. Now the indifference of the Gravemaker suggests to him that death is cut of common cloth. Shrouds and coffins fit lawyers, courtiers, politicians, my Lord Such-a-one, even the jovial Yorick, even the fair Ophelia. Men die, as Hegel said, as a matter of habit.

Hamlet's own "habit," his sea-cloak, with its suggestion of serviceability and action, is thus in accord with his verbal mode, stripped as it now is of soliloquy and antic dishabille and styled to direct and functional utterance. His parodies of the excesses of others—Laertes' graveside rant, the statists' Ciceronianism, Osric's rhetorical sawings of the air—sharply contrast to his own verbal restraint which culminates in the speech on readiness. For that entire passage is almost as barren as the *it* of whose little he makes so much. Its skeleton of plain sense is not dressed in figures; it sports none of Hamlet's puns even. Its repetition and antithesis seem in the service not so much of rhetoric as of a ruthless logic that systematically closes each of life's temporal gates. It is appropriate that such unadorned stoic simplicity should end with the words "Let be," because it itself so plainly "is."

4. The Fit of Death

In *Measure for Measure* Isabella says that by telling her condemned brother Claudio of the alternative to his execution, namely a loss of her own chastity, she will "fit his mind to death" (2.4.186). She soon discovers that as far as Claudio is concerned death in any form is unsuitable. Hamlet takes a somewhat similar view until late in his play when his language and his clothing jointly announce his readiness for what is to come. Unfortunately he is not alone in his readiness, for Claudius has most carefully prepared a final drama, a play of swords in which Hamlet is cast in a tragic part. At the same time Claudius has unwittingly fashioned a part for himself that he has the talent but not the desire to play. Let us go back a bit, however, to observe how Shakespeare himself makes ready for all of this.

Much earlier, in the Prayer Scene, Hamlet passed up an apparently perfect opportunity to kill the King because, thinking him deep in prayer, the justice or rather injustice of it displeased him:

> And am I then revenged,
> To take him in the purging of his soul
> When he is *fit* and seasoned for his passage?

Fit, like ready, has obvious sartorial implications. Fearing that the kneeling Claudius is spiritually ready for a journey that would nullify his revenge, Hamlet postpones his departure until a time when he will be fit for a less lofty destination. That time arrives when the preparations for the duel have been made and the King sends an anonymous Lord to Hamlet "to know if [his] pleasure hold to play with Laertes, or that [he] will take longer time" (5.2). Hamlet replies:

> I am constant to my purposes; they follow the King's pleasure. If his *fitness* speaks, mine is *ready*; now or whensoever, provided I be so able as now.

Hamlet speaks as though he were to duel with the King rather than fence with Laertes, and of course in a sense he is. At any rate his readiness is dependent on the King's fitness. If the King is at his pleasure, spiritually disarmed—if he is, as Hamlet said in the Prayer Scene, "about some act / That has no relish of salvation in it" (executing a plot of murder would seem to qualify)—then Hamlet is inwardly armed for what must be done. His readiness consists in a poised alertness that does not force opportunity but awaits it "now or whensoever," by contrast with Laertes' enraged charge for revenge on his return from France (4.5) and with Claudius's sly stirrings of poisonous plots.

This line of imagery continues when Horatio urges Hamlet not to fence if he has misgivings: "I will forestall their repair hither, and say you are not *fit*." But Hamlet insists. Earlier he had told the actors to prepare for their stage-play by saying "Go, make you ready" (3.2); now as he is about to perform his part in the sword-play, he has himself made ready in the tiring house of thought. That he is inwardly appareled for his role is confirmed by his speech, and is outwardly reflected also if, as seems likely in the heat of which Osric complains, he has removed his cloak, robe, or coat to fence more freely in shirt sleeves.

In a larger sense Hamlet's readiness involves a willingness to be clothed by the situation, to fit himself to circumstance. Until this last act the world has been unfit for him and he for it, and the friction between the two has chafed his mind. At the end, however, his discontent, his "irritable reaching after fact and reason," in Keats's words, has given way to that ability to abide amid uncertainties, mysteries, and doubts that Keats called negative capability. His experiences at sea and in the graveyard, where for a few violent moments with Laertes he wore Ophelia's grave as a shroud, have brought him to terms with death.

The first indication we have of this fitting of the mind to death comes shortly after Claudius receives Hamlet's cryptic message about arriving naked on his kingdom. Deciding that Hamlet must be killed, Claudius fumbles for a plan, and finds it in Hamlet's presumed envy of one of Laertes' "parts." Laertes asks "What part is that, my lord?" and Claudius couches his reply—that the envied part is Laertes' skill in fencing—in sartorial terms:

> A very riband in the cap of youth,
> Yet needful too, for youth no less becomes
> The light and careless livery that it wears
> Than settled age his sables and his weeds,
> Importing health and graveness. . . .
>
> (4.7)

The stress is clearly on suitability, on fit and fashion. And the epitome of the fashionable, Claudius goes on to say, is the visitor who spoke so highly of Laertes in Hamlet's presence—a master horseman who fit his mount to perfection. "A Norman was it?" Laertes asks, and when Claudius says it was indeed a Norman, Laertes exclaims "Upon my life, Lamord." "The very same," Claudius affirms.

This Norman cavalier Lamord is almost as mysterious as the messenger Claudio who helped convey Hamlet's letter to Claudius. Each has inspired much throwing about of brains.[9] As Harold Jenkins says,

> The apparent irrelevance of the horseman has led many to suspect a personal allusion. The favourite candidate is the cavalier mentioned in Castiglione's *Courtier* whose name, Pietro Monte, is rendered by Hoby (Tudor Trans., p. 58) as Peter Mount (cf. F *Lamound*). Dowden connects Q2 *Lamord* with Fr. *mords*, a horse's bit. But if we suppose some purposeful association in the name (and why, otherwise, should it be given at all?), will it not suggest La Mort?[10]

Will it not indeed? Especially when Laertes' line of recognition, "Upon my

life, Lamord," seems deliberately designed to play off life against death.
And is there not a suggestion, then, that Hamlet's envy of Laertes is inspired
by or associated with this cavalier of death, the recollection of whom inspires
in Claudius the plot that will result in Hamlet's death? Death comes to
Elsinore and particularly to Hamlet not in a cape of solemn black, an alien
figure, but as "the brooch indeed / And gem of all the nation," as Laertes
says of Lamord—indeed, it seems, the observed of all observers. At any
rate, something in Hamlet quickens to the words of this masterful dandy
La Mort, so that it is no surprise that Hamlet's own passage toward death
leads from Lamord through the graveyard to the swordplay that Claudius
says is such fashionable livery for young men.

Being ready for death, dressed for the fatal appointment, entails being
equipped also for life—"Upon my life, Lamord"—for the kind of life in
which even death answers to a higher concept of fitness. If Hamlet is ready
for his role in the King's play of swords, he is also ready for his role in the
play of Providence, in which all men play a part and even sparrows suffer
their brief tragic falls.[11]

Thus readied, Hamlet awaits his cue to act. When it comes, he improvises
a death that is fit for Claudius. Indeed he fashions not one death but two,
patterning his acts on those of the King. If Claudius has made a fatal thrust
at Hamlet with the blade of Laertes, then Hamlet must deliver an equally
fatal riposte with the sword poisoned by Laertes. Because the poison on
the bated blade yields "not half an hour's life," as Hamlet is told, his second
killing of Claudius is pragmatically superfluous. But in symbolic terms, as
part of the decorum of revenge, which requires re-venge to be suited to
venge, it is the fit fulfillment of Hamlet's vow to avenge his father's death;
the leprous distillment poured by Claudius into the ears of old Hamlet flows
into the stoup of wine that he himself is forced to drink. For these deaths
the King's "fitness speaks," and for the King's offenses Hamlet's revenges
are most ready.

In this context of inner and outer attire, it is appropriate that when he
comes to speak of Hamlet's story Horatio will speak, he says, "Of deaths
put on by cunning and forced cause." Death too, it seems, may be worn;
and we can be sure that whether suitable or not it is always in fashion.
Death, then, is the final dark clothing of Hamlet's life, the mortal habit for
which he has been readying himself throughout the play. Invested thus,
his body carried aloft by the four captains to the "stage," he is again, if not
the glass of fashion and the mold of form, at least (like La Mort) the observed
of all observers, as he continues to be.

VIII Immortal Money in
The Merchant of Venice

1. Gold and the Devil

Since death is a costly way to purchase immortality, the truly rich—men like Timon and Shylock—prefer to pay in gold. Gold is the god men worship, and the Exchange is their church. If, as this implies, the contents of your purse are sacred stuff, then all you need do is to put money in it again and again, as Iago advises Roderigo, and you can purchase the secular equivalent of immortality in Venice, the divine Desdemona.

In *Twelfth Night* Feste fools with the divinity of money when he amuses Duke Orsino by making gold migrate from the Duke's pockets to his own:

DUKE.   Thou shalt not be the worse for me. There's gold.
CLOWN. But that it would be double-dealing, sir, I would you
        could make it another.
DUKE.   O, you give me ill counsel.
CLOWN. Put your grace in your pocket, sir, for this once, and
        let your flesh and blood obey it.
DUKE.   Well, I will be so much a sinner, to be a double-dealer.
        There's another.   (5.1)

And of course Feste tries for a third but is put off. Here, then, we find religious and aristocratic grace played off against the sinful flesh and its hankerings after gold. Feste's "put your grace in your pocket" means for his Grace to put his hand in his pocket but also for his ethereal "grace" to disappear and for gold to materialize in its stead. In the religion of aristocracy practiced by dukes like Orsino, divine grace quite naturally incarnates itself in the shape of *his* Grace; but in Feste's religion of postlapsarian flesh and blood it should descend one step further and become coins for clowns.

Feste's substitution of gold coins for grace forecasts Timon's labeling gold a "visible god" (5.2). According to Kenneth Burke, gold and money have an air of divinity about them because they substitute for God as a common denominator of human motives. A common deistic faith once dissolved cultural and international differences: God represented "the universal substance in which all human diversity of motives was grounded."[1] Money can compete with such a faith because it too serves "as a universal symbol, the unitary ground for all action." Antonio and Shylock can scarcely speak to each other across the barrier dividing Christian from Jew, but one is a merchant and the other a usurer, and so for both of them money talks.

But according to Luther it talks with a diabolic accent. For him, money does not substitute for God directly; the Devil does that. Money is simply the medium of the Devil, and capitalism is his creation. "Money," Luther declares, "is the word of the Devil through which he creates all things, the way God created through the true word." If gold is a visible god, then the god is not God but the Devil; and he who worships gold worships the Devil: "usury lives securely and rages, as if he were God and lord in all lands. . . . There is therefore no worse enemy of mankind on earth, next to the Devil himself, than the covetous man and the usurer, for he wishes to become God over all men."[2] Covetous men like Shylock are bound by money into the Devil's cult. But then most economies are bound together by money; certainly that of Venice is. Business activities like buying and selling, loaning and borrowing bring men together as members of a common society, even if only for the duration of a contract. However appalling the bond between Antonio and Shylock, it does bind them despite their hatred, just as their common language binds them even when they use it to "trade" insults.

In fact one might argue that precisely because he lends money for interest, Shylock is more bound into Venetian society than the Christian Antonio, who lends money gratis and conducts his trade abroad. For the same reason, the philanthropic Timon is as alienated from Athenian society as the misanthropic Timon he later becomes. He does not loan but gives money, and in the spirit of Aristotelian magnanimity he espouses pure giving with no expectation of repayment. This idealistic one-way practice militates against "bonds," the essential feature of which is reciprocation. Thus when Timon's money runs out and he looks to his friends for relief, he makes the unhappy discovery that pure giving creates pure receiving—receiving devoid of a sense of moral indebtedness—and this discovery sends him into the wilderness where he digs up gold and identifies it as a visible god, a god that cannot "redeem" or atone mankind but can circulate the diseases that will bind men in their common mortality.

In *The Merchant of Venice* at any rate, money binds not merely the devilish Jews into a tribe but the Christians as well. Antonio's unholy bond to Shylock must be honored because the law will have it so; but the law itself is bound to higher masters, as even Antonio acknowledges:

> The Duke cannot deny the course of law;
> For the commodity that strangers have

> With us in Venice, if it be denied,
> Will much impeach the justice of the state,
> Since that the trade and profit of the city
> Consisteth of all nations.   (3.3)

With trade and profit enthroned over all, the boundaries between Christian and Jew begin to blur, and Luther's fears about the threat of capitalism to religion appear to have some basis, at least in Venice where Christianity seems little more than a social shibboleth. Where, after all, are the other magnanimous Christian merchants when Bassanio goes forth to "try what [Antonio's] credit can in Venice do"? Of course Shakespeare has got to get Antonio indebted to Shylock, but he does not even trouble to suggest a reason for Bassanio's failure to try the Christians first. Ducats are ducats; they weigh as much in the Jew's pocket as in the Christian's.

Because money binds men in such unholy alliances, capitalism for Luther is a thoroughly devilish business. And devilish business is for him fecal business. As Norman O. Brown says, "the anal character of the Devil is sensuously perceived and sensuously recorded by Luther (in his *Table-Talk*) with a gross concreteness that latter-day Protestantism cannot imagine and would not tolerate."[3] Let us forgo the illustrations and merely agree that from Luther's point of view money is both fecal and devilish. As such it becomes, like the Devil, the visible god of a degraded materialistic world.

This Lutheran equation, though often endorsed by psychoanalysts, does not appear in Shakespeare, so far as I can tell, except on one significant occasion in *King Lear*.[4] Instead Shakespeare seems to side with those who argue that money represents a reaction formation to the unfortunate presence of feces in humans. Norman O. Brown and Ernest Becker, for instance, say that "money is god" because it "negotiates immortality" —because it symbolizes, not feces, but "the denial of feces" and what it represents, "physicalness, animality, decay, and death."[5] In other words, if the body in its material repellence betrays us to death, and if the most repellent feature of the body is feces, then one way to transcend both is to accumulate gold and buy our way to greatness.[6] The compulsion to deny death and the body acts as a philosopher's stone to transmute base feces into the gold that can purchase immortality.

Money is especially conducive to these high-flying aspirations because it generates disembodied desire. That is, purely bodily needs can be satisfied, at least temporarily. We can eat and drink our fill, engage in sex, sleep, get warm or cool off. But the desire for money compounds like interest itself, more begetting more.[7] Like the mystic yearning for the City of God with its streets paved with spiritual gold, the capitalist dreams of an El

Dorado forever situated just beyond the horizon. If we run a little faster, work a little harder, get a little luckier, then grace will come to us as it does to Feste. But, alas, we can never get our fill of the sacred stuff. The insatiate trafficker in gold, Luther complained, will not content himself until he has become "God over all men." And to become a god is to become immortal. Let the Dow-Jones average rise just one more point and I can buy all the indulgences I will need for the sin of possessing an animal body.

One great virtue of money as a means of denying death is, as Timon noted, its visibility. As an external recognizable sign for elusive internal qualities, it quantifies our worth, for our own benefit as well as for others. Terms of value like *value, dearness, worth, price, estimate, wealth,* and so on are indispensable, but even they lack the measurable precision of money, which can tell me to the penny how much more I am worth than Jones and how much I need to catch up to Smith. In this respect money has the additional virtue of being hierarchically ordered, ranging upward from pennies to crowns and sovereigns, and therefore reflects and reinforces the hierarchical gradations and degrees in the socioeconomic chain of being.[8] A penny will make you a pauper, but crowns may make you a queen; at least they will buy you country estates and servants and all the livery of wealth. Which is to say that in the immortality market God, being invisible, finds it hard to compete with the devilishly visible god whose pockets jingle with sovereigns and crowns and nobles by the score. Divine signifieds are merely so much celestial vapor without signifiers of highly visible substance. It is names, icons, churches, and rituals that keep the pews full. And that means dealing in the Devil's coin. For great cathedrals betoken not only great spiritual worth but also lots of tithes. So too with people. Who can spot a Joan of Arc, an Albert Schweitzer, or a Martin Luther King on the boulevard? and who can miss Midas, the Aga Khan, or a Rajneesh with his ninety Rolls Royces? For that matter who can miss Portia, the wealthy heiress of Belmont?

2. Midas and Portia

Before turning to Portia, let us take a look at Midas, the very symbol and personification of wealth. He came by his golden touch by doing Dionysus a service and getting his choice of a reward. In choosing gold it is as though he said to Dionysus "If you can't immortalize me as a god, do the next best thing: make me the richest of men." But Midas's fate reveals that an obsession with symbolic immortality may lead to the very death it seeks to transcend. Men deny their bodily nature at their peril, as Ovid makes clear when he tells us how Midas's pleasures take a painful turn:

> Then whither his hand did towch the bread, the bread was massy gold,
> Or whither he chawde with hungry teeth his meate, yee might behold
> The peece of meate betweene his jawes a plate of gold too bee.[9]

The attempt to satisfy the spirit, it appears, is inimical to the satisfaction of the body; if the soul surfeits, the belly must fast. This is evidenced by the fact that the distinction between Midas's own body and spirit is paralleled by that between gold as metal and gold as money. For in his hunger for the symbolic value of gold, its sacred power, Midas unwisely ignores its material nature. His fate foretells the fate of all immortality projects: a demystifying return to the body and death.

To elaborate: the Midas story illuminates as I say the difference between gold and silver metals and gold and silver money. The metals in themselves are as useless as dog's teeth, beads, shells, currency, cheques, and so forth. "In money," Marx says, "the value of the things is separated from their substance."[10] Of course as malleable metals gold and silver can be transformed into artifacts, but even then they exist primarily as works of art, better for disinterested contemplation than for hard service over time. The wise king will use gold for his crown, not for his helmet, and silver for his scepter, not for his sword. And the wise suitor for Portia's hand in *The Merchant of Venice* will distinguish between Portia's symbolic commercial value as a woman of wealth and her human value as a woman of beauty and virtue — the kind of distinction she herself makes in assuring the Prince of Morocco that his black exterior is irrelevant to his inner worth (2.1).

Portia's first two suitors should have taken instruction from Portia and Marx, because in choosing the gold and silver caskets they both misvalue the lady and misunderstand money. If gold and silver are to graduate from useless metal to precious money, they must be assigned an arbitrary value, and in this play that suggests a kind of lie or presumptuous superficiality of which the precious metals are guilty and lead is innocent. Lead is a good honest metal; it takes on no glittering airs but appears as plain and valueless as in fact it is. It is therefore an appropriate stand-in for the virtuous Portia, who exhibits a leadlike maidenly modesty in saying "You see me, Lord Bassanio, where I stand, / Such as I am" (3.2).

Thus before Bassanio rejects the gold and silver caskets he muses at some length about false appearances and true realities, and exhibits an awareness of the distinctions Midas could not grasp. In fact, he turns from the golden casket murmuring "gaudy gold, / Hard food for Midas, I will none of thee"

(3.2). He chooses metal instead of money, material object instead of symbol, and Portia such as she is instead of Portia as she appears in the eyes of the avaricious world. In doing so he escapes the "carrion Death" that lies within the gold casket (2.7).

Bassanio's conception of human worth runs counter to that of Shylock. Later when Bassanio proposes that Shylock loan Antonio a thousand ducats, the noncommittal Jew observes that Antonio is "a good man" (1.3). Bassanio replies haughtily "Have you heard any imputation to the contrary?" and Shylock hastily corrects him: "Ho, no, no, no, no! my meaning in saying he is a good man is to have you understand me that he is sufficient" (1.3). For the usurer it is not moral worth but collateral that counts. Besides, what evidence has the Jew had of Antonio's moral or simply human goodness? Antonio's mode of valuation is no more attractive. "Many a time," Shylock says, "and oft / In the Rialto you have *rated* me" (2.1). "You call me misbeliever, cut-throat dog, / And spit upon my gaberdine," and Antonio replies that he is like to do so again if the opportunity presents itself (1.3). The "dog" epithet makes it clear that Antonio's sense of his own personal worth derives largely from the superiority of the "human" Christian to the "animal" Jew and, as he (and everyone else) says again and again, to the "devil" Jew. From the perspective of the Christians Shylock more than qualifies as Luther's diabolical money god seeking to rule over a manure-heap world.

3. Denying Death by Choosing Death

Let me pause at this point and return briefly to the "Theme of the Three Caskets." In an article of this title,[11] Freud argues that because dumbness often represents death in myth and psychoanalysis the plain speechlessness of the lead casket, which Bassanio says "doth move me more than eloquence," associates it with death. This view is somewhat misleading because the play specifically associates the gold casket with death when Morocco opens it and discovers a skull within—"O hell! What have we here? / A carrion Death" (2.7). Still, Freud's instincts are right. Actually all three caskets can be said to represent potential death, even the lead one. Caskets, after all, are caskets—i.e., coffinlike—and Portia tells Bassanio "I am locked in one of them" in the form of a picture that is her "shadow." Moreover, for Bassanio to "give and hazard all he hath" on the lead casket clearly implies a willingness to risk his life. In making such a choice, Freud suggests, Bassanio "chooses" death and transcends it at the same time, for to choose potential death is to reverse the natural scheme of things in which

death chooses us. Bassanio's choice represents the ultimate in wish fulfillment, an occasion on which we triumph over our mortal victimage and
transform death into Portia—into life and love, not to mention a substantial
dowry.

In any event, as Bassanio gathers himself for the choice, both he and
Portia insist that they are liminally poised between death and life. Let me
choose quickly, he says, "for as I am, I live upon the rack"; and Portia
declares "I stand for sacrifice" and hopes that Bassanio can rescue her from
imminent death as Alcides did Hesione when she stood for sacrifice before
the sea monster. "Live thou, I live," she says, as though he, and she as well,
confronted death. Of course Christians have always maintained that the
way to everlasting life is by choosing death, by dying to the world. Bassanio
and Portia do not risk death to attain eternal life but to attain the symbolic
immortality offered by a love that conquers death—or, in this trade-domi-
nated play, a love that bargains with death and wins life.

4. Portia as Apportioner

In a recent article on *The Merchant of Venice* Lars Engle perceptively
notes that Portia's name implies the "portion" brought to her marriage by
an Elizabethan bride, a portion that Bassanio can employ to relieve his
debts.[12] This certainly helps account for what Portia *is*, a prize. I wonder if
a supplement to this symbolism might also help account for what she *does*.
I have in mind the fact that the Greek concept of fate, Moira, is expressed
in terms which imply that human lives are alloted, shared out, or, in our
present context, apportioned. Clotho (the spinner), Lachesis (the apportioner), and Atropos (the inflexible) combine to distribute shares of life to
humans as though they were dividing the spoils of a victory or portioning
out food for a meal. It is not we who choose our lots but the Moirai who
assign them to us.[13] That Shakespeare may have had this or a similar notion
in mind is suggested when Portia associates *lot* and *destiny* in telling Morocco

> In terms of choice I am not solely led
> By nice direction of a maiden's eyes;
> Besides, the *lott'ry of my destiny*
> Bars me the right of voluntary choosing.
> (1.3)

Although Shakespeare probably did not have the Moirai in mind, Tyche (or
Ananke), the mother of the Moirai, is equivalent in Roman religion to For-

tuna, a goddess Shakespeare was quite familiar with and likely to associate with this lottery of life and life's goods.

If we think of Portia as being not only a portion in her own right but also an apportioner, then she would appear to fulfill her destiny by insisting on a strict accounting of the portion of Antonio due Shylock:

> If thou tak'st more
> Or less than a just pound, be it but so much
> As makes it light or heavy in the substance
> Or the division of the twentieth part
> Of one poor scruple, nay, if the scale do turn
> But in the estimation of a hair,
> Thou diest, and all thy goods are confiscate.
>
> (4.1)

Shylock's lot—his life and all his goods—depends on his taking no more than his just share of Antonio's flesh; and needless to say, Antonio's lot hangs in the same balance, in the scales of Fortune.

Fortune unfortunately is fickle and unfair. She spins out more life from her wheel of fortune to some than to others, and pours forth more goods, health, and happiness from her cornucopia of plenty to some than to others. Because of these discrepancies in physical, social, economic, and mortal status, some men envy others, and the others are often apprehensive of being envied. It is part of the business of culture to foster systems of belief that will reduce envy or justify it and hence reconcile men to their unequal lots—by creating, for instance, myths that make goddesses like Tyche and Fortuna responsible for the discrepancies, or by calling on the spurious analogies of social Darwinism to legitimize having and not-having as the inevitable consequences of natural selection.[14]

Surely the envy generated by inequality plays a powerful role in *The Merchant of Venice*. In an Iago-like speech Shylock says he cannot or will not explain his insistence on his bond—

> So can I give no reason, nor I will not,
> More than a lodged hate and a certain loathing
> I bear Antonio.   (4.1)

That tells us next to nothing. Gratiano seems closer to the mark when he observes Shylock whetting his knife:

> Not on thy sole, but on thy soul, harsh Jew,
> Thou mak'st thy knife keen; but no metal can,

> No, not the hangman's axe, bear half the keenness
> Of thy sharp envy.   (4.1)

Helmut Schoeck points out that no society seems immune to envy, certainly no Western one, and yet envy is almost always repressed as a motive.

> It is remarkable how seldom the vernacular forms of different languages permit one to say directly to another person: "Don't do that. It will make me envious!" Instead, we tend to talk in abstract terms of justice, saying that something or other is intolerable or unfair, or we relapse into sour and bitter silence.[15]

That seems an apt description of Shylock, who prefers to cite an unmotivated hatred and loathing than to admit that he envies the Christian merchant whose lot in Venice is so much more fortunate than his own.

Might this not have some bearing on Antonio's mysterious sadness? The ethic of the New Testament is designed to protect Christians against the envy and hostility built up by social and economic inequalities. It insists that we should love our neighbor as ourself, expunging all envy, that in the eyes of God we are all spiritual equals, that the poor inherit the earth while the rich are stuck like camels in the eye of the needle, and so on. But because even Christian societies retain discrepancies in status, particularly those as devoted to commerce as Venice, the handsome, the brilliant, the powerful, and perhaps especially the wealthy must be made to carry a burden of guilt for being so favored by Fortune. If you envy me, it is my fault, not yours. If I am greatly fortunate, then I am greatly at fault. Everyone I pass who is less fortunate than I stares back at me with the evil eye. They hate and revile me. I must do something to ward off the evil eye, to rid myself of guilt, to atone for my being so favored. "Guilt-engendered activity," writes the psychoanalyst Gerhart Piers, "is at best *restitution* (sacrifice, propitiation, atonement) which rarely frees, but brings with it resentment and frustration rage, which in turn feed new guilt into the system."[16]

Perhaps Antonio's unaccountable sadness is a symbolic product of Shylock's unaccountable hatred and loathing, his secret envy. If so, if Antonio feels mysteriously guilty, then he is by the logic of metaphor in debt. This metaphorical debt owed the despised Jew by the Christian is as it were taken literally by Shakespeare, who quickly converts it into monetary debt and then bodily debt. It would be in keeping with such a view that when his bond falls due Antonio accepts its consequences with resignation and patience, as though some part of him welcomes the opportunity to pay the debt and hence to atone for his criminal superiority. Having had more than his fair share of Fortune's gifts, he yields to the Jew who will gladly take more than his fair share of vengeance. Only Balthazar the apportioner can rescue him by pointing out that the law of Venice measures the financial transactions of its citizens with scrupulous exactitude, however unequally their lots in life may weigh in Fortuna's scales.

5. Metaphoric Trade

As Sigurd Burckhardt first observed, the patriarchal "law" that governs Portia in Belmont is as harsh as the (equally patriarchal) law that governs Antonio in Venice.[17] Both laws appear to prescribe death, Venetian law literally, Belmontian law figuratively; both, properly interpreted, make apparent death yield life; and both are subordinate to a higher law, Trade. As Antonio's lines quoted above indicate, the law in Venice must be upheld for the sake of Venetian trade. By the same token, the paternal law in Belmont must be upheld for the sake of a marital and sexual trade—vows and bodies—that is also grounded in money (Portia's) and debt (Bassanio's). Both laws, in other words, must function in such a manner as to promote exchanges, whether of money, goods, or love.

Thus despite the differences between Belmont and Venice the two laws are metaphorically interchangeable. Which suggests that if money is the principal medium of exchange in Venice, metaphor is the principal medium of exchange in Shakespeare's play. As such, metaphor closes gaps and dissolves differences. Metaphor is Shakespeare's money.

Who for instance could be more different and antagonistic than Antonio and Shylock? Yet Shakespeare takes pains to dissolve the differences between the two men. Each invests his immortality overtly in his religion—where else should immortality come from?—and yet as we have seen their common god is money. After all, Antonio expects from his oceanic ventures a "return / Of thrice three times the value of this bond" (1.3). And the point of his accumulating these sacred ducats is to deny death and the body. Hence by substituting a pound of flesh for ducats, Shylock demystifies the money god, demonstrating just what it is that the money they share and the religions they do not share repress and transcend. That is part of the driving force behind Shylock's most famous speech:

> I am a Jew. Hath not a Jew eyes? Hath not a Jew hands, organs, dimensions, senses, affections, passions; fed with the same food, hurt with the same weapons, subject to the same diseases, healed by the same means, warmed and cooled by the same winter and summer, as a Christian is? (3.1)

As Shylock has demonstrated, the religious differences between Jew and Christian are bridged not only by money, their shared immortality symbol, but also by the body, their shared mortality symbol. No wonder Shylock can make money and flesh interchangeable, substituting the one for the other in his bond with Antonio. And no wonder Portia-as-Balthazar asks on entering the courtroom "Which is the merchant here, and which the Jew?" (4.1). Like Portia's erring suitors, the two financial venturers are mis-led by the glitter of religious and social symbolism into regarding one another merely as stereotypes of those hateful abstractions, the Christian and the Jew, when the symbolism of the play itself suggests that they should present themselves to one another as Portia presents herself to Bassanio: "You see me . . . where I stand, / Such as I am."

But Shakespeare is not so naive as to think the Jew and the Christian can divest themselves of their culture. That sort of thing is proper to Belmont and romance, not to Venice and materialism. Hence the abstract money dealings of the two men devolve into a murderous bodily bond, just as Midas's greed for sacred power led back toward death. Even more obviously than, say, honor or patriotism or kingship, money is exposed as a form of false immortality, the god that always fails. And yet in *The Merchant of Venice* money metaphorically points the way to what Shakespeare regards as a true or at least a more humanly satisfying immortality. It is a matter of breeding.

As Shakespeare presents it, the artificial symbolic value that converts gold from metal to money is a kind of interest or "use." As Aristotle said, as the laws against usury said, and as Antonio says, gold and silver, like lead, are "barren metal" (1.3).[18] On being converted into money, however, they acquire a capacity to breed and multiply: money makes money whether through usury or mere trade. By that account Portia's wealth, her symbolic value, is an inherited product of her father's use of money to make money. But it is just that kind of use that the casket scheme rejects. Of the three equally barren metals Bassanio chooses the one that modestly presents itself as it is, and thus he wins Portia as she is. But as she is, apart from her wealth, Portia, far from being barren, derives her greatest value from her natural ability to breed. Not to breed money, like Shylock's "use," but off-spring, like Laban's "ewes." Such as it is, the human solution to death is for Bassanio and Portia to "get the ring upon [Bassanio's] finger that never will come off," as the phallic riddle in *All's Well* puts it, and to show "a child begotten of [Portia's] body" (3.2).

Thus as Marc Shell has shown,[19] the procreativity of Belmont stands in opposition to the barrenness of Venice, where the mysteriously sad Antonio is by his own denomination a "tainted wether" (4.1)—i.e., castrated ram—

and where Shylock metaphorically suffers the same fate when Jessica makes off with his money, including "two sealed bags of ducats / Of double ducats . . . / And jewels—two stones, two rich and precious stones" (2.5). Bereft of his "two stones"—the "family jewels," as the familiar pun aptly puts it—Shylock, like Antonio, is gelded and reduced to the human equivalent of barren metal. Money and the body are metaphors for one another in this play, but to take the metaphor literally, as Shylock does, is to take a great risk. For in losing ducats and jewels he also loses both his body's ability to increase (the stones) and indeed his body's increase (Jessica herself). As a result the infertility represented by his and Antonio's commercialism points to the fertilities of Belmont as a truer medium of immortality.

At the same time we have to admit that Shylock is not entirely barren. Unlike Antonio he has married Leah, he has begotten Jessica, he makes money breed money, and he makes language breed meanings. The essence of his verbal style is metaphor, the medium through which words and meanings are exchanged. The fact that his metaphors beget most of the truly eloquent speeches in the play suggests that we should not dismiss him or his values out of hand, for he may tell us something about Shakespeare's sense of verbal value in this play.

For words, after all, are Shakespeare's money. Like Portia's wealth they are as good in Venice as in Belmont, as "sufficient" as Antonio's collateral, as binding as Shylock's bond, as all-governing as the will of Portia's father or the law of Venice. Words are not only Shakespeare's money but his bonding agent, and metaphor is his special medium of exchange. By virtue of the playwright's penchant for metaphoric trading, money, the body, guilt and innocence, religion, law, and sexuality circulate here and there throughout *The Merchant of Venice*, assembling all of the play's different themes in the marketplace of art.

Before Bassanio chooses the lead casket he launches into a long speech repudiating the silver and gold caskets for their deceptiveness. They are ornamental, superficial, and dangerously seductive—the visual equivalent to the gilded Cicernonian style of Shakespeare's day. The equivalent, indeed, to Shakespeare's own style in a play like *Love's Labour's Lost*: self-consciously playful, verbose, full of fire-new sesquipedelian phrases and sentences that turn obediently inside-out like cheveril gloves. Unfortunately for the scholars, such a style proves "use-less" inasmuch as it fails to generate a bond, a "world-without-end bargain" between them and the French ladies. Therefore, in penance Berowne vowed to tailor his language more simply in the future, discarding "taffeta phrases [and] silken term precise" in favor of "russet yeas and honest kersey noes."

In *The Merchant of Venice* Shakespeare makes good as it were on Berowne's promise. Like Bassanio he chooses the lead casket and the plain style. Not of course that he now writes a leaden style or one in which words are as literally exact as those of the Venetian law, but that he employs the plain style procreatively, to multiply meanings, to promote metaphoric trading, to create finer verbal bonds. Even the lead casket, after all, is not just barren metal but a visual metaphor for sincerity, honesty, and modesty—and, as I am arguing, for a literary style that embodies these qualities. If it illustrates the Puritan precept that "every man," as Stephen Gosson claimed, "must show him selfe outwardly to be such as in deed he is,"[20] still it also violates that precept by being figurative, by being more than it appears to be. In this respect the lead casket, the metallic parallel to Portia's modest virtues, forecasts her later figuration, or transfiguration, of herself as Balthazar. That is, if we think of Balthazar as the vehicle of a metaphor whose tenor is Portia, and think of this exchange of identity as part of a geographical metaphor in which her journey to rescue Antonio carries the meaning of Belmont to the signifier Venice, then it is by means of these metaphoric exchanges that the two otherwise discrete worlds of Shakespeare's play are beneficently bound together.[21]

Because of its network of metaphors, then, *The Merchant of Venice* brings about marriages not merely among its characters but among its own parts. The result is a denial of artistic death analogous to the denial of actual death by the marriages of the lovers. We can phrase it in ringlike terms. Portia rebukes Bassanio for losing the ring which was "a thing stuck on with oaths upon your finger, / And so riveted with faith unto your flesh" (5.1). The faithful riveting of flesh to ring bawdily metaphorizes the sexual fidelity of husband and wife. To give the ring to another, as Bassanio does, is to become guilty of wantonness. Thus Portia-as-Balthazar performs a ring trick analogous to the bed tricks performed in *Measure for Measure* and *All's Well* later. When the rings are revealed to be in the proper feminine keeping, and go back on the proper masculine fingers, the jeopardized bond is sealed. The promiscuity of Venice is thus redeemed by the chastity of Belmont.

Inasmuch as the ring represents the womb, it is a source of life. From such a ring Bassanio and Portia will take new life in the form of the children in whose veins their blood runs. From such metaphors Shakespeare's play takes new life also. If Venice is redeemed by Belmont, the lovers will be redeemed by children. Children are the "use" of sex, the interest earned by a faithful keeping of the marital bond. This multiplication of meaning is likewise the interest earned by Shakespeare's richly metaphoric but more than ornamental use of language. Bodies breed like ewes, ewes breed like interest, interest breeds like metaphor, and metaphor breeds like bodies. Such circular exchanges of meaning bond *The Merchant of Venice* into a ringlike shape, a magic circle enclosing a wealth of meaning, and capable of keeping such envious devils as time and death outside its circumference.

Part 2
Tragedy and Death

IX Tragedy and the
Denial of Death 1

1. Tragedy, Comedy, and Immortality

Tragedy is not the genre in which we would expect to find death denied very effectively. Nor is it. Still, one could argue that the denial of death is central to the form of both tragedy and comedy. If we start with the notion of man the self-conscious animal—the creature that alone knows it has a body, and knows therefore that it will die—we can sketch out some rudimentary distinctions between the two genres. For the consciousness of one's body can be either comic or tragic. The mind may think, like Satan's, that it is its own place and can make a heaven or hell at will, but it ultimately collides with the body that encases it, and then it can either laugh or cry. In tragedy it cries, having discovered like Swift's unfortunate philosopher that while your eyes are on the stars you may be seduced by your lower parts into a ditch. The Greek version of this dangerously narcissistic star-gazing, the *hubris* of the tragic hero, is not merely the insolence that attends power and status but also the spiritual obtuseness of those who can no longer distinguish themselves from gods—that is, of those who have become oblivious to their bodies and hence to death. Oedipus goes blithely on his way, proud of his riddle-solving intellect and unconscious of his limping foot. Compelled at last to glance down and acknowledge the bodily truth, he weeps blood. By the time Prometheus learns a similar truth he has become bait for vultures. What Aristotle calls *anagnorisis* is most fundamentally a recognition of creaturely death, whether it is Pentheus torn apart in the forest or Ibsen's Master Builder plunging into the rock quarry. And somewhere behind all these deaths and recognitions, the ritualists tell us, is the tragedy of the Year-Daemon that arrives in the spring, waxes great with vegetative life, commits the sin of *hubris*—believing the grain and grapes he lives in will grow forever—and then is slain at the harvest.

Comedy sublimates the tragic vision; in it the collision of soul with body is less a reminder of mortality than a source of laughter. In comedy man is immortal by convention. Comic characters are often on the verge of death, and some of Shakespeare's heroines may even seem dead, but in the end they will all be rescued or resuscitated by their life-nourishing genre. Because comedy celebrates the communal, and because the community survives, comic man survives along with it. This accords with the fact that the social order is normally a fortress against death, a place where the naked individual puts on cultural armor. Or, more accurately, it is a sanctuary from death, a religious place where the individual, guilty of being alone and vulnerable, is baptized in the sacred pool of immortality. If I am weak and afraid and conscious of being a short-lived creature—that is, if I am human—I find salvation from death in becoming part of a grand and enduring communal project. When I kneel within the nave of society's great church, how could lightning ever strike me? That is how the alienated lovers in *A Midsummer Night's Dream* must feel when they return from the confusions of the forest to orderly Athens and merge their marriages with that of Duke Theseus, the high priest of reason.

But if the social order loses contact with the sacred, then my immortality is threatened, and I shrivel spiritually, as primitives do when the gods seem no longer to champion them. This is the point at which many of Shakespeare's comedies begin, with a societal church presided over by dying priests. In *All's Well*, for instance, the older generation is either already dead, like Helena's and Bertram's fathers, or dying, like the King and the Countess. The King puts it well when he says of Bertram's father and himself: "But on us both did haggish age steal on / And wore us out of act" (1.2). Other comic characters are also for one reason or another worn out of act when their plays begin. The scholars of Navarre have died to the world by virtue of their academic sequestration; the aging and isolated Prospero is dead to Milan; Olivia in *Twelfth Night* is deep in mourning for her brother (and "care," Sir Toby says is "an enemy to life" [1.3]); and Portia's father is dead but still governing in Belmont, while Antonio is a "tainted wether," his life in jeopardy. Even the Vienna of *Measure for Measure* is "worn out of [the procreative] act" by virtue of being too much worn *into* the promiscuous act.

Far from denying death, then, these societies are sterile and moribund, in desperate need of reestablishing contact with the sacred powers. In comedy of course these powers are sexual, because comedy has never completely lost contact with the *komos* and the satyr plays, where hairy beast-men caper about in what classicists call the ithyphallic state. Comedy may force indignities on the human body, converting tragic falls into pratfalls, but in the end the body is found to have one great and redeeming virtue: it can reproduce. Bodies not only collide, we finally discover, but they embrace; and so we are all, characters and audience alike, swept up in the collective saving embrace of comedy.

This view of comedy is familiar enough to go without extensive illustration. But the denial of death in tragedy may deserve a closer look. Briefly and oversimply, then, let me suggest how several of Shakespeare's tragedies appear if we adopt this perspective, regarding them as plays in which various forms of immortality are mortified.

2. Unfathering in *Romeo and Juliet*

A helpful way of looking at tragedy is to focus on what Freud called the child's wish "to be the *father of himself*,"[1] that is, the male child's Oedipal urge to act as a father-substitute with his mother and hence to transcend not only his childish but also his mortal limitations. "The essence of the Oedipal complex," as Norman O. Brown says, "is the project of becoming God—in Spinoza's formula, *causa sui*; in Sartre's, *être-en-soi—pour-soi*."[2] With this megalomania, man denies death by denying birth, liberating the self from the genetic process and especially from the state of dependency it entails by, paradoxically, identifying himself with his genetic origins. If I am my own father, then I am self-caused and hence immortal. For as George Santayana said, "The fact of having been born is a bad augury for immortality."[3] If we had never been born, if we had remained in a heaven of Platonic ideas instead of being ignobly imbruted in these dying bodies, we would have lived forever. Or if we could somehow divest ourselves of our bodies without dying, we would live forever. But because neither of these options is likely, we must resort to other tactics. The most popular means of allaying our anxieties about death is by taking shelter behind something much more durable than our bodies, preferably something sacred to our culture like God, king, flag, money, possessions, books, and so forth. This is a subtle cultural version of confusing death by merging ourselves with the herd, the pack, or the tribe. A riskier method is the *causa sui* project in which we submit to the narcissistic delusion that we are so splendidly special and independently virtuous as to be one of a kind, self-created. According to this strategy, we can dispense with the tribe or society, indeed even with the species, because we are in effect a species all to ourselves, much as the initials of the immortal HCE in *Finnegan's Wake* can be taken as "Here comes everybody."

An amusing historical example of the *causa sui* project is the story told of Andoche Junot, one of Napoleon's generals, who after conducting a brilliant campaign in Portugal was made Duke of Abrantes and is said to have announced "I am my own ancestor." The hero conquers death on the battlefield and is rewarded with an exalted social identity that erases his natural family line and institutes a new one coextensive with himself. A similar process takes place, as John Blanpied has shown, when Prince Hal becomes Henry V. In announcing Hal's reformation by saying

> The breath no sooner left his father's body,
> But that the wildness, mortified in him,
> Seemed to die too; yea, at that very moment
> Consideration like an angel came
> And whipped the offending Adam out of him,
> Leaving his body as a paradise
> To envelop and contain celestial spirits.
>
> (*HV* 1.1)

the Archbishop "leapfrogs the implications of lineal succession, the son's dependency from the father, by the baptismal theory: an angel has scourged the father, the offending Adam, out of the son."[4] When Hal's father dies, all his fathers die, for Adam and Falstaff are soon to follow. His reformation erases not only his own past but postlapsarian time itself so that during his reign England recapitulates paradise. Not of course that Shakespeare is content with this pious interpretation; but the Archbishop's view is useful here in showing how a kind of princely unfathering conduces to a royal self-fathering. Shakespeare has not forgotten the brevity of King Harry's reign—"Small time," he says in the epilogue, "but in that small most greatly lived / This star of England." Such great living, albeit brief, transcends death. Not only Harry but anyone who hitches a wagon to his royal star will have booked passage to eternity, an eternity that will cast its glow over England again each year on St. Crispian's Day.

King Harry's England is some distance from the Italy of Romeo and Juliet, but the militant king and the Veronese lovers are linked by this same un-fathering experience. Unfathering in Verona, however, does not consist in Oedipal massacre or even in a premature self-crowning at the bedside of a dying king; it is accomplished simply by climbing over an orchard wall and gazing up at the starlike radiance of Juliet. From the beginning the play warns us that Juliet's celestial light will be darkened by the glow of their star-crossed love, but in the interim its dazzle is enough to eclipse not only the mysterious Rosaline of Romeo's lovelorn past but even Romeo's identity as well. And for that matter, Juliet's too. For as Romeo is risking life and limb getting over the orchard wall, Juliet is intoning to the night her famous speech about names—

> O Romeo, Romeo, wherefore art thou Romeo?
> Deny thy father and refuse thy name!
> Or, if thou wilt not, be but sworn my love,
> And I'll no longer be a Capulet.   (2.2)

To refuse a name, whether Montague or Capulet, is to deny one's father, one's family, one's genetic inheritance. This unfathering, or unfamilying, leaves the self free for a kind of special creation: "Call me but love," Romeo says, "and I'll be new-baptized; / Henceforth I never will be Romeo." As his last clause here indicates, love's baptism is negative; Juliet does not give Romeo a new name, she merely scrubs away his old one, and hers as well. What remains are two nameless, infinitely private, almost inexpressible selves: the "I" and "thee" of love.[5]

This marriage of true minds dispenses with public forms. Its pledge is not made with depersonalizing names, not "Romeo takes Juliet," but simply "I take thee." The two pronouns are, as the linguists say, shifters; unlike that of names their reference changes as the speaker changes. In their conversational passage back and forth they reflect the reciprocity and intimacy of love as it bridges the social distance between two people that is otherwise maintained by their discrete public names. *I* and *thee* also make a gesture in the direction of immortality because they represent the secret inward spring where the sense of life and meaning is renewed. As Erik Erikson says, "No quantifiable aspect of this experience [of the "I"] can do justice to its subjective halo, for it means nothing less than that I am alive, that I *am* life."[6]

Moreover, because the identity of the "I" is constant, it sustains this sense of life-fullness in a way that names cannot. "Romeo" and "Juliet" are tags pinned on the "I" from the outside; hence they can be modified, discarded, changed or exchanged. Rosalind and Celia in *As You Like It* can disguise themselves as "Ganymede" and "Aliena," and Caius Martius can become "Coriolanus"; but in each case the identity of the "I" remains the same. That is why Juliet, who would dispense with all names, forestalls Romeo's vow to "the inconstant moon" and says

> Do not swear at all;
> Or, if thou wilt, swear by thy gracious self,
> Which is the god of my idolatry,
> And I'll believe thee.

Names for Juliet are as distant and mutable as the moon. Only a love as inward as the "I"—presumably as sequestered from the public streets of Verona as the Capulets' walled orchard—can hope to survive.

From this point on, the lovers reenter the world of family and feuding, the world of names, only in disguise—as "Romeo" and "Juliet"—whereas their true selves flower in the garden of "I" and "thee." Together, they transcend the transient and associate themselves with stars and timelessness, defying death for "one short minute" in one another's sight, as Romeo tells the Friar: "Do thou but close our hands with holy words, / Then love-devouring death do what he dare" (2.6). But the world pauses only briefly for young love, and Romeo must return from the immortality of the orchard to the death-ridden streets where Tybalt strides about looking for a grave.

In an excellent chapter of a book in progress on play-death and apocalypse Kirby Farrell charts the sad consequences of Romeo and Juliet's attempt to abandon a patriarchal system that "like religion, acts to secure the self in the world by providing master and follower [especially such followers as children] a symbolic transcendence of death."[7] In other words partriarchy is a sacred source of immortality for parents and children. Shakespeare's testy fathers are his sexually insecure young men grown old. For just as the young men assert their masculine identity by distinguishing themselves somewhat desperately from inferior females (see chap. 4), so the old men assert their patriarchal status by suppressing their families, especially their children. Thus from the child's point of view, if you stand obediently under the patriarchal canopy you are safe; but dare to venture forth on your own and you die (or are threatened with death, disinheritance, and similar calamities). As Carolly Erickson observes of the repressiveness of the Elizabethan family,

> Failure to observe "honorable esteem" toward parents had extreme consequences. Disobedient children were thought of as unnatural beings, "cruel murderers of their parents," who would at the very least be harshly punished by God for their impiety. Sometimes a magistrate was called in to impose a father's penalty on his son or daughter. But most parents would have found this excessively nice, preferring to follow the simple maxim "Whip the devil out of them!" for all misbehavior. Whippings, thrashings, severe spankings were everywhere incident to Tudor child rearing. Beating was seen as a sort of behavioral purgative, driving out the child's inborn inclination to wantonness and vice. Even the best-behaved children were pinched and cuffed and slapped when their perfection faltered; insensitive parents teased and threatened their tortured sons and daughters almost past endurance in the vague belief that affectionate treatment bred wrongdoing.[8]

There stands Capulet to the life—to *his* life, that is, but to Juliet's death should she disobey him.

In *Romeo and Juliet* the immortality that normally attends patriarchy is compromised by the deadliness of the family feud which the lovers also inherit from their fathers. This places the lovers in the Antigone situation—

dead if you do (remain within the patriarchy), dead if you don't. When they abandon the feud and deny their names, they renounce their genetic inheritance, death, but also forgo the death-denying benefits of patriarchy. As apostates, they are on their own. But they are oblivious to the risks of apostasy, having become acolytes in a religion of love that, they feel, transcends death. Like Henry V with the offending Adam whipped out of him, they have purged themselves of their postlapsarian past and transformed the orchard into the original Paradise where death has yet to put in an appearance.

In the privacy of their counter-religion they turn not merely from Montague and Capulet to "I" and "thee," but also from their genetic fathers to a "ghostly father," Friar Laurence. The fact that the priest is a Father associates him with the patriarchal system the lovers have left behind; but the fact that the Father is a priest dissociates him from that system and implies that the lovers have placed their love under the aegis of a kind of spiritual sterility. If a priest-father is a contradiction in terms, so is a private marriage. Perhaps it is appropriate that when they confess their love to Friar Laurence and attempt to convert the marriage of true minds into a wedding they come to grief. This displaced acknowledgment of the father, even in the form of a Father who stands for inward peace, not outward street clashes, seems an invitation to death. In accord with the (il)logic of causative contiguity, in the following scene Mercutio dies, Romeo kills Tybalt in an act that realigns him with his family, and banishment follows. The magic circle of immortality the lovers sought to draw around themselves is broken.

Friar Laurence is a pale spiritual version not only of the lovers' genetic fathers but of Verona's political father, Prince Escalus. It seems there is no escape from fathers or from the death that having a father implies. In the political world, seeking to terminate the feud, the paternal Prince banishes Romeo, thereby "killing" him—"And sayest thou yet that exile is not death?" (3.2) In the spiritual world, also seeking to terminate the feud, Friar Laurence gives his potion to Juliet, thereby "killing" her. So it goes in plague- and feud-ridden Verona where, because unmannerly children "press before [their fathers] to a grave" (5.3), only amorous Death can bring about a permanent if not immortal union of the lovers and an enduring end to parental feuding.

3. Divinity in *Richard II*

Richard II is a mortifying play. In fact it begins at such a pitch of ceremony that mortification is almost inevitable. Only in King Harry's speech on Ceremony (*HV* 4.1) is it more apparent than in the ritualistic opening scenes of this play that the primary purpose of Ceremony is to deny man's creaturely insignificance, clothing him and his actions in pomp and dignity to help him forget that he is what Richard ultimately discovers himself to be—nothing. In the opening scene, however, Ceremony—the almost planned formalization of charge and countercharge—has a more specific task, to create an aura of majesty that will help disguise the fact that Richard has violated the sanctity of his patriarchal line. As everyone knows, he has arranged for the death of his uncle Gloucester, and in so doing symbolically spilled his grandfather's and hence his own father's blood. As Gaunt says,

> O, spare me not, my brother Edward's son,
> For that I was his father Edward's son.
> That blood already, like the pelican,
> Hast thou tapped out and drunkenly caroused.
> My brother Gloucester, plain well-meaning soul,
> Whom fair befall in heaven 'mongst happy souls!
> May be a precedent and witness good
> That thou respect'st not spilling Edward's blood.
>
> (2.1)

This severance of self from patriarchal past is generalized when Richard's seizure of Bolingbroke's patrimony arouses the ire of his uncle York:

> Take Hereford's rights away, and take from time
> His charters and his customary rights;
> Let not tomorrow then ensue today;
> Be not thyself; for how art thou a king
> But by fair sequence and succession?   (2.1)

But Richard shapes his identity in terms not of sequence and succession but of Divine Right, and Divine Right creates in his view a kingship invulnerable to time and rebel armies:

> For every man that Bolingbroke hath pressed
> To lift shrewd steel against our golden crown,
> God for his Richard hath in heavenly pay
> A glorious angel; then if angels fight,
> Weak men must fall, for Heaven still guards the right.

A king with angels in his camp must surely be immortal. However, if there are angels behind Richard, there are angels *before* Bolingbroke, as he indicates in an address to his followers:

> All my treasury
> Is yet but unfelt thanks, which more enriched
> Shall be your love and labour's recompense.
>   (2.3)

Crowns coin angels, and the prospect of golden angels generates more militancy in Bolingbroke's army than the supposed presence of spiritual ones does in Richard's. Shortly after Richard's exhortations, he and Bolingbroke meet at Flint Castle, where Richard's divine but unmilitarized right encounters Bolingbroke's unsanctioned but overpowering might (3.3). As a result His Highness is compelled to descend to the "base" court and make his humbling way from thence to London where in full presence of the commons he deposes himself.

Richard's belief in the divine rightness of his kingship constitutes a denial of death and hence of royal succession. The association of kingship with death denial can be made in terms of Richard's royal title, as a quote from Kojéve's commentary on Hegel suggests. According to Hegel, naming a thing "murders" its particular existential reality and substitutes in its place a universal symbolic being. Symbolizing is a reflection of the mortality of things, even as it attempts to transcend that mortality:

> If the dog were eternal, if it existed outside Time or without Time, the Concept "dog" would never be *detached* from the dog itself [it would be a "natural sign," univocal]. The empirical existence (*Dasein*) of the Concept "dog" would be the living dog, and not the *word* "dog" (thought or pronounced). . . .[9]

The credulous Richard, however, attempts to live only within the symbolic mode, where death has no dominion. For him the words *King* and *Richard* merge to form one name—his own. Unlike Juliet, he is unable to separate the enduring private "I" from the transient public name. As Richard III proclaimed "I am myself alone," so Richard II proclaims "I am the King alone." As such, he is as immortal as a Platonic idea. But of course neither Shakespeare nor Bolingbroke will have it so, as even Richard senses. Dismaying news lets him down from Platonic heights to corporeal depths, where his words do not deny but dote on death: "Let's talk of graves, of worms, and epitaphs / . . . [and] sit upon the ground / And tell sad stories of the deaths of kings" (3.3).

The play redefines Richard and his kingship by extracting the one from the other, by driving a wedge between the title and the man. Instead of being the Platonic idea itself, Richard is merely an instance of it. The name of *King* will prove as hospitable to the words *Henry IV* as it has to *Richard II*. And instead of being gathered into the artifice of regal eternity, Richard is cast into Pomfret Castle where the realization is forced upon him that Time has made him, like all men, its mortal numbering clock:

> But whate'er I be
> Nor I nor any man that but man is
> With nothing shall be pleased, till he be eased
> With being nothing.   (5.5.)

Thus Richard descends from divinity to mortality to nothing, which is a good place to pause before moving on to Elsinore where the Danish hero undergoes a similar experience, falling like man himself from princely heights ("How like a god") to corporeal depths ("this quintessence of dust").

Tragedy and the
       Denial of Death   2

1. Fathers in *Hamlet*

Some heroes, Coriolanus and Macbeth most notably, illustrate the self-glorifying effect of surviving death, the primitive exhilaration of standing over fallen bodies and feeling "They're dead, I'm alive!" However, precisely the opposite effect is possible when death strikes down someone they revere, someone to whom they have entrusted their own symbolic immortality. By a revered figure I mean one possessing what Jung calls a "mana-personality," who gives off that special air of potency that causes others, anxious "to find a tangible hero somewhere, or a superior wise man, a leader and father, some undisputed authority, [to] build temples to little tin gods with the greatest promptitude and burn incense upon the altars."[1] Having burned his own share of incense at Freud's altar, Jung knew a good bit about the mana-personality, and also about the feelings of those who have been expelled from the temple. In the psychoanalytic subculture, Paul Roazen says, it was "readily believed that if Freud dropped a man it could lead to his self-extinction. Exclusion from the revolutionary community was an annihilation greater than any physical death."[2] The loss of symbolic immortality that takes place when one is no longer protected by a superior source of power is made explicit in the words of an apostate from fundamentalist Christianity: " 'You get the feeling that someone has died,' says Niall Lynch, 26, who abandoned fundamentalism after 10 years in its ranks, 'and that someone is you' " (*Newsweek*, September 9, 1985). In these cases the loss of the immortality project annihilates the ex-believer. Of course the same effect obtains when the mana-personality dies, leaving the apostle abandoned and stripped of his symbolic immortality, as suggested in a quote from a young Chinese journalist recording his feelings on learning of the death of Mao: "I was shocked. Mao dead? The first words we learned to speak were 'Long live Chairman Mao.' The first words we learned to write were 'Long live Chairman Mao.' He was God. God never dies" (*Los Angeles Times Magazine*, September 7, 1986, p. 10). But when the god does die, then his survivors are, if not dead, grievously fallen into the mortal condition.

Which gets us roundaboutly to Hamlet. For when Hamlet's royal father dies the Prince responds not by trumpeting in Coriolanus tones "He's dead, I'm alive!" but by lamenting "He's dead, I should be too"—or as he puts it, "O that this too too sullied flesh would melt." Hamlet's flesh does not cooperate but his symbolic immortality has clearly dissolved. For him, as for Nietzsche and the Chinese journalist, God is dead; and Hamlet makes little distinction between God the Father and Old Hamlet *his* father, as he indicates when he describes Old Hamlet's portrait to Gertrude in the Closet Scene:

> See, what a grace was seated on this brow:
> Hyperion's curls, the front of Jove himself,
> An eye like Mars, to threaten and command,
> A station like the herald Mercury. . . .   (3.4)

Thus even before Hamlet hears the Ghost's tale about murder and "incest" he experiences the symbolic death of a son abandoned by his divine father and cast out of the cult formed by his father's reign—a reign based on the chivalric virtues evident in the combat between Old Hamlet and Old Fortin-bras.[3] This cult of the past—a medieval world of arms and good fellowship where Yorick was wont to set the table on a roar and Hamlet himself glittered as the glass of fashion and the mold of form—has been his unconscious immortality project, and with his father's death it disappears. What remains is an "unweeded garden" inhabited by things "rank and gross in nature," like Claudius, like Hamlet.

The inevitablility of death, that fundamental aspect of anagnorisis that other tragic heroes acquire only at the end of their plays, is forced upon Hamlet at the beginning of his. Until the arrival of the Ghost he has led a life of "bestial oblivion," the kind of life Richard II, Brutus, Othello, Lear, and Coriolanus lead for a much longer time. Fallen from grace, however, Hamlet dies spiritually. But he can also die physically. After all, if gods can die, he can die. With Claudius popped in between the election and his hopes—not to mention in between incestuous sheets—Hamlet is now a disinherited prince and an abandoned son, one who is "too much in the sun" in the Elizabethan sense of being exposed to death (or "out in the cold," as we would say). Hence prior to his meeting with the Ghost, Hamlet exists, like the Ghost itself, between two worlds, not dead but not fully alive either.

From this persepective *Hamlet* is a play about discovering death—and coming to terms with that discovery. The discovering is easier than the coming to terms. When Hamlet meets the Ghost and receives its command-ment "Remember me!" he momentarily recovers life and purpose. Properly to "remember" the Ghost would mean to restore the past in the collective recollection of Denmark by erasing the present—the reign of Claudius with its fashionable Osrics, its duplicitous schoolfellows hastened home from Wittenberg, and its inexplicably changed mother. But the reasons why the present should be obliterated—murder, betrayal, luxury, damned incest— are so appalling that they merely intensify Hamlet's disillusionment: "The time is out of joint. O cursed spite, / That ever I was born to set it right!" Thus his initial passion for revenge succumbs to an antic disposition that does not get the King killed, though it confuses him, and us, and Hamlet himself.[4]

Instead of killing the King, Hamlet obsessively explores the corporeal dimension of man's life, as though for the first time he has reached out and touched death—or it him—and he cannot rid his imagination of the revolting yet fascinating experience.[5] If you peel away bestial oblivion, he discovers, you expose the wormwood of decay and dying, the "hidden imposthume" that erupts inward and shows no cause without why the man dies. And he alone, he seems to feel, is privy to such information. Thus he sees death and degeneration everywhere. Life itself is bred of death, as maggots are bred in a dead dog's body. To shield herself against such corruptive "conception" Ophelia should flee to a nunnery from fellows like him, lustful cynical creatures "crawling between earth and heaven" like animals. Whether "The Mouse-trap" reveals the King's guilt or not, Hamlet's wit's diseased and his "imaginations are foul / As Vulcan's stithy" (3.2). What except a diseased imagination, thinking too precisely on halved and quartered thoughts, would cause him to forfeit an available revenge when the King is at prayer in favor of a "more horrid hent" in an imagined future, when the King might be drunk or raging or 'twixt incestuous sheets (3.3)?

Contra Socrates, then, for Hamlet as for most men the unexamined life seems worth living, the examined one not worth the candle. How does he get from such a bleak position to the stoic sense of "readiness" he exhibits in the last act? Oversimply: by negotiating between two radically dissimilar attitudes toward death, his mother's and the Gravemaker's, both of which represent the bestial oblivion that so repels him. Puzzled by his grief, Gertrude blandly remarks that death is "common" since "all that lives must die, / Passing through nature to eternity" (1.2). Her platitude constitutes a denial of death, particularly the death of Hamlet's father, by spreading it invisibly thin over "all that lives" and then by spiritualizing it out of existence into eternity. At the other extreme the Gravemaker denies death by corporealizing it out of existence. In his equally oblivious view, death as a fearful human experience disappears into pocky corses and whoreson dead bodies and the technical problems of "laying in." Both see death as "common"—Gertrude as a universal passage toward eternity, the Gravemaker as a vulgar descent into clay.

Both versions of death are repugnant to Hamlet, though he characteristically swings between the two. From death as abstract and universal—the unimaginable "not to be" of his famous speech— he moves toward acknowledging its concrete particularity when he fingers the King's packet aboardship and looks upon his own death warrant. Still, even at this point, death remains symbolic. In the graveyard, however, he profits from the vulgarity of the Gravemaker's casual corporeal view, which puts flesh on death's bones while stripping it from humans. Death for Hamlet is now simply a body. Not just any body or all bodies. He can speak with wry humor about the skulls of politicians and courtiers and lawyers and even Lord Such-a-one. But these give way to one skull, Yorick's, which teaches the prince of cerebration what a bony house thought inhabits; and then to one body, Ophelia's, which teaches him that death is more, and less, than ghostly reports from another country or an abstract theme for soliloquizing. This personalizing of death brings Hamlet to terms with himself, enabling him to stand forth and announce his name and address: "This is I, / Hamlet, the Dane!" In the place where bodies decompose, Hamlet forms an identity. Unfortunately, identities are always dangerous. They tell death who and where you are. They get you killed.

As Hamlet exposes himself to death, however, he makes what seems a compensatory retreat in the opposite direction. He speaks of the shaping force of divinity in men's affairs and of a providence so conscientious that even the sparrow's role in the cosmic plot is accounted for. Thus as he acquires a "readiness" of mind that will permit him to revenge his father, he also takes shelter under the umbrella of a paternal divinity. In other words, his metaphoric deification of his father earlier is now literalized by his assumption that he has come under the aegis of God the Father. The fusion of the two deities occurs when he tells Horatio how on his ocean voyage he intercepted the King's packet and rewrote his death warrant, at which point Horatio asks "How was this sealed?" and Hamlet replies—

> Why, *even in that was heaven ordinant.*
> I had *my father's signet* in my purse,
> Which was the model of that Danish seal;
> Folded the writ up in the form of the other,
> Subscribed it, gave it the impression, placed it safely,
> The changeling never known.

Following so hard upon a mention of heavenly ordinance, the phrase "my father's signet" may cause us to wonder whether "father" means "father" or "Father." The two coalesce in the fortuitous but divinely ordinant presence of the death-sealing life-saving ring. When Hamlet presses the signet into the wax of the rewritten document, both of his fathers give their imprimatur to his enterprise.

This implies that at the end of the play Hamlet accomplishes a kind of regressive progression from father-worship to Father-worship, from one immortality project to another. It is regressive inasmuch as Hamlet reidentifies himself with his dead father. Of course he identified with his father to begin with, as his grief in act 1 indicated. But later, his failure to sweep to his revenge as he had promised constituted a failure, as the Ghost put it, to "Remember me," a failure in effect to keep the father alive. It is analogous to Romeo's abandonment of his filial duties as a feuding Montague when he falls in love with Juliet. And just as the two lovers retreat from paternally sanctioned death and public names into a seemingly deathless love founded on the immortality of "I" and "thee," so Hamlet defers his deadly assignment, annuls his nominal identity with Hamlet his father, and retreats during the middle of the play into the labyrinths of perhaps the most private and elusive "I" in literature. For Hamlet, that "I" is life, however painful, whereas to assume his role as "Hamlet, the Dane" is death. Now, however, as he moves toward a sense of readiness, he again establishes a bond with his father. Thus his "This is I, / Hamlet, the Dane!" echoes his address to the Ghost at their first meeting—"I'll call thee Hamlet, / King, father, royal Dane" (1.4).

But as the providential ring episode suggests, "father" now includes God as well as the Ghost. Hamlet has not simply regressed to an earlier stage, ending where he began, because the route from "father" to "Father" has passed through the graveyard. His "readiness" now is not the naive death denial of those who simply "sleep and feed" (4.4), but a clear understanding that "If it be now, 'tis not to come; if it be not to come, it will be now; if it be not now, yet it will come" (5.2). That is a knowledge he can live with, or if necessary die with: "Let be."

To summarize: on this reading the death of his father destroys Hamlet's naive symbolic immortality—what he calls in others "bestial oblivion"—and sets him off on a neurotically obsessive exploration of death in its various and most repellent forms. The grisly knowledge he acquires at first reduces all life to absurdity and himself to paralysis. Gradually, however, in a somewhat shrouded manner, his study of corporeal meaninglessness leads to a détente with death. In fact, his leap into the grave of Ophelia can be taken as a synecdoche of his experience throughout the play. Ever since his father's death he has been tenting graves and lying in coffins. The graveyard and this grave, we see in retrospect, are a kind of vortex that has been pulling the entire action of the play down into it.

But the grave is not entirely in death's service. If Hamlet enters it, he also issues from it—with a newborn sense of resignation, knowing somehow that in the entelechies of providence what-is-to-be will be with or without his willing it: "Let Hercules himself do what he may. / The cat will mew and dog will have his day" (5.1). The grave then is not merely destructive—My Lady Worm's eatery—but instructive as well, perhaps even in a grim sense life-enhancing, albeit the kind of life-enhancement peculiar to tragedy.[6] For Hamlet has had to take the mortal leap into the grave in order to tent the human wound to the quick. The life of death, its "quick," consists in man's wry awareness of it. Without that, he "is but a beast, no more"; with it, he is the "quintessence of dust" but also the subject of divine consideration. At the end of the play, that is, Hamlet reverses the direction of his speech "What a piece of work is a man!" (2.2), seeing man not merely as a god that descends to dust but as dust that ascends toward God. The final ascent cannot be made, it seems, until one has experienced in person the preparatory descent. Then death becomes a part of one's life, and spiritual paralysis is transformed into "readiness," into a willingness to revenge if occasion presents itself—and it will—and to die if providence ordains—and it will.

Despite the transcendent turn of Hamlet's mind at the end of the play, once his revenge is accomplished and he lies dying, he seems indifferent to the flights of angels that might sing him to eternal rest, and passionately anxious that Horatio tell his "story" in such a way as to restore his wounded name in Denmark. As Otto Rank observed, men are more concerned to ensure their immortality than to preserve their lives.[7]

2. Fetishism in *Othello*

Othello's immortality centers intitially in what he calls "My parts, my title, and my perfect soul" (1.2), all of which derive apparently from a past characterized by "battles, sieges, fortunes, / That I have passed" (1.3) in which he repeatedly met death and triumphed. But surviving among the Anthropophagi and men whose heads "do grow beneath their shoulders" does not necessarily prepare a black general for survival in white super-subtle Venice among the likes of Iago. Othello's naive romanticism, especially after Hamlet, strikes one as a form of bestial oblivion. And indeed there is a beast in Othello that will out as the play progresses. In the meantime he insures his perfect soul by investing its immortality in the "divine Desdemona" — an irrational almost religious act of faith[8] — only to lose his investment when he is persuaded by Iago that "the wine she drinks is made of grapes."

Torn between Desdemona's divinity and Iago's diabolism, Othello exchanges soul for body in keeping with the Iago principle. For what Iago "really stands for," Robert B. Heilman says, "is the destruction of the spirit," and thus he repeatedly "states the counterpoint of *immortal* and *bestial* that runs implicitly all through the drama."[9] In Othello's absolutist mentality this counterpoint takes the form of a radical either/or. A man is either human or beast, and a woman is either platonically pure or viciously corrupt. Thus what he calls the "business of [his] soul" is dependent on Desdemona's chastity, and when this is supposedly sullied he is bestialized, as he unwittingly predicted to Iago:

> To be once in doubt
> Is once to be resolved. Exchange me for a goat
> When I shall turn the business of my soul
> To such exsufflicate and blown surmises,
> Matching thy inference. (3.3)

In a desperate effort to recover his immortality, Othello must kill off the beastly goat in himself, and what better means to do so than by making Desdemona a scapegoat sacrifice? By demystifying her divinity — "strumpet," "whore," "Cassio did top her," "she was foul" — he transforms his jealous lack of faith into a holy cause ("it is the cause, my soul"), himself into a priestly confessor ("Have you prayed tonight, Desdemon?"), murder into sacrifice ("[you make me] call what I intend to do / A murder, which I thought a sacrifice"), and their marriage bed into a death bed.

Of course he is doing away not only with a strumpet but with the wife on whose love his image of self and his status in Venice depend. Throwing away the jewel of his existence is a sacrifice that should endear him to the gods. His virtue runneth over. But on learning the truth he discovers where the true animal resides, and after a final rhetorical bid for a share in the immortality he has so rashly thrown away ("Then must you speak / Of one that loved not wisely but too well") he kills the subhuman in himself, the "uncircumsized dog," and the faithless non-Christian "Turk."

Othello's either/or rigidity of mind amounts to a kind of fetishism whereby the full human reality, with its mingled yarn of complex goods and ills, is reduced to a single trait. Fetishism is not necessarily the mark of a deranged mind. It is a form of synecdoche whereby an unfamiliar whole is reduced to a manageable part, a not uncommon method for the foreigner to acquire a pseudofamiliarity with a new locale. From this standpoint fetishism helps explain Othello's motives as an outsider in Venice. The black African mysteriously set down in Europe among super-sophisticated Venetians clearly risks disapprobation and mere sufferance. As long as his military skills are useful he is tolerated; when he loses his occupational value he may well be spurned. How better to survive, even to gain access to the cultural immortality bank of Venice, than to court and win Desdemona, who as virtuous, beautiful, and not least of all white is a human fetish representing Venice at large. Her total acceptance of him, confirmed in court, authenticates his right not merely to exist but to be prized as a black man in a white society. It seems significant in this regard that Othello says of Desdemona, "She loved me for the dangers I had passed, / And I loved her that she did pity them" (1.3), which suggests that his love is for a feminine symbol of his acceptance in Venice as much as it is for the flesh and blood Desdemona.

If Desdemona is a fetishistic representation of the love of Venice for the stranger, then it is appropriate that another fetish, the handkerchief, should be instrumental in his loss of that love. But what he loses is more than love. The handkerchief is a fetish the possession of which magically brings Othello's and Desdemona's love under the aegis of his own African past, and especially under the aegis of his parents' love. For as he tells Desdemona, the handkerchief was given his mother by an Egyptian charmer who

> told her, while she kept it
> 'Twould make her amiable and subdue my father
> Entirely to her love, but if she lost it,
> Or made a gift of it, my father's eye
> Should hold her loathed and his spirits should hunt
> After new fancies.   (3.4)

Since his mother never lost it, the handkerchief embodies the perfection of his parents' married love and thus bridges the gulf between Africa and Venice and reassuringly canopies the present under the past.[10]

In addition, however, the fetishistic handkerchief with withchcraft in its warp emblematizes the irrational element in Othello's love. It sums up all the superstitious efforts among Venetians to account for an amorous experience that, at least throughout Shakespeare, is as resistant to explanation as Iago's hatred of Othello. The handkerchief weaves together talk of witchcraft, magic, charms, dark arts, conjuration, and so forth.[11] Love, and especially Othello's love, will not submit to the shows of reason; it is, as humors psychology would have it, a mysterious stirring in the liver or, more romantically, an enchantment of the imagination. Othello falls in love, Iago falls in hate. Each is an absolute experience, a case of either/or. You have it or you do not, as you possess a handkerchief or you do not. Neither experience will abide our questions.

Thus the magic in the web of the handkerchief condenses the mystery of Othello's and Desdemona's love—a mystery like the mystery of religious faith ("My life upon her faith"). In fact the handkerchief defines love *as* faith, since you must believe in its magical properties as Othello must believe in Desdemona for marriage to prosper. The handkerchief, then, is a fetish of a fetish, compacting several faiths. It substitutes for Desdemona's chaste faith in Othello, which is a synecdoche of Venice's acceptance of the black general, which substitutes for Othello's own faith in his past heroic self and perfect soul. When Desdemona loses the handkerchief, Othello loses a sense of self formed in pre-Venetian days when he made conquests of death and fashioned his perfect soul. Hence,

> Farewell the tranquil mind! farewell content!
> Farewell the plumed troops, and the big wars
> That makes ambition virtue! O farewell!
> Farewell the neighing steed and the shrill trump,
> The spirit-stirring drum, the ear-piercing fife,
> The royal banner, and all quality,
> Pride, pomp, and circumstance of glorious war!
> And, O you mortal engines, whose rude throats
> The immortal Jove's dread clamors counterfeit,
> Farewell! Othello's occupation's gone!   (3.3)

Othello's lament is not merely for his lost occupation but for the loss of the immortality vested in a military life whose glories transcend death.[12] The storm that destroys the Turkish fleet destroys the general as well, leaving him disarmed of his occupation and facing a storm far worse than the sea can generate.

The swiftness with which Othello's elegy shifts from the loss of Desdemona's love to his own loss of occupation, past, and self forecasts a similar movement at the end of the play when he attempts to erect a monument to himself on which his role as one who "loved not wisely but too well" is superseded by a heroic image of himself out of the past, "in Aleppo once." There is considerable pathos in his final appeal for approval as one who revenged a Venetian against a milignant Turk, and a perceptive rightness about it too, since he casts himself simultaneously as the servant of the Venetians and, stabbing himself, as the offending foreign dog. He makes a bid for immortality in the process of killing himself. In a sense that is what all tragic heroes do.

XI   Tragedy and the
        Denial of Death   3

1. Patricide in *Macbeth*

In *Totem and Taboo* Freud argued that the archetypical father is more formidable dead than alive. The hypothetical primal horde, he conjectured, was dominated by a father whose sexual monopoly drove his sons to kill him, as in the myths of Uranus and Cronus. But guilt soon overcame the sons, who agreed that henceforth no one should be allowed the freedom the father once had. The dead father is thus associated with Law and the Superego, with restraints upon impulse that are prerequisites of civilized life.

Fathers have comparable status in Shakespeare. Like gods they must be obeyed and placated, and like gods they have the power of life and death. Titus Andronicus strikes down his son Mutius for getting between him and his wrath and kills Lavinia to seal up her shame. Lear banishes Cordelia, and Gloucester orders Edgar killed on mere suspicion. In *Romeo and Juliet* and *A Midsummer Night's Dream* Capulet and Egeus insist their daughters marry men of their choice or die the death; and even Prospero turns stern and threatening with Miranda. Indeed so powerful are fathers that not even death can still their desire. Like Freud's *Ur*-father, from beyond the grave they continue to assert their will, perhaps beneficently, as in the cases of Portia and Helena (*All's Well*), and sometimes selfishly, as when the Ghost issues commands to Hamlet to forget all else and "remember" him.

All fathers and father figures in Shakespeare are akin to the Ghost inasmuch as living or dead they demand that their offspring remember them. Failures of memory in the younger generation—whether these take the form of simple disobedience, neglect, or an actual assault—are symbolic versions of Freud's primal patricide, especially in the tragedies and tragic history plays. Richard Crookback proclaims "I am myself alone!" and demonstrates his contempt for all greybeards by hacking down Henry VI. Richard II suborns Mowbray to do away with the Duke of Gloucester, and in so doing spills the blood of the great progenitor Edward III. Romeo and Juliet simply disregard old Montague and Capulet and their cherished feud. Brutus hacks down Caesar in the forum; Hamlet, lapsed in time and passion, lets go by the important acting of his father's dread command; Lear's pelican daughters bleed him to death; Macbeth slays Duncan; and Timon is abandoned by those he nurtured. But fathers have much mana; they bestride the world like colossi. To violate their law or their bodies is to defile the temple and, joining hands with Lucifer and Adam, to swell with pride even as you exile yourself from paradise.

Macbeth falls under the prediction. If self-fathering is a form of genetic substitution, a means of converting "son" into "father," then it cancels the process of lineal descent. Or, rather, it makes a psychological attempt to cancel lineal descent—which brings it within Macbeth's purview. For Macbeth is fundamentally opposed to the lineal, to succession, to process. But that is only after he has come into power by lineal means, by inheritance. Let me address the issue of patricide and linearity by saying something first about the role of entropy (undifferentiation) and difference in the creation of social meaning for Macbeth.

Macbeth's famous bleak elegies for the death of meaning—his "My way of life" and "Tomorrow" speeches—suggest a primitive state of entropy from which meaning, like a human life, emerges and into which it again falls. Meaning and meaninglessness, order and disorder, make a pendular swing throughout the play. The battle with which the play begins is a product of a rebellion against the most meaningful difference in Scotland, that between king and subjects; and in its effort to elide that difference it is characterized by entropy. It dissipates meaningful human differences, even the differences between friend and foe, in a sea of blood. Incarnadined at this font, Macbeth emerges as a special creature endowed with basic meaning—first, as one who continues to breathe and, second, as one who like Romeo is new-baptized. Still washed in the blood of his enemies, he hears from Ross about his new title and from the Witches about titles yet to come, and in accents far more ominous than Romeo's he declares in his heart "Henceforth I never will be Glamis."

Unlike Romeo, Macbeth wants not to retire from a death-ridden world but to immerse himself more deeply in it, since in Scotland generally and in his experience particularly violence and blood are sacred, the ultimate sources of meaning. After all, death has made him its favored heir. Upon the death of the Thane of Glamis he has become Thane of Glamis, upon that of Cawdor he has become Thane of Cawdor. How else should he become King of Scotland if not by the death of Duncan? Death may be the great eliminator of differences, as Hamlet discovered from the Gravemaker, but it is Macbeth's avenue to difference and meaning, especially to the grandest difference of all, "greatness." And this difference is brought into possibility for him when death eliminates the differences between him and Cawdor. "Glamis, and Thane of Cawdor! / The greatest is behind" (1.3).

Cawdor, we are told, dies well; but in a sense, of course, he does not die at all, since he lives on nominally and treasonously in his successor.

The "greatest" may be behind Macbeth when Cawdor dies, but "greatness" still lies ahead. Only an old man's body lies between him and it, and Macbeth is a veteran unseamer of bodies. Still, this is a special body; it belongs to the King, to the man who, as royal father, represents the paternal father below and the divine Father above. To kill such a multiple father is to put an end to origins, to place oneself outside the genetic process that attends mortality, and to father oneself in an ambiance of deathlessness. But what about consequences?

As I have argued elsewhere, the unwitnessed unstaged act in Duncan's chamber is metaphorized as a grotesque fusion of patricide, incest, and birth.[1] Macbeth shies away from identifying the act as anything more specific than *it* ("If it were done," etc.)—a pronoun Freud personified as the Id—and insofar as "it" is meant to be a king-killing, Macbeth would have it "done," crystallized as "the be-all and the end-all here," and consigned to the past even before it is performed. But in its incestuous aspect, as a displacement of the sexual act of procreation of which the Lord and Lady are incapable, "it" has, despite Macbeth's contraceptive rhetoric, "consequences." The act that kills the father proves fertile and fathering; it begets subsequent murders—of Banquo and of Macduff's family—that are designed to trammel up the consequence of the primal murder.

Thus despite Macbeth's efforts to terminate time and procreation—even if doing so entails tumbling all of "nature's germains" together in sickening destruction—the genetic process flourishes in macabre and sterile forms, springing even from death. He who once held the head of McDonwald in his hand while his own was on his neck, who stood breathing amid fields of corpses, who could claim immortality as "Bellona's bridegroom," and who was proclaimed immune to death from one of woman born, even he cannot escape the mortal implications of having been fathered. His act of killing the father figure Duncan enables him to substitute politically for that father, but it does not do away with the father. "The time has been," Macbeth complains, "That, when the brains were out, the man would die / And there an end" (3.4).

But Banquo is not the only man who refuses to die. Duncan survives death because the act of patricide itself survives death, refusing, as Macbeth feared, ever to be "done." The murders of Banquo and of Macduff's family and heirs are repetitions of the murder of Duncan, efforts, that is, to get the terrible deed done once and for all, to terminate genetic and political succession. But death, perversely procreative, refuses to be terminal. The murder of Duncan begets the revengeful Malcolm, the murder of Banquo

begets Fleance and a line of kings leading to James I, and the murder of
Macduff's family begets the killer of Macbeth. Unchilded in a childed world,
Macbeth sees nature's germains reproducing in a line stretching out to the
crack of doom. But despite promises of immortality, he alone, it seems, can
truly die. At the end the only immortality he registers is an endless nothingness revivified from day to day along the dreary route toward eternity.

2. Death Devotion in *Coriolanus*

Like Macbeth, Coriolanus is a conqueror of death on the battlefield,
but his is a rather different case. He is a good example of what Erich Fromm
calls the necrophile—not because he takes an erotic interest in corpses but
because he is enamored of force—and force, Simone Weil claimed, is the
capacity to transform a man into a corpse. As Fromm puts it:

> Just as sexuality can create life, force can destroy it. All force is, in the
> last analysis, based on the power to kill. I may not kill a person but only
> deprive him of his freedom; I may want only to humiliate him or to take
> away his possessions—but whatever I do, behind all these actions stands
> my capacity to kill and my willingness to kill. The lover of death necessar-
> ily loves force.[2]

For the lover of death, for Coriolanus, there are only two species of men—
not the Romans and the Volsces but simply killers and their victims. Hence
in the midst of battle Coriolanus can turn upon his own soldiers and shout
"Mend and charge home, / Or by the fires of heaven I'll leave the foe / And
make my wars on you" (1.4). If his phrase "charging home" has a faintly
sexual connotation that seems incongruous in this context, it is because
Shakespeare has reversed the usual bawdy metaphor depicting sex as a
military engagement in which man assails feminine virginity (as in the
conversation between Helena and Parolles in *All's Well* 1.1). For Coriolanus,
war is a substitute for sexuality, a flight from the dominating feminine world
of his mother to the engagements of the field. Thus when he encounters
Cominius immediately after the battle he cries jubilantly—

> O, let me clip ye
> In arms as sound as when I wooed, in heart
> As merry as when our nuptial day was done
> And tapers burned to bedward!   (1.4)

The point here—and in his "embracing" love for Aufidius later—is not
homosexuality but a kind of death intoxication, the sexual arousal produced

in Coriolanus when he kills and survives and hence conquers death. Thus when his men *"take him up in their arms,"* as the stage direction has it, he says breathlessly "O, me alone, make you a sword of me?" The phallic symbolism is obvious. Not virility and the creation of life but martial prowess and the shedding of blood are sacred to him. He comes fully alive only in the presence of death.

A major reason for this is his need to escape the domination of Volumnia. Coriolanus has no father in the play, only Volumnia the masculinized female. In a sense she and her son are in competition to replace the lost father. As Christopher Lasch says of fatherless families,

> In the child's fantasies it is not the mother who replaces the father but the child himself. . . . The child imagines that the mother has swallowed or castrated the father and harbors the grandiose fantasy of replacing him, by achieving fame or attaching himself to someone who represents a phallic kind of success, thereby bringing about an ecstatic reunion with the mother.[3]

In a case reported by Annie Reich a young woman whose father had died when she was an infant believed secretly that she was a genius who would, in her words, "suddenly reveal herself and stand out as an obelisk."[4] The phallic symbolism of the obelisk parallels that of Coriolanus as sword. Caius Martius has assaulted, besieged, penetrated the gates, and made a sexual conquest of Corioli, whose name he is given as a sign of masculine power. Surely now he is not merely a legitimate substitute for his father but an autonomous phallic force rising above Corioli and death, perhaps even above the formidable Volumnia.

His efforts to become autonomous by satisfying his blood lust are both a result of and a reaction against the child-rearing practices of his mother. For Volumnia makes it clear that she has raised her son for one purpose only, to acquire honor. As a comely but still unblooded boy, he was for her no better than a picture of manhood "if renown made it not stir" into life. Honor is life itself. Yet on the battlefield Coriolanus is not so much seeking honor but, as I have suggested, conquests of death. The applause of honor, after all, is worthy of receiving only from an audience worthy of bestowing it; and we know Coriolanus's opinion of the plebeians, which readily extends to all men. "Trust ye?" he says:

> With every minute you do change a mind,
> And call him noble that was now your hate,
> Him vile that was your garland.   (1.1)

To invest one's immortality in "report" when the market is so mercurial is to risk spiritual bankruptcy at any moment. So Coriolanus goes off to war to build his immortality account, less by accumulating honors than by courting and conquering death—by emerging from Corioli alive and victorious, by scotching and notching Aufidius like a side of beef and if not actually eating him, nevertheless ingesting his mana ("An he had been cannibally given, he might have boiled and eaten him too" [4.5]). By such means he becomes death's most passionate courtier, risking himself again and again for her favors.

This death devotion of Coriolanus helps explain the curious episode following the battle of Corioli when he begs deliverance for a captured Volscian who had befriended him. He says to Cominius:

> He cried to me—I saw him prisoner—
> But then Aufidius was within my view
> And wrath o'erwhelmed my pity.
>   (1.9)

But when Cominius agrees to spare the Volscian and asks his name, Coriolanus replies, "By Jupiter, forgot!" It is not just that wrath overwhelmed his pity or that his memory is faulty but that at the most fundamental level he exists to kill men, not to restore them to life. As a human sword his business is to hack and slash bodies. In doing so, he transforms individuals into "them," the enemy, and makes no distinctions. Thus later, when he stands on the verge of destroying Rome, and Cominius tries to "awaken his regard / For his private friends"

>   his answer to me was,
> He could not stay to pick them in a pile
> Of noisome musty chaff. He said 'twas folly,
> For one poor grain or two, to leave unburnt
> And still to nose the offence.   (5.1)

When it comes to sparing men's lives, Coriolanus's memory always fails.

Without death, then, Coriolanus would die. And that is precisely why he does die. When he returns from banishment at the head of the Volscian army, he has become the perfect exemplar of the *causa sui* or self-fathering project, which, to repeat Norman O. Brown's remark, is at bottom the desire to be God.[5] By this time Coriolanus has become even more obviously a machine for murder, not just a man who kills but death incarnate:

when he walks, he moves like an engine, and the ground shrinks before his treading. He is able to pierce a corslet with his eye; talks like a knell, and his hum is a battery.   (5.4)

More than that, he is, as Cominius says, "their god":

> He leads them like a thing
> Made by some other deity than Nature,
> That shapes men better.   (4.6)

These intimations of immortality are reaffirmed by the fact that his greatest victory, the destruction of mother Rome, would leave him unfamilied.[6] He would stand, he says, "As if a man were author of himself / And knew no other kin" (5.3). To be author of oneself—or to be made "by some other deity than Nature," by Mars for instance—is to deny one's mortal paternity and conquer time. As Menenius says "He wants nothing of a god but eternity and a heaven to throne in" (5.4).

However, as so often in Shakespeare, it is precisely the magnet of mortality—the appeals of mother, wife, and son—that persuades him to spare the life of Rome, and jeopardize his own. To relocate oneself in the genetic process is to become not merely humane but human, and the price of becoming human is death. "You have won a happy victory to Rome," he tells his mother,

> But for your son—believe it, O believe it—
> Most dangerously you have with him prevailed,
> If not most mortal to him. But let it come.
>
> (5.3)

This is as close as Coriolanus ever comes to anagnorisis: not just his realization that the Volscians may kill him but his knowledge that his immortality structure has been sheared away.

Thus when he faces the Volsces in the final scene Coriolanus's plight is analogous to Macbeth's when he encounters Macduff and learns he was not of woman born. He is wholly corporeal now, a scarred body to hack and notch. When he cries "Cut me to pieces, Volsces—men and lads, / Stain all your edges on me"—he seeks to transcend, not death, but an ignominious death by calling on an image of himself in former times, triumphantly, superhumanly alone, "like an eagle in a dove-cote" fluttering "Volscians in Corioli." He is not so much issuing a challenge to combat—making a sword of himself as in grander times—as inviting a Roman suicide. It is he now who makes of the Volsces a sword to fall on.

3. Immortality in the Globe

Before leaving the subject of death denial in tragedy, let me append a few remarks on the role played by the audience. One way to do this is to cue on the role of the audience within the play. They—those who attend and depend on the hero—have invested their immortality in his account. His role as the repository of the sacred is most apparent in Greek tragedy where the chorus is a weather vane of the hero's fortunes, not merely marking their direction but being blown about in the process. When the sons and daughters of old Cadmus gather in supplication before his palace Oedipus takes on the status, if not of a god, as the Priest says, then of "the first of men / in all the chances of this life and when / we mortals have to do with more than man."[7] And why not? It was he who conquered death both as an infant on Mount Cithaeron and as a solver of riddles on the outskirts of Thebes—even as the home-coming Agamemnon conquered death at Troy, and Macbeth at Forres, and Coriolanus at Corioli. But these are primitive heroes whose mana comes from the battlefield. As Ernest Becker says: "The hero is the one who can go out and get added powers by killing an enemy and taking his talismans or his scalp or eating his heart. He becomes a walking repository of accrued powers. Animals can only take in food for power; man can literally take in the trinkets and bodies of his whole world."[8] In other words heroic humans have the dubious virtue of being able to kill not merely for self-protection or food but for higher reasons; we fat ourselves on symbols, absorb power, transcend death. The trinket of greatest interest to the Shakespearean hero is the crown, the possession of which unites him to divinity and yields him the body of England. Now, as His Highness, he acquires the royal touch; he can cure the evil in those who otherwise would die. And so his subjects line up before him to be sanctified, feeling, as Alan Harrington phrases it, "I am making a deeper impression on the cosmos because I know this famous person. When the ark sails I will be on it."[9] Hence as long as the king lives his followers live; if he dies they die. Obviously therefore, he cannot be allowed to die. This difficult feat was accomplished in medieval and Renaissance England, as Ernst Kantorowicz has shown, by creating the fiction of the king's two bodies, which gives rise to the popular expression "The king is dead, long live the king."[10] In his corporeality the king may be mortal, but in his regality he is "a Corporation himself that liveth ever." By becoming shareholders in this royal corporation the king's subjects also liveth ever.

If heroism in life has any bearing on heroism in art, we would expect the tragic hero to be, somewhat like the king with his two bodies, a combination of god and *pharmakos*. As such he is more exalted than us but also more degraded. As audience to his great affairs, we yearningly identify with his godlikeness; in his seeming immortality our own deaths evaporate. By the same token our pity and fear are aroused by the hero's fall from immortality, because the cease of majesty, Rosencrantz says, "dies not alone but like a gulf doth draw / What's near it with it" (3.3)—and it is we who are near it. Exposed to death along with the hero, we must sacrifice him to save ourselves, which means that we must load him with sins to account for the disillusioning fact that he is as mortal as we are. We thought him a canopy of saving greatness, but he betrayed our trust, and gods who fail must be killed.

But we never kill gods, we kill impostors and sinners. So we discover in retrospect that the hero was evil like Richard III and Macbeth, self-indulgent like Richard II, too stiffly righteous like Brutus, self-absorbed and inefficient like Hamlet, imperious like Lear, and in general too foolishly given to risk-taking, to raising his head presumptuously or venturing beyond the safety of the pack. Translating Aristotle's *hamartia* as "moral failing" reflects our need to come to terms with our own loss of symbolic immortality by condemning the hero for being, after all his claims and our high hopes, merely mortal. But we, whose immortality consists in protective coloration—outside the arc of the footlights, we are safely invisible—we deserve to live. Or at any rate we *do* live, which is surely the same thing.

We survive the hero because we are still alive after he dies, but also because we were greater than he to begin with. By the grace of theater we are outside and above his world. We know more than he does. We know the folly of his absolutism, the irony of his grand moments; we see the shape of his destiny. His greatest achievement, the moment of anagnorisis when he looks within himself and realizes how what he is has issued from what he has done, represents the point at which his knowledge catches up to ours. But he can never catch up completely. He cannot watch his own death.

But on the other hand we do not die with him, and so our knowledge cannot catch up to his. As he is both above and below his followers, we are above and below him. Above him by virtue of our godlike status as audience, which grants us a knowledge greater than his and an immunity to the perils of his experience; and below him by virtue of our ordinariness, our reassuring lack of involvement. As mutes and audience to his acts, we survive the hero, and hence are ennobled and degraded at once. We bear an uncomfortable likeness to the Common Man who comes forth at the end of Robert Bolt's *Man for All Seasons* and announces:

> I'm breathing. . . . Are you breathing too? . . . It's nice, isn't it? It isn't difficult to keep alive, friends—just don't *make* trouble—or if you must make trouble, make the sort of trouble that's expected. Well, I don't need to tell you that. Good night. If we should bump into one another, recognize me.[11]

Shakespeare's tragedies end similarly, with someone—Horatio, Lodovico, Edgar, Malcolm, Aufidius, or even Caesar—coming forward to say to a cluster of survivors in England or Rome but also in the Globe, "I'm breathing—are you breathing too?" By naming his character the "Common Man" Bolt suggests what Shakespeare already knew, that despite Arthur Miller's essay on "Tragedy and the Common Man" the common man is not a tragic hero, he is a survivor. He survives by staying with the herd, by not making trouble, by not sticking his neck out or his head up—in short by not really living at all, like Willy Loman, perhaps like us.

Still, why not? Let the tragic heroes do our living for us; they do it so well. They have the courage to stick their heads up, and we do not. But then we keep our heads where they belong, attached, and they do not. So let them do our dying for us too. Let them climb high and court death and prove themselves exceptional, distinct, greater-than. As long as they are in contact with the powers—as long as Oedipus's luck holds and Antony is large with Egyptian life—the audiences within the plays and those in the theater are content to bask in the shadow of their greatness. But tragic greatness ultimately pays a fearful price. Who hath this honor? as Falstaff asked—"He that died o' Wednesday." So when we see the drawbridge of the hero's destiny shutting behind him, we prudently turn our backs like Timon's friends, or disappear in the night like Lear's Fool and Enobarbus, or simply avert our gaze like the Theban chorus. And so we live to place our palm upon our chest and announce "I'm still breathing—are you still breathing too?" The answer is always a relieved "Yes." With our foot on the corpse of the tragic hero, we know for certain that common men never die.

4. Death Demeaned and Dignified

This would suggest that tragedy is an amulet the audience acquires in the theater to ward off death. One of the ways this occurs is by taking the terror from death through humor.[12] The murder of Henry VI is cold blooded and vicious, and yet immediately before it, Richard (if he is at all the Richard of the next history play) supplements Henry's speech describing his monstrous birth and deformities with a clownish pantomime, especially at a line like

> Teeth hadst thou in thy head when thou wast born,
> To signify thou cam'st to bite the world.
>
> (3 HVI 5.6)

And immediately after Henry's murder, Richard parodies himself with lines like

> The midwife wondered and the women cried
> "O, Jesus bless us, he is born with teeth!"

The focus here is clearly on the playful killer, not the dying victim. Bracketed between two farcical performances by the toothy Richard, Henry's death loses some of its theatrical bite, much as Polonius's does when Hamlet, discovering who he has killed, merely says

> Thou wretched, rash, intruding fool, farewell!
> I took thee for thy better. Take thy fortune.
> Thou find'st to be too busy is some danger.
>
> (3.4)

Polonius is simply dismissed as a slip of the sword, and Hamlet goes on to the really serious business of piercing Gertrude's conscience, "If it be made of penetrable stuff." The last indignity is Hamlet's parting remark to his mother as he spots Polonius on his way out, "I'll lug the guts into the neighbor room." Alas, poor Polonius; his unlamented fate is like that of Rosencrantz and Guildenstern, of whom Hamlet, on hearing they have gone to it, says

> Why, man, they did make love to this employment;
> They are not near my conscience.   (5.2)

Like Polonius, Hamlet's schoolfellows make the mistake of getting "between the pass and fell incensed points / Of mightly opposites" like the Prince and the King. If death in their case is not humorous, it is not serious either, merely a pause in the greater action.

Even more serious deaths are lightened by wit and comic action—most famously perhaps the death of Duncan. For no sooner has the royal father gone ungently into his good night than the comic Porter comes beating at tragedy's door. In this case the deed of death is triply buffered, both during and after its commission. First, because the murder itself is unstaged, our attentions are focused on Lady Macbeth and her fierce imaginings as she listens outside the chamber. Second, in the moments following the murder, after Macbeth emerges full of the agenbite of inwit, the emotions we might have expended on Duncan are displaced onto his horrified killer. And finally, our attention is diverted to the irreverent Porter who in his own unwitting way, in speeches and metaphors of such relevant irrelevance, thumbs his nose at death much as Richard did.

In *Antony and Cleopatra* the gravity of Antony's death, like the gravity of his and Cleopatra's tragic stature throughout the play, struggles against comic crosscurrents. First his botched suicide has an almost Falstaffian or Gloucester-at-Dover-Cliffs aspect to it when he inspects himself and discovers he is not in Elysium:

> To do thus
> [*Falls on his sword.*]
> I learned of thee. How, not dead? Not dead?
> (4.14)

There follows the grotesquery of his effort to achieve a grand romantic death while the uncooperative Cleopatra keeps hedging her romantic bets with realistic self-interest. Refusing to leave the safety of her monument for a dying kiss, she comments ungenerously about how heavy her lord weighs as they haul him skyward, and when he dies at last—almost, one would think, as much from embarrassment as from his wounds—she reproaches him for not taking her feelings into account (5.15). If death is not quite denied in all of this, its gravity is surely compromised, in keeping of course with Shakespeare's practice of compromising all high claims in this play.

Antony is the only hero whose death is so ungraciously dealt with. When death is belittled, it is normally the deaths of minor characters. Still there is a sense in which even the deaths of tragic heroes are denied. Let me return briefly in this connection to *Richard III*.

Richard's mockery of murder at the end of *1 Henry VI* is continued throughout *Richard III*. From his impatient point of view, brothers, lord, dukes, and princes are merely so much material stuff, so many annoying tubs of guts blocking his path to the crown; their deaths are not real deaths, merely the removal of impediments. And in some degree we share his attitude. Richard seduces us as he seduces Lady Anne, and by the same device—by announcing his desire. He has, he tells us, a goal to achieve, a crown to gain, and plots to gain it by. By keeping us informed of Richard's plots Shakespeare arouses in us the desire for form, for the completion of an aesthetic pattern. "Form," Kenneth Burke said years ago, in what is still the best definition we have of the elusive concept, "is the creation of an appetite in the mind of the auditor, and the adequate satisfying of that appetite."[13] When Macbeth speaks of how "withered murder" moves "towards his design" like a ghost, his phrasing echoes the sense of aesthetic form implicit in the Witches' prophecies and Macbeth's wicked imaginings on the heath, both of which forecast his movement throughout the play toward the completion of murderous designs. Whatever or whoever frustrates this teleology frustrates us as well as the hero, and must be gotten rid of if the proper end is to be attained. Aaron, Iago, Edmund, and Macbeth all make us long perversely for the successful prosecution of forbidden acts.

In a larger sense, Shakespeare the tragic dramatist plays as villainous a role outside his plays as his Machiavellian plotters do within them. He too has murderous desires and designs. Tragedy, after all, is a killing kind of play, and it is the dramatist's dark business to see that this killing takes place, to try conclusions. Hence, like Richard III and the others, he establishes an appetite in us for a formal completion not just of the villains' plots but of his own tragic plot, whether there are villains or no. He creates in us an appetite for death the satisfaction of which compensates us for the pity and fear we have been made to suffer. Yet death is not truly death when it is reduced to playing a culminating part in the plot, a part we expect it to play and, in our aesthetic perversity, want it to play.

Death in tragedy is denied, demeaned, and diverted. It is also dignified beyond its due. To be touched with a poisoned foil like Hamlet or stabbed by one's own dagger like Othello is not the same thing as coughing and retching one's way to the grave like Keats. Most deaths are ugly, pathetic events, and Shakespeare must have seen his share of them in bodies tettered by the pox, made noseless by syphilis, or festering blackly from the plague. Tragic death transcends all of this. When the Player in *Rosencrantz and Guildenstern Are Dead* speaks well of histrionic killings and dyings, Guildenstern is indignant:

Actors! The mechanics of cheap melodrama! That isn't *death*! (*More quietly.*) You scream and choke and sink to your knees, but it doesn't bring death home to any one— it doesn't catch them unawares and start the whisper in their skulls that says—"One day you are going to die."

(*He straightens up.*) You die so many times; how can you expect them to believe in your death?

To which the Player replies "On the contrary, it's the only death they do believe."[14] Both are right. Theatrical death *is* the only death they believe, because it lends an aura of vitality and excitement to the drab deaths outside the theater that they dare not believe in because to do so sets off those fatal whispers in the skull. From this standpoint theater itself becomes an immortality system, not merely because it sands the rough edges from death but because it intensifies and glamorizes all human behavior, superimposing on life a grander life replete with grander deaths.

Until now we have examined various Shakespearean versions of the denial of death, passing from the cruder tactics of self-preservation—feeding, fighting, fleeing, hiding—to more sophisticated strategies in which the narcissism of the individual, which left to itself would be socially destructive, is transformed into chauvinism, the narcissism of the pack. By joining the pack the individual not merely enhances his or her chances of physical survival but gains access to symbolic immortality. However, in tragic heroes the narcissistic impulses of the self resist merging with larger groups. I may absorb some of the bigness of the pack I join, but I can grow perhaps even bigger if I survive my pack, if I am the last one left standing on the field. In a sense that is what some of the tragic heroes we have just examined attempt to do. By rejecting or symbolically killing fathers, they become father to themselves. They vacuum up their genetic past and stand as the lone survivor, self-created, independent of God and human lineage. Needless to say, such immortality is short lived. Fathers do not go gently into that good night or remain content there for long. They require vengeance. And in the hero who has so grandly announced his unique and autonomous identity they find a target ready-made for death.

Of course the playwright can invert the tragic focus and depict not the defeat of sons by fathers but that of fathers by sons. Or of fathers by daughters, which would bring us to *King Lear*. Here it is the father who absorbs time into himself, not the past but the future. Lear's division of his kingdom is paradoxically an act of giving that is also an act of taking. In a symbolic version of the *sparagmos* of Dionysiac ritual he dismembers his political body and divides it among his daughters in return for their worshipful love. Instead of substituting for his own father, Lear the father will substitute for his daughters' husbands. He liberates himself from the cares of kingly office, but he refuses to liberate his daughters from caring for him. The effect is the same as before: denying death, he takes total command of genetics, a point made even clearer by Shakespeare's deletion of a mother from the play's genetic structure.

Lear would take total command of genetics if he had more cooperative daughters. But of course Goneril and Regan are even greater takers than Lear. They may fatten him with flattery at the beginning, but only to make their feeding more filling. By the time they are done, their pelican parent is an O without a circle, and they have become fathers of themselves—hard-hearted and self-sufficient creatures whose organs of increase, if Lear had his wish, would shrivel inside them. Their fate is forecast by Albany:

> That nature which contemns its origin
> Cannot be bordered certain in itself.
> She that herself will sliver and disbranch
> From her material sap, perforce must wither
> And come to deadly use.   (4.2)

However, *King Lear* further complicates the relationship between patriarchy and Oedipal self-fathering as immortality projects. At first Cordelia, caught in the Antigone situation, tries to do justice both to her daughterhood and her selfhood by dividing her love fifty-fifty between Lear and her husband. But of course Lear regards this as one hundred percent betrayal and, in effect, condemns her to death with very nearly the enmity displayed by Capulet toward a rebellious Juliet. In the other camp, Edgar is made to appear a usurping patricide, and in return is condemned to death by Gloucester. However, the appearance of self-fathering impulses in the opening act is nullified later by a reversal of roles that reinstates the patriarchy. In the Dover Cliffs scene Edgar assumes the role of father to the blind Gloucester, not to kill him and become his own ancestor, but to return his life to him. Similarly, Cordelia plays a motherly succoring role in freeing Lear from his wheel of fire and returning his life to him. As substitute parents the two children "father" their own fathers, repaying them life for life. But of course the play does not end on that redemptive note.

My theme here, however, is not the denial of fathers but the denial of death—or, rather in *King Lear*, the breakdown of cultural defenses against death. For insofar as culture is an attempt to fend off nature, it is an attempt to fend off death. It may conduct us to death faster even than nature can, but when we die it is nature that does us in. Culture dresses up our deaths. It dresses up our sexual conduct too. Sex and death are weak points in culture's effort to surmount nature, because neither of them allows of a clear-cut distinction between us and the "lower" creatures. Of course it is not just sex and death but the place where sex and death take place—the human body—that must be dressed up if we are to transcend our origins. In Shakespeare's time the metadramatic implication was clearer because culture was thought of as "art," and art was usually opposed to nature. So what I am largely concerned with is the extent to which Shakespeare's art in *King Lear* is a reflection of the broader cultural effort to deny death and the human body.

1. The Truth—More or Less

If endings are largely arbitrary, so are beginnings. Let me begin with the crudely corporeal. As the mad Lear is about to enter the hovel on the heath he pauses to address the poor naked wretches of the world and his own failures:

> O, I have ta'en
> Too little care of this! Take physic, pomp;
> Expose thyself to feel what wretches feel,
> That thou mayst shake the superflux to them
> And show the heavens more just.   (3.4)

The arresting word here, it seems to me, is *superflux*. It means superfluity, and the superfluity to be shaken to the poor is the excessive riches of the wealthy. However, following the command to "take physic," the word inevitably calls attention to its component *flux*—i.e., the excremental product of a cathartic or purge—and presents us with an embarrassing excess of meanings associated with excess itself. As waste matter, flux is a bodily excess, so unnecessary and unnatural as to constitute a risk to health. To add *super* to *flux* then is to add excess onto excess, both semantically (*super* meaning above, over, beyond, exceeding) and morphologically (*flux* can stand by itself, whereas *super* supplements a suffix). The result is a transcendence of flux. By means of its prefix, *superflux* represses the crudities of the body and ascends to the abstract level of mere excess or superfluity. But the sublimation is not total; given the right context ("Take physic") we have a return of the repressed.

What does this mean for the poor naked wretches who go without? At a purely economic level Lear is arguing for a policy of monetary redistribution. So the blind Gloucester suggests a bit later when he gives money to Poor Tom and, as though glossing Lear's speech, says

> Here, take this purse, thou whom the heavens' plagues
> Have humbled to all strokes. That I am wretched
> Makes thee the happier. Heavens, deal so still!
> Let the superfluous and lust-dieted man,
> That slaves your ordinance, that will not see
> Because he does not feel, feel your power quickly;
> So distribution should undo excess
> And each man have enough.   (4.2)

In Gloucester's more decorous terminology, *superfluous* and *excess* supplant Lear's *superflux* so that "shaking the superflux" means no more than distributing. This solves an awkward problem, because Lear's earthier way of phrasing it might well leave us wondering whether the poor are to be enriched by the wealthy or shat upon by them. Perhaps both. Perhaps at this point in Lear's experience wealth seems, as the psychoanalysts maintain,[1] a form of cultural aggrandizement that is at bottom excremental. This uneasy conjunction of the sacred and the profane in money reflects the fact that as Norman O. Brown and Ernest Becker—and before them, Luther and Swift—uneuphemistically put it, man is the god who shits.[2] Thus at an appropriately dismal moment in Lear's wanderings he—or rather Shakespeare, because this is one of those expressions whose secondary meanings seem to issue more from the playwright than from the King—suggestively employs a word that sums up not only his but the general human plight. We are suppressive, repressive, self-deluding creatures, as Freud insisted; how else could we live with ourselves?

In this connection we should note that Lear and Gloucester both assume a connection between the divine and the economic, though not the same connection. Lear says "the heavens [will show] more just" if the wealthy begin giving to the poor. That is an oddly upsidedown way of putting it. Normally we should expect justice in the heavens to inspire an emulative justice on earth; but here earthly justice is called upon to create a heavenly counterpart. Gloucester's speech presents the more orthodox position. He condemns luxurious, self-indulgent man for violating the ordinance of heaven and urges reformation. Surely this is the proper view of the matter, and we might well be inclined to think Gloucester right if he had ever been right before. But, alas, he has been the very pattern of the deluded man; and even now, as he gives his purse to Poor Tom, he is buying his way to Dover "Cliffs" and a suicidal death that will prove his greatest delusion yet.

In Lear's lacerated consciousness, however, and certainly in his experience, the heavens are to all practical intents superfluous, if not nonexistent. Yet in another sense they are absolutely necessary, because they are a product of man's desperate need to create a transcendent source and pattern of justice. If this need is irrational, then "reason not the need!" Lear would cry, as he does cry when his hundred knights are reduced to none (2.4). The knights are superfluous too, but to the dispossessed Lear they symbolize royal status, prestige, authority, immortality; they protect his psyche, not his person. Without such trappings of self-esteem, he says, "man's life is cheap as beast's." And what is the grandest source of human self-esteem, the ultimate armor for the psyche, if not the belief that we are the favored ones of the gods and that heavenly justice is disposed in our behalf?[3] Without that, or some cultural substitute, life *is* cheap as beast's.

At this point in *King Lear* a cultural substitute can be envisaged, though not universally applied. In the speeches of Lear and Gloucester the distribution of money substitutes for the dispensation of divine grace. Wealth is an earthly compensation for human suffering brought on by the indifference of the gods. Money is substitute manna. Its "heavenly" aspect consists in its symbolic transcendence of its material nature. In its merely metallic form it is altogether useless stuff. The gold in Gloucester's purse will not warm Poor Tom's hands or fill his belly. As long as he is alone on the heath it is so much dead weight in his pocket, merely so much . . . well, Luther and Swift would find a name for it. But the alchemical business of culture is to transmute yellow metal into money, and money into the sacred—or in Lear's terms, to transform flux into superflux.

We seem then to have a hierarchy of superfluities. At the level of nature we find unaccommodated man with his unfed sides and houseless body. This unhappy creature is "the thing itself," a lump of breathing matter on the earth, as useless and meaningless as the lumps of yellow metal it finds in the earth. But even the thing itself is excessive: it has a brain far beyond its practical needs. When a beast lacks sensory stimulation, it loses interest and falls asleep; man in the same situation loses interest in outward affairs and falls to thinking—among other things, about what can prevent his life from being as cheap as beasts'. So he creates a symbolic world to live in. He adds value and meaning to yellow metal, he adds culture to nature, the heavens to culture, and *super* to *flux*.

Needless to say *King Lear* does not proceed upward in this way, by vertical addition, but downward, subtracting one excess from another until it reaches that existentially unaccommodated creature from which nothing further can be subtracted except its life. Let us see how this bears on Lear's experience.

To begin with, Lear himself is excessive: "They told me I was everything," he says after he has come dangerously close to being nothing, "'Tis a lie, I am not ague-proof" (4.6). Clothed in ermine, crowned in gold, housed in a palace, fed as he chooses, and possessed of all England, Lear is beyond bodily want; he needs nothing more, he is already the most. In this state of satiety he cannot *feel* the world or himself, like Gloucester's superfluous man who "will not see / Because he does not feel." For him the physical world has been consumed by symbols. England's "shadowy forests and champains rich" have dissolved into cartography, so that with a gesture toward an unfolded map Lear can slice through mountains and divide rivers. He is similarly alienated from his body. Small wonder, when he cannot feel heat or cold, hunger, pain, or thirst. For him at this point "ague" is merely a pair of cryptic syllables without a referent. He thinks his shoes are his feet, his clothes his body. His one remaining need is not bodily but spiritual, to be loved. However, because he cannot distinguish between symbols and referents, words and feelings, he cannot distinguish between love and flattery. There is a kind of poetic justice in the fact that if his daughters give him so many empty words he gives them in return so much empty space on a map.

Flattery clothes the naked truth in the ermine of words. In the case of Goneril and Regan the truth hidden by this clothing is hearts so hard that there seems to Lear no cause in nature that could have made them so. The truth in Cordelia's case is a love that should not be hidden yet cannot be expressed in a language corrupted by lies. If she could, Cordelia would dispense with language altogether; she would, as she says, merely "Love, and be silent." For her on this occasion the least of speech would be superfluous compared to silence, the "thing itself." But because silence will not do here, instead of saying nothing, she does the next best thing and says "Nothing." She lends naked silence a rag of the thinnest cloth, but it will hardly keep out the cold. Of course Cordelia goes on to deliver a carefully measured speech setting forth the balance sheet of her affections. Love is not love, she says, if it admits excess. Fifty percent to a husband, fifty percent to a father, and not a trace of superflux to shake even to the poor Fool. All of this adds up in her view to one hundred percent of the truth.

Cordelia's puritanical truth may seem the verbal antidote to her sisters' flattery. But in defining truth so strictly, as a rigid bond between words and feelings, she antedates the Coriolanus of whom Menenius says,

> His nature is too noble for the world;
> He would not flatter Neptune for his trident,
> Or Jove for his power to thunder. His heart's his mouth;
> What his breast forges, that his tongue must vent.
>
> (3.1)

Cordelia's heart's her mouth too, and hence she like Coriolanus suffers banishment. Her fate should remind us that the principle of decorum sensibly insists that there is no right style as such; there are only right styles for right occasions. On this view truth is not simply a binary correspondence between words and feelings but a complex adjustment among words, feelings, and shifting occasions. Truth, which cannot exist outside of language, cannot exist entirely inside it either; like words it has a social dimension. When words are too compliant to the occasion, they lie and truckle and wanton promiscuously; when they are too compliant to felt facts, and dismissive of the occasion, they turn terse and silent and ungenerously chaste. Between these extremes, a proper marriage of words and feelings can be made before the altar of occasion, but it is a delicate procedure. That it can be done, however, is implied by Kent when he says later on, "All my reports go with the modest truth, / Nor more nor clipped, but so" (4.7).

In the meantime, however, Cordelia's devotion to the bare truth implies that it is sufficient unto itself. But truth is more complicated. For her in her situation the truth can only be "Nothing." But Lear says "Nothing will come of nothing." That means on the one hand that "nothing" is self-sufficient in its emptiness. After all, the truth is the truth; it cannot be more or less than itself. Turned another way, however, Lear's remark implies that truth can be more than itself, that nothing can multiply, creating more nothing. In which case there can be too much truth, Cordelia's truth. Attempting to avoid the superfluities of flattery, she attains a superfluity of truth.

If Cordelia's style is the verbal equivalent of unaccommodated man, it is appropriate that because of it she herself should be rendered as poor and bare as the thing itself. "When she was dear to us," Lear says to Burgundy,

> we did hold her so;
> But now her price is fallen. Sir, there she stands.
> If aught within that little seeming substance,
> Or all of it, with our displeasure pieced,
> And nothing more, may fitly like your Grace,
> She's there, and she is yours.

Cordelia stands before her suitors as Portia did before hers when she said "You see me, Lord Bassanio, where I stand, / Such as I am" (3.2). Cordelia's price so radically reduced, she has diminished to nothing, like gold money returning to the "little seeming substance" of yellow metal. Except of course that to the discerning suitor she, like Portia, has the kind of instrinsic value that Gresham's Exchange cannot register. France accepts the "unprized precious maid," and she is rescued from her nothingness.

In effect, of course, what Lear does to Cordelia, his daughters do to him—or rather he does to himself, because it is he who enfranchises them. But whereas Cordelia has only briefly to suffer her swift fall from grace to cultural nothingness—the sudden "dismantling," as France puts it, "of so many folds of favor"—Lear's divestiture is long and painful. By the time Cordelia, taking a cue from France in the opening scene, acknowledges the old man's intrinsic worth at their reunion, his brains are cut beyond cure.

Because in the opening scene Lear receives too many words from Goneril and Regan and too few from Cordelia, the truth is lost and tragedy commences. The remedy, it seems, is to discover the lost truth of Goneril and Regan's malignity and Cordelia's love. For Lear to learn the truth about his flattering daughters, however, is to learn a larger truth about himself and overcivilized man—namely, that culture taken too readily on faith is merely flattery writ large. To learn this truth Lear must be stripped of his cultural garb. He undoes the first button himself by giving away the more substantial properties of kingship—the land and "the sway, revenue, and execution of the rest"—and retaining nothing but its symbols, "The name and all the addition to a king." Then he loses his knights, then his Fool, and at last his clothing and his mind. At this point he becomes what he takes Poor Tom to be, the truth, or what he takes the truth to be—man stripped bare of culture. If earlier he was alienated from his body through satiety and symbolism, now he is nothing but body—shivering flesh and aching bones, a dirty, stinking creature who must wipe his hand before letting Gloucester kiss it because "it smells of mortality" (4.6).

Lear thinks Poor Tom is the thing itself, when it is only Edgar pretending to be. The sweep of his pendular experience has taken Lear as far wrong in the direction of nature as it had at the start in the direction of culture. It seems Shakespeare sets up oppositions of this structural sort, only to dissolve them with subtle mergers and gradations and supplementations. Edgar *looks* like the truth of mortifying nature Lear seeks, but is actually suspended above it by a shred of culture: between him and Nothing is his role as Poor Tom. Similarly his brother Edmund calls on nature to be his goddess and defend him against the plague of custom. His goddess would dissolve all distinctions between himself the bastard and Edgar the legitimate, and so he ends up crying "Now, gods, stand up for bastards!" Yet he is a bastard and "natural" child not by grace of nature but only by the disgrace of culture. Legitimacy and illegitimacy being purely arbitrary cultural distinctions, there are no natural children in the nature he valorizes. But of course it is not a leveling nature he wants anyhow, but the cultural distinctions he lacks—legitimacy, property, power, love.

Whatever Edmund says and however Edgar looks, they will not cast aside the mediations of culture and plunge naked into nature's storms.[4] But Lear does. He wants to find the truth in all its immediacy. And of course he finds more truth than man can bear. On the stormy heath nothing comes of nothing for Lear, and comes again and again until it batters him mad. By the time he speaks the truth he does not know what he is saying. He says "Come, come, I am a king, / Masters, know you that?" (4.6). He has proved a natural king, as he always assumed he was, crowned now with thorns and arrayed in weeds, but he is also a man o'ermastered. To be a "natural king" is a contradiction in terms, there being no more kings in nature than there are bastards. Thus Lear unkings himself in the act of proclaiming his kingship.

It is not truth Lear needs now but love, and Cordelia offers him both at once, for her truth is her love, expressed in the simplest yet dearest of terms: "And so I am, I am. . . . No cause, no cause" (4.7). Love, however, like truth, can be excessive in this play. At the end, when Lear stares frantically into the face of Cordelia and dies, we cannot tell whether he dies of too much truth or too much love—his heart bursting either from the despairing knowledge that she is dead or from an exultant misimpression that she is not.

2. Poetic Truth—More and Less

Let me take a step now in the metadramatic direction by asking how all this bears on the poet, particularly the one who is writing *King Lear*. Surely in some degree Shakespeare is in the position of Cordelia, called on to speak the truth in a language of lies. If so, then like her he can hardly say nothing; and yet to follow her example and say no more than "Nothing" is to be puritanically close with the truth. Can he afford to indulge himself in her somewhat self-righteous concern for honest speech?

On the other hand, if Shakespeare shares Cordelia's plight, must he not also feel some affinity to Goneril and Regan? After all, poetry has more in common with lies and flattery than it has with the naked truth. The russet yeas and honest kersey noes to which the reformed Berowne dedicates himself at the end of *Love's Labour's Lost* yield little poetically; we are lucky we met him before he grew so blunt and countrified of speech. And who but a mule would want Falstaff an ounce lighter if it meant jettisoning his lies? Poetry is Falstaffian, thriving on surpluses—more words than the facts require, more meanings than strict truth demands. Reason not the need, the poet cries, there are needs and needs. Lear needs a hundred knights, Goneril a wardrobe of ermine. He would die of shame without retainers, she of the cold if she wore wool. So poetry would shrivel into prose if it were confined to the literal, the utterly plain style. We should remember that although Goneril's and Regan's speeches are most egregious flattery, they are also most excellent poetry.

Still, if poetry has a lot to do with lies, it surely has a little to do with truth. But as there are needs and needs, so there are truths and truths. Cordelia's truth is a loving one; it needs saying. Yet what she says is "Nothing." Shakespeare's truth in *King Lear* is not so loving, yet he manages to say it at great length and with marvelous eloquence. When he came to write the play, however, he must have had some reservations. He must have wondered what a poet should say if the truth is that there is no truth, if the truth is "Nothing." Did he ask himself, as Lear asks, "Is man no more than this?" — simply the thing itself caught out of doors in a maddening storm? And if so, should he be told this truth, or should he be flattered into believing the gods are just, life full of meaning, and he himself the paragon of animals?

Who would want to answer such questions? Not Shakespeare, I think. If it is the responsibility of the playwright to answer them, then in *King Lear* Shakespeare gives every indication of wanting to abdicate from that responsibility. But abdication, he discovers, is not as easy as it looks. If we consider the play from a metadramatic perspective we find the playwright formulating the issue and unformulating it at the same time, by creating a play whose subject is uncreation.

XIII *King Lear* 2

As I suggested in the previous chapter, in *King Lear* the denial of death takes a broad cultural form. More than in any other of Shakespeare's tragedies the play calls in question the nature and purpose of society. Lear's concept of *superflux*, in which the Renaissance notion of hierarchical order collapses into the scatological struggle of man's divine upper functions to transcend his devilish lower ones, is reflected in various ways in the play, most obviously perhaps in Lear's depiction of woman as a centaur, fine above but foul below. At this point the foulness of humanity gives every indication of overcoming its fineness; and Albany sums up the general disintegration of social order and meaning with his image of humanity metamorphosing into monsters of the deep gliding randomly about in search of prey.

In this and the following chapter I want to expand the focus of death denial to include not only the plight of characters within *King Lear* but the plight of *King Lear* itself. That is, I want to give death denial a metadramatic turn by exploring, as I think Shakespeare does, the notion that a play is itself a product and a reflection of culture. As such it is a tenuous and somewhat arbitrary effort to create meanings out of the crude stuff of human experience, meanings that, like Albany's "humanity," are always in danger of slipping down into the monstrous depths. To keep this from happening is the business of the playwright, and in this play, I think, Shakespeare dramatizes the burdens and dilemmas entailed by that responsibility.

1. Abdication and Authority

Throughout his career, from the saintly Henry VI sitting on his molehill during the battle of Towton to Prospero breaking his staff and drowning his book, Shakespeare was apparently fascinated with the concept of abdication and truancy. Prince Hal plays truant from his royal studies, Hamlet from his revengeful duties, and Antony from his Roman wars. The academicians in *Love's Labour's Lost* retreat from the world and women, King John tells the Bastard Faulconbridge "Have thou the ordering of this present time," Richard II deposes himself with histrionic relish, Duke

Vincentio retreats into dark corners, and Lear formally abdicates. Perhaps we may sense in these depictions of royal withdrawal an impulse on Shakespeare's part to abandon, not necessarily London for the rusticity of Stratford, but his own responsibility as playwright exercising authority over his theatrical subjects. In any event, on at least one occasion, when he composes the choruses of *Henry V*, we find him explicitly renouncing his authority as sole creator and regarding the play as issuing from the cooperative imagination of his audience as well. What then of *King Lear*, where the formal abdication of the hero might suggest a similar abdication on the part of the playwright? Examining the play from this standpoint suggests, I think, that Shakespeare is engaged in a kind of creative uncreation.

First, some qualifications. Obviously Shakespeare can never wholly abdicate from his role as creative authority. Because forms and meanings do not fall from the sky, not even from an intertextual sky, he remains responsible for his art and for what it does to us. We are inevitably his subjects in the Globe—not slaves, as Brecht would have it, but subjects obliged by our bond to honor his authority (at least as long as he gives us no just cause for rebellion) and by an act of poetic faith to endow his illusions with an air of reality. Hence when I say that Shakespeare uncreates *King Lear* I can hardly mean that, swept up by a passion for entropy, he abandons his play to disorder, and us to early sorrow. The patterns of imagery, the double plot, verbal echoes, and structural parallels, all the biblical allusions, proverbs, aphorisms, sententiae, and other suggestions of communal wisdom testify to Shakespeare's ordering presence. Still, while remaining within the bounds of artistic form, Shakespeare manages, I suggest, both to unmake as well as to make *King Lear*.

Whether you simply create or creatively uncreate depends on whether you begin with order or disorder. The traditional procedure is assumed to begin, like God in Genesis, with disorder, which is then ordered into art. "Life," Samuel Beckett says somewhere, "is a mess," and it is the writer's business to clean it up. Or if life or nature is not entirely a mess, still it can profit from artistic "gilding," as Sidney believed, or from being "methodized" in the approved neoclassic manner. On the other hand, you can begin with order and "disorder" it into art. When a culture reaches the point where reality has been definitively charted—when fluid forms have petrified into institutions, and live meanings deadened into clichés—the artist may feel it is high time for turbulence, in which case he will seek to "defamiliarize" with the Russian Formalists, to "alienate" with Brecht, or in other ways to liberate the energy of what Morse Peckham calls "man's rage for chaos."[1]

With this in mind, let us glance again at Lear's act of uncreation, his division of an ordered (even well-mapped) kingdom in which the differences that plague men have been incorporated into the hierarchical chain of societal being under the unified rule of a king. Lear's uncreating act of division may remind us of God's creative divisions in Genesis when beginning with chaos he divided the land from the sea, the sky from the earth, the day from the night, Sunday from the week, and eventually Eve from Adam's rib cage. Shakespeare's upsidedown glance at the Creation is repeated from a different angle in the opening scene if we recall that God did not think or craft but rather *spoke* the world into being with the magical utterance "Let there be." Surprisingly, in the mouths of Goneril and Regan speech has a similar creativity as their flattering words materialize into acreage. Here in parodic accord with the doctrine of ex nihilo, which William Elton labels "a keystone of the accepted theology of Shakespeare's day,"[2] and despite Lear's announcement to Cordelia that "nothing will come of nothing," from the nothing of flattery issue "shadowy forests . . . with champains riched," "plenteous rivers and wide-skirted meads," and other signs that like Osric the ladies have become spacious in the possession of dirt.

Something frequently comes of nothing in *King Lear*. From the nothing of his lies and forged letter in act 1, scene 2, Edmund gradually creates himself Duke of Gloucester and head of the armies of England. And if lies and flattery are unreferential nothings, so are disguises. When Edgar assumes his disguise he says "Edgar I nothing am" (2.3). From that nothing emerges Poor Tom. But by the same token, remove the rags of his disguise and Edgar would have to confess "Poor Tom I nothing am." Thus Edgar leaves various nonidentities behind as he creates new somethings—Poor Tom, the "fiend" at the top of the cliff, the gentleman at the bottom, the "most poor man" who aids Gloucester after the meeting with Lear, the thick-spoken peasant who cudgels Oswald to his grave, and the knight who kills Edmund. Each is a kind of nothing or "not this" from which at last the real Edgar magically issues as prospective king. But Edgar's most spectacular creation of something from nothing is at Dover "Cliffs," where his empty, unreferential words create the most dizzying height in literature. Moreover, if we back away from this precipice, we see that Shakespeare is far more inventive than Edgar in fashioning out of nothing the heights and depths, not of Dover, but of *King Lear* itself. He ushers us into the "wooden O" of the theater and seats us in front of a barren stage, he brings forth two men, has one of them say "I thought the King had more affected the Duke of Albany than Cornwall"—and before we can say "ex nihilo" the world of pagan England stands before us.

My theme, however, is uncreation—not the something that comes of nothing but the nothing that comes of something. As everyone knows, "nothing" is a kind of vortex that draws the ordered world of *King Lear* downward, reducing Lear to nakedness and madness and Gloucester to blindness.[3] However, Shakespeare does not merely divest Lear of his clothing; he also strips his own theatrical art to a kind of nakedness as "near to beast" as Poor Tom. As various critics have shown,[4] he forces his language down the great chain of stylistic decorum from a richly appareled high style to an honest kersey plainness, and then by means of repetition—e.g., "Kill, kill, kill, kill, kill, kill," "Sa sa sa sa," "Help, help, O, help," "Run, run, O, run," "Howl, howl, howl," "No, no, no life," "Never, never, never, never, never" (4.6; 5.3)—obliges it to descend one further step, to the point at which words are shorn of meaning and become again merely savage cries, the wild phonic stuff of which we suppose speech to have been originally formed. Clearly this is an aesthetic dead end. The play can go no further in this direction unless the entire cast begins to howl, transforming Shakespeare's Globe into Artaud's theater of cruelty.

At this extreme of verbal nothingness, where words run together in a jumble of undifferentiated noise, we reach a point of maximum entropy, a black hole of speech from which no meaning can emerge. However, language is merely one, albeit a major, instance of how Lear's uncreating act causes ordered differences to collapse into chaotic undifferentiation. His line "They told me I was everything; 'tis a lie, I am not ague-proof" illustrates his own fall from an eminence conventionally created ("They told me") to that ague-prone condition which comes all too naturally to everyone. To be meaningful in language or in culture generally, difference must be arbitrarily ordered—a fact of which Lear was formerly oblivious but which he now registers most painfully:

> See how yond justice rails upon yond simple thief. Hark in thine ear: change places, and, handy-dandy, which is the justice, which is the thief? Thou hast seen a farmer's dog bark at a beggar?
>
> GLOUCESTER. Ay, sir.
>
> LEAR. And the creature run from the cur? There thou mightst behold the great image of authority; a dog's obeyed in office. (4.6)

Remove the distinctions, subtract necessity from luxury, and on the heath all are "poor naked wretches," "none does offend," king and beggar shiver alike, and the bastard is as rich in dirt as the legitimate. As Edmund's leveling "dear goddess" Nature implies, when difference falls from its ordered vertical hierarchy onto a horizontal plane, it becomes the random "differences" of creatures governed only by a common need to devour. As Albany puts it,

> If that the heavens do not their visible spirits
> Send quickly down to tame these vile offenses,
> It will come,
> Humanity must perforce prey on itself,
> Like monsters of the deep.   (4.2)

This entropic Hobbesian state ruled only by appetite cannot be said to mean; it simply is. The distinction between meaning and "is" is frequently made in this play, most notably perhaps by Edgar when he witnesses the moving meeting of his blind father and the mad King: "I would not take this from report; it is, / And my heart breaks at it" (4.6). Edgar's term *report* is convenient to my purpose here since as a secondary verbal account it may be contrasted with the primary "it is" of direct experience. These two modes might be regarded as dividing up *King Lear* itself, or any play — the mediated *re*-presentation of past affairs, the "there and then" mode we call narrative, and the immediate *present*-ation of the "here and now" we think of as dramatic. Edgar is no doubt right to suspect report, which in its "re-carrying" of events in speech may subtract from them for easier portage or add to them to increase their value. It is rare indeed when one can truly say with Kent, "All my reports go with the modest truth, / Nor more nor clipped, but so" (4.7). But in all cases, whether more or clipped or so, reports are interpretations — verbal orderings of immediate experiences that in themselves do not "mean" but simply "are."

In this broad sense of interpretation we might argue that in subjecting *King Lear* to a state of entropic uncreation Shakespeare is stripping it of "report" en route to the naked "it is" of immediate experience. It is almost as though, abdicating from his task of presenting his audience with made meanings and fashioned forms, he were requiring us to return with him to a point of creative origin, the unshaped, meaningless stuff with which he began. If so, then this regressive undoing of the play seems to accord with its historical regression to ancient England — to a primitive period before Christianity imposed its form and meanings on the presumed chaos of pagan times.[5] For Shakespeare's Jacobean audience Christianity would have constituted a Kent-like true report of the condition of man, a redemptive supplement to paganism. Even within the play, which is explicitly pagan, Christian values are often expressed — repentance, expiation, humility, patience, forgiveness, the sin of despair and suicide, the recurrent hope that the "heavens" like a just and merciful God will send down "visible spirits" to tame offenses before it is too late. But men's hopes count for very little in this play. Lear cries "O, let me not be mad, not mad, sweet heaven!" and subsequently goes mad (1.5), or he calls to the heavens "Make it your cause; send down, and take my part" and has his soldiers reduced to zero (2.4). [6] Our own hopes of mercy seem happily fulfilled when with Lear and Cordelia reunited a spirit of grace appears regnant. We are prepared to accept such a Christian report as "so" and to rejoice in the gentle conquest of pagan suffering. But within two hundred lines Lear makes his dreadful entrance with Cordelia dead in his arms, and we are compelled to agree with Edgar on seeing his father blind:

> Who is it can say "I am at the worst"?
> I am worse than e'er I was.   (4.1)

The consolations of Christian philosophy are temptingly offered but cruelly withdrawn. [7]

Edgar follows his remark about the evolution of "the worst" with another even more significant:

> And worse I may be yet. The worst is not
> So long as we can say "This is the worst."

It is fitting that Edgar should present this brief report on the relation of report to the grievousness of "it is" inasmuch as he is himself so given to reportage. In fact as Bridget Gellert Lyons suggests, [8] the subplot of which Edgar is a part can be regarded as a report on the main plot. Of course the main plot has its own reporter, the Fool. But whereas Edgar judges men by moral standards, the Fool measures them against his own role. His critique of Lear, Kent, and all "lords and great men," is that they imitate what he appears to be ("they will not let me have all the fool to myself" [1.4]), instead of what he is, a wise fellow. Yet the wise fellow is foolish enough himself to follow Lear to kennel in the storm instead of having the good sense to stand by the fire like Lady Brach and stink (1.4).

The Fool's report, which yields a world of undifferentiated foolishness, tells the truth, but tells it slant and incomplete. If the same actor doubled as Fool and Cordelia, then we may see each character embodying merely part of the truth. [9] In the opening scene Cordelia's truth is not "allowed" and she is banished. But she returns later in the role of the Fool, now "allowed," and tells Lear the abrasive truth about his own folly. But the Fool cannot tell Lear the whole truth. When the King's wits begin to turn in earnest, passing beyond the range of mere folly, the Fool's fooling pales by comparison. Lacking employment, he grows more and more concerned with practical affairs—the coldness of the night and lack of shelter (3.4)—says less and less, and at last abdicates his fool's cap by disappearing from the play. His disappearance, however, makes foolish sense. When Lear has absorbed the Fool's truths and begins to utter them himself, the Fool becomes redundant.

After all, the Fool's function is to tell subversive truths to a court society foolish enough to think its own truths are *the* truth. Thus he is a liminal figure, the "outsider-within," living at the borders of accepted reality, issuing alternative reports on "what is." When Lear crosses those borders he enters uncharted regions of mind where much madness is divinest sense and the Fool has no business. The Fool can tell the court that much sense is the starkest madness, but it is a violation of foolish function to tell the starkly mad Lear the redundant truth that he is mad. Perhaps that is why the Fool, in an early forecast of his later abdication, said "I would fain learn to lie," only to have Lear insist that he stay true to his calling: "An you lie, sirrah, we'll have you whipped" (1.4). Unable in the storm either to lie or to tell the truth, the Fool appropriately falls silent and disappears. Or, if the doubling theory is true, he metamorphoses into Cordelia, representing what Lear now needs more than the truth—love. But not even love can save him in this harsh world. Ultimately he must announce "My poor fool is hanged"—both his poor fools. Perhaps in "The Phoenix and the Turtle" Shakespeare found the right requiem for this doubly sad hanging: "Truth and beauty buried be."

Even with this complex Fool, then, the main plot still calls for interpretation, for report. The subplot on the other hand tends to supply its own. Lear's dying moments, for instance, are harrowing to an audience in part because they are presented as immediate, uninterpreted experience. We must make of them what we can. But Gloucester's death comes to us more comfortably because its rawness has been filtered, ordered, and endowed with meaning by Edgar's long report of it (5.3); and even though Gloucester's "suicide" is dramatically immediate, it is accompanied by Edgar's reassuring commentary and followed by his interpretive summing up.[10] Thus the subplot, whose actions are so familiarly formed and morally coherent, is a kind of cultural paradigm that illuminates by contrast the disintegrations of the main plot.

Yet if the subplot constitutes a dramatic/narrative report, a gloss in the margin of the main plot, it is not a very enlightening commentary. Indeed, even its reports on its own actions clip a good deal from the modest truth of Kent's "so." For instance, kindly as Edgar's intentions may be, his saving of Gloucester from despair at Dover has been justly called a "pious fraud."[11] Denied the comfort of ending his suffering (4.6), Gloucester is made to believe himself miraculously rescued by the "clearest gods," presumably so that the entrance of the mad Lear a few moments later—"O ruined piece of nature!"—can be inflicted on him. Gloucester's experience in general is given the reassuring form of a Christian tragedy. His moral blindness about the begetting of Edmund and the betrayal of Edgar leads to a physical blinding which is spiritually compensated for by his inner illumination—"I have no way, and therefore want no eyes; / I stumbled when I saw" (4.1). Then at Dover redemptive faith, inspired by miracle, makes a conquest of despair. However, this providential pattern is not merely irrelevant to Lear's experience but is, like Edgar's charade at Dover, a kindly cruel misrepresentation of what Gloucester himself has suffered. In its large way it is as trivializing as Edgar's moralistic remarks attributing the blinding of his father to his dark and vicious beggetting of Edmund.

Edgar, though himself a victim of Edmund's spurious reports, is nevertheless the principal reporter in the play. Everything is grist for his moral mills. He witnesses the most appalling things—the bleeding fact of his blinded father, his attempt at suicide, Lear mad on the heath, the meeting of the two old men, his father's death, the deaths of Cordelia and Lear—and through it all he marches steadily forward behind a shield of sententia and aphorism. In his reportorial role he specializes in second-hand experience in a way somewhat like that of the poet. That is, his suffering is not direct but at a slight remove, mediated by his suite of disguises; and his reports recapitulate the experience of others—Lear, Gloucester, Kent. As a *poète manqué*, however, he settles too readily for conventional forms and ideas. Like the Fool, he cannot accompany Lear into what Conrad calls the heart of darkness, though like Marlow he can return to tell us about it in words we know are incommensurate to their subject. Lear does Edgar's living for him, as Kurtz does Marlow's for him. Because Lear is truly mad, Edgar need only pretend to be. Lear says "I am bound upon a wheel of fire" and is entitled to believe it true. For Edgar it could never be anything but metaphor.

In the final lines of the play Edgar uncharacteristically says "Speak what we feel, not what we ought to say"—thus saying both what he ought to say and presumably also what he feels.[12] More often, however, he simply says "what we ought to say"—what is prescribed by moral decorum and makes sense within known frames of reference. Not that Edgar lacks feeling. After all, it is he who says of Lear, "My tears begin to take his part so much / They mar my counterfeiting" (3.6), who speaks of the horrors of "the worst," and who concludes his remarks about not taking the meeting of Lear and Gloucester from report by saying "And my heart breaks at it." It is not that Edgar doesn't respond to painful situations but that he keeps his pain in place. For ultimately he is more a man of action than an artist. However inadequately he may account for things, he does evade a sentence of death, protect Lear on the heath, save his father's life from both suicide and the ambitious Oswald, fight in battle and survive, kill Edmund in combat, and stand ready at the end to rule England. Edgar cannot afford to think, or feel, too precisely on the event; he must keep an eye out for hovels and cudgels, roots, berries, bounty hunters, malevolent brothers, and propitious moments. We might even take the incommensurateness of his "reports" as an index to his competence and resourcefulness as a man. Edgar will not create a new order or discover the previously unapprehended relations of things, but he will keep the world intact for one more day.

It goes without saying that Shakespeare's art is a far cry from Edgar's. Edgar makes practical use of conventional forms, employing the morality play to save his father and the chivalric romance to kill his brother. Shakespeare begins with conventional forms also: the chronicle play of *King Leir*, Sidney's pagan romance *Arcadia*, and of course more broadly the form of tragedy. However God may have accomplished his Creation, the doctrine of ex nihilo has no place in the artistic practice of Shakespeare, who throughout his career relies on prior textual somethings to generate a greater intertextual something. Nevertheless, "nothing" has its role in this process. Unlike Edgar, who preserves conventional forms, Shakespeare warps and undermines them. The plots of *King Leir* and of Sidney's episode in the *Arcadia* may supply the framework of Shakespeare's action, but their original import is nullified as much as their form is displaced. To construct his main plot Shakespeare divests *King Leir* of its Christian trappings, and to lend his subplot a morality structure he erases the paganism of Sidney's story.[13] And finally, as Stephen Booth emphasizes, he brings the tragic form of the play to an apparent conclusion only to turn the rack a bit further.[14]

In other words, Shakespeare's treatment of prior forms is analogous to his treatment of language, which he puts on the rack to compel it (by troping) to forgo its conventional lies and tell the truth. Less figuratively, although we know language is differential, the poet, like the rest of us in our ordinary dealings with it, experiences signifiers and signifieds as naturally bound together within the sign. Thus the first act of the poet will be to decompose this unity, breaking words free from their conventional significations in order to endow them with new and greater meanings. This process is suggested in Shakespeare's treatment of Lear, whom he portrays at the beginning as a man caught up in the supposed naturalness of speech when he honors the apparent bond of signifier and signified in the flattery of Goneril and Regan. Though Lear divides his kingdom, he unites words and meanings. Then, having empowered flattering words, he gradually discovers that there is no natural bond between what is said and what is meant. The result for him, as for the poet who consciously breaks this bond, is chaos—a breakdown of all familiar meanings and expectations. This period of chaotic nothingness, in which the old meanings have been abandoned and new ones not yet formulated, constitutes the poet's storm, the confusions and discomforts of which he must endure as he makes his way toward a new order, the forging of new bonds between words and meanings.

It is this stormy interim of creative madness that the Fool cannot endure or Edgar suffer at first hand. So the Fool escapes madness by disappearing, and Edgar by holding tight to the prefabricated forms and artificial truths of his social order. Only Lear confronts this storm wholly unaccommodated, and it kills him. Lear's madness is not the poet's madness. Lear does not return from madness with words of illumination; he knows only that he does not know, for "to deal plainly," he says, "I fear I am not in my perfect mind" (4.7). He entertains fantasies of a safe withdrawal from suffering for him and Cordelia, and thinks "the gods themselves throw incense" on "such sacrifices" as them (5.3). After all he has experienced, we feel at this point like demanding as Kent did in the opening scene, "See better, Lear!" Perhaps at the very end, when he cries "Look there, look there!" after his five "nevers," we are meant to think he does see somewhat better. Not that he sees Cordelia's living breath but that he registers the sheer human necessity of continuing to insist on life in the process of dying, for without this he and she and we are already dead.

Only Shakespeare enters the storm and (in the most meaningful sense of the phrase) lives to tell about it. To be sure, it was he who created the storm in the first place, willfully disjoining the form and content of texts he might have preserved intact had he been Edgar, and dissolving the "something" of prior words into "nothing" by fragmenting the sign. Still, it requires more courage to volunteer for storm duty than to be conscripted to it like Lear; the winds are no less cold and mind numbing. But the poet must leave the palace of received meanings and enter the uncharted heath, to bare his mind and shiver and chatter like the thing itself, before he can frame chaos into shapes of sense accessible to us in the theater. In a large act of metaphoric naming he abuses and violates language, rips words from their meanings, scatters sense in all directions, lets signifieds be ravened up by signifiers, until the deconstituted stuff of his art, like humanity itself in Albany's prediction, "must perforce prey on itself, / Like monsters of the deep" (4.2). Yet out of this madness and nothingness Shakespeare at last emerges, unlike Lear, in even more than his right mind, indeed so marvelously "mad in craft," as Hamlet put it, that he can write *King Lear* as a play that dramatizes this very experience.

1. Report

In *King Lear* Shakespeare not only puts his creative materials on
the rack but employs a mode of development that is itself racklike as well.
As Michael Goldman and William Matchett have shown, Edgar's remarks
when he sees his blinded father—

> O gods! Who is it can say "I am at the worst"?
> I am worse than e'er I was . . .
> And worse I may be yet. The worst is not
> So long as we can say "This is the worst"
>
> (4.1)

—underscore a basic rhythm of defeated expectation in the play.[1] Like the
characters, the audience is obliged to pass from one painful "it is" to another
even more searing. Punctuating this degenerative movement are the interpretive reports—e.g., "This is the worst"—that issue periodically from
various characters but most often from Edgar, who seems to speak for
everyone including the audience in voicing the hope that we have come to
the end.

Edgar's word *report*, as I mentioned earlier, is useful because it helps us
score a basic rhythm of the play as it first presents and then records experience. Edgar records his own response to the sight of Lear and Gloucester
meeting on the heath by saying "I would not take this from report; it is, /
And my heart breaks at it" (4.6). The immediate "it is" of *King Lear* is often,
as here, heartbreaking. Report—i.e., narration, interpretation, representation—is by comparison, Edgar implies, more comforting. It stands to "it is"
as "super" stands to "flux," transcending not man's corporeal grossness but
the gross immediacy of his suffering. Report cushions the impact of immediate experience because it re-presents it at some distance in time, but
also because, however scant it may be, report is still a made meaning, a
transformation of rawness into the once-remove of speech, and hence of
coherence, sequence, order, and form.[2] Even a stark depressing statement
like Edgar's "This is the worst" voices small the large institutionalized say-

ings of culture without which we hear nothing but William James's blooming buzzing confusion.

In the context of *King Lear* these periodic sayings constitute moments of arrest within a current of worsening. At their simplest they do no more than register the "it is" of pain, as in the extraordinary emphasis on "hearted" feeling:

> O, madam, my old heart is cracked, it's cracked! (2.1.92)
> O, how this mother swells up toward my heart! (2.4.55)
> O me, my heart, my rising heart! (2.4.119)
> Wilt break my heart? (3.4.4)
> [It is,] And my heart breaks at it. (4.6.141)
> O, that my heart would burst! (5.3.186)
> Break, heart, I prithee, break! (5.3.317)

In addition to these bare recordings of pain, so thinly separated from pain itself, characters make gestures toward meaning that range from Lear's baffled questionings — "Is there any cause in nature that make these hard hearts?" (3.6.76) — to his mad trial in search of truth and justice, and his random pronouncements on the heath about the human plight. As Lear's search for sense returns to elemental states of nakedness, homelessness, helplessness, and madness, the sense he madly discerns makes fewer and fewer distinctions: all are wretched, all go to it, none is guilty. On the other hand, the subplot begins with generalities and undifferentiations — Gloucester's astrological determinism, his claim to make no distinction between his sons, Edmund's leveling goddess Nature — and proceeds toward formal clarity as it takes on the character of a morality play at Dover Cliffs, a chivalric romance in the trial by combat, and, finally, a definitive report when Edgar moralizes his father's blinding and narrates his death.

There is a suggestion then that the two plots, though parallel in some respects, are moving in opposite directions — the main plot toward maximum entropy, madness, and the unspeakable "it is," the subplot toward order, meaning, and the mediations of report; the one broadly uncreating, the other creating. Thus the overall thrust of the play is a racklike intensification of pain briefly arrested by moments of report that differ from plot to subplot. All the transient reports by characters participate in the overall report that is the developing form of *King Lear*, a form we begin to sense as the play proceeds on its painful way.

That way of putting it implies that report is comforting, a haven of order and meaning amid a world of suffering — and in some degree it is. Unfortunately, however, the form that is taking shape is that which is identified by

Edgar's statement, "The worst is not / So long as we can say 'This is the worst.' " The act of saying "This is the worst" offers some slight consolation inasmuch as it re-presents rather than presents us with the worst: yet it is merely a verbal anesthetic for a pain that, as the saying itself guarantees, will recur and deepen. Thus report shields us from present pain with, paradoxically, a promise of worse suffering in the future.[3]

2. Bearing Affliction in the Globe

Before seeing where all this pain is taking us, let us glance at two famous episodes that illustrate the relation of "it is" to "report." I mean the blinding of Gloucester and his salvation at Dover, both of which have meta-dramatic overtones. What stands out in the blinding scene, of course, is the sheer brutality of the evil confederates as they grind out Gloucester's eyes and leave him "all dark and comfortless" (3.7). This mercilessness is punctuated on three occasions when Gloucester twice invokes the "kind gods" and once explicitly cries "Give me some help! O cruel! O you gods!" But the gods are silent; and we are left with two questions: "Would a charitable God permit Gloucester's eyes to be ground out?" and "Would a charitable playwright violate classical decorum by staging this action?" In both cases the answer is clearly "No." If there is no mercy for Gloucester, there is none for us either. To paraphrase Edgar, we would happily have taken this from report, but we are not given the opportunity; it is, and we, like Gloucester, are tied to the stake and must stand the course. Shakespeare grinds this scene into our eyes as viciously as Cornwall grinds his boot into Gloucester's.

Few scenes in dramatic literature better exemplify Edgar's "it is" than this one. By the same token few scenes better exemplify his term *report* than the one at Dover Cliffs. In each scene the audience is compelled to experience what Gloucester experiences. We share his pain during his blinding, and we share his blindness during his fall. As Levin and Matchett have shown,[4] a first-night audience to the Dover Cliffs scene would be as deluded initially by what Shakespeare says to us as Gloucester is by what Edgar says to him. According to theatrical convention the time and location of an action are dictated not by what we see on stage but by what we hear from characters. The words "This is Illyria, lady" waft Italian sea breezes across the bare English stage; and "By the clock 'tis day / And yet dark night strangles the traveling lamp" shadows the afternoon sun in the Globe as well as in Scotland. We must suppress the evidence of our senses, and especially at Dover where we are on the same (non)cliff as Gloucester. Like him we *hear* that he is on a fearful height, though we see only a flat stage ("Methinks the ground is even"); we hear that the sea is surging below, though no sound tells of it ("do you hear the sea?" — "No, truly"); and we hear that from the extreme verge crows and choughs can be seen winging the midway air, and fishermen moving like mice on the beach, though we see no such things on stage. We do know that Edgar has a stratagem when he says "Why I do trifle thus with his despair / Is done to cure it," but it is not until Gloucester has sprawled forward and Edgar says "Had he been where he thought, / By this, had thought been past" that we know for certain he is not on a cliff and we have been as blind as he.

What to make of this? Why at a moment of such high dramatic intensity should Shakespeare strain plausibility to and beyond the breaking point? Why introduce a scene that inevitably provokes some members of the audience to laughter and invites Shakespeare students to harass their instructors with scoffing questions?

Let us work our way toward an answer by assuming to begin with that Shakespeare has deliberately paralleled our theatrical with Gloucester's fictional situation in this scene. For if we share his blindness we will wonder what else we share with the old man. The not so obvious answer would seem to be a loss of faith leading to salvation, since that is what we see Gloucester experiencing. In his case the pattern is clear. When he asks Edgar to lead him to Dover he has lost faith, as he had also, to a lesser degree, when he listened to Edmund's lies in act 1. But at that point he needed no faith because he lacked no eyes; indeed he vaunted his sightedness ("Let's see. Come, if it be nothing, I shall not need spectacles"). Now, however, unable to compare what he hears with what he sees, he must take Edgar's words on faith. He does, and he is saved.

Edgar's text for Gloucester is faith; so is Shakespeare's text for us. However, if we are to share Gloucester's faith we must first share his despair. Thus Shakespeare perpetrates his theatrical hoax on us, leading us against all the evidence of our senses to accept stage conventions and believe in Gloucester's fall, and then exploding our belief. A lamentable betrayal. For after all, we have been obedient believers until now. We accepted the fairy-tale opening scenes, the stagey deception of Gloucester, the unrealistic iniquities and virtues of the children. Even when the fairy tale turned nightmare on the heath we still believed. We even believed against our will that Gloucester was being blinded. At that point disbelief would have been a blessing. Had we despaired of theater then — smiling like Duke Theseus at the mechanicals' play and murmuring "The best in this kind are but shadows" — we would have been spared the pain of seeing what we saw. But even with all this, Shakespeare is not through with us. In the Dover scene he insists that we believe the most outrageous stuff and then, when we do, he pulls the rug of illusion out from under us and leaves us sitting on our backsides, not on the beach below the cliff, but down among the groundlings while the players stand and smirk.

So for an instant *King Lear* seems as fraudulent as Edgar's morality play—and less kindly motivated. Where does that leave the audience then? Are we supposed to get to our feet, dust ourselves off, smile at our gullibility, and then view the rest of the play in the skeptical spirit of Theseus? Hardly. For even as the scene destroys our grounds for theatrical belief, it calls on us to believe. At the moment of theatrical despair—when we have taken our version of Gloucester's fall—we are asked to emulate Gloucester in *his* moment of despair. What he does is to roll over incredulously, explore his crushed body, voice his doubts, and then allow himself to believe not only in Edgar's new role but in the miracle of his own redemption. "Think," Edgar says, "that the clearest gods, who make them honors / Of men's impossibilities, have preserved thee"—and Gloucester does, and he is saved. And, to pursue this logic, we too will be saved if we resume our willing suspension of disbelief, our poetic faith.

But what does it mean for the audience to be saved? Well, we have only Gloucester's experience to go on; let us bear it out with him by asking the meaning of his salvation. It means, bluntly, being condemned to life, as he laments upon discovering himself still intact:

> Is wretchedness deprived that benefit
> To end itself by death? 'Twas yet some comfort
> When misery could beguile the tyrant's rage,
> And frustrate his proud will.

Salvation, if that is what it is, comes heavily compromised when it means no more than a prolongation of wretchedness and misery. Yet that is precisely the form salvation takes in this play—not a redemption from suffering but an extension, even an intensification of it.

Thus I suggest that Shakespeare staged this scene to strip his audience of the comforts of skepticism. At first glance, just the opposite seems true—that the scene is designed to relieve our distress by debunking theater and reassuring us that however painful the play may be, it is still merely a play. From that standpoint the blinding of Gloucester was every bit as fraudulent as his phony fall—just more convincingly, and hence more dishonestly, accomplished. From this standpoint the entire play is a fraud. But the playwright can hardly want us to adopt this view, which would be fatal to the theatrical life of the play and false to our experience of it.

Instead I think Shakespeare presents this scene as a metadramatic lightning rod. It functions with respect to human suffering in *Lear* the way Mercutio and the Nurse do with respect to high romance in *Romeo and Juliet*. Shakespeare knows that the play is as much an ordeal for us as it is for his suffering characters and that we, like Gloucester, will be tempted to escape from that ordeal, to commit theatrical suicide as it were by subjecting our imaginations to the self-slaughter of skepticism. Recognizing this, he presents us with Dover Cliffs, saying, "Here, if you cannot endure realism any longer, I give you a sacrificial offering: this ludicrously unrealistic scene which as blatantly invites you to escape from pain as the blinding scene compels you to suffer it. This is your chance—in fact your last chance—to obtain release through mockery. But that done, I challenge you, as Edgar challenges Gloucester, to forgo escapism in the future, to reinstate your poetic faith, and henceforth to bear affliction to the end."

So, with our cynicism purged and our ability to "feel what wretches feel" restored, Shakespeare returns us and Gloucester to the ordeal of pain by ushering in the mad Lear and forcing us to endure the meeting of the two old men that prompts Edgar to say "I would not take this from report; it is, / And my heart breaks at it." That is our reward for suspending disbelief; we are granted the opportunity of having our hearts broken repeatedly, by this reunion, by the reunion of Lear and Cordelia, by their reunions in death at the end.

3. Worse Still

In the scene at Dover we see the comforting aspects of "report"—Edgar's gloss of Gloucester's experience—gradually erased both for him and for the audience. The scene provides us a momentary relief from pain, only to return us to it with our nerve ends more rawly exposed. Thus the scene follows the paradoxical logic of Edgar's statement "The worst is not / So long as we can say 'This is the worst.'" Shakespeare honors this paradoxical principle to the end of his play. With the chivalric combat over and Edmund dying, he spares us the immediate experience of Gloucester's death and of Kent's arrival by having Edgar narrate both events. Edgar speaks with self-conscious formality. "List a brief tale," he says, and tells how his father died. Then Edmund says "But speak you on; / You look as you had something more to say." Albany demurs:

> If there be more, more woeful, hold it in,
> For I am almost ready to dissolve,
> Hearing of this.

In other words, let this saying of the worst *be* the worst, for by this point "saying," which shields the audience from the immediacy of the deaths it tells of, also becomes a destructive, or at least for Albany a "dissolving," agent. Nevertheless, Edgar proceeds with his story, telling how he encountered Kent, who "having seen me in my worst estate [i.e., as Poor Tom] / Shunned my abhorred society," but who then, recognizing him as Edgar, "fastened on my neck" and wept, then cast himself on the dead body of Gloucester and told so piteous a tale of him and Lear on the heath that "the strings of [his own] life / Began to crack." By now the fact that Edgar can "say" he was formerly in his "worst estate" should set him and us both wincing. Sure enough he is brought to a worse state yet—in part by what he has said. For Edgar's report of these affairs inspires Edmund to order a reprieve for the condemned Lear and Cordelia—"This speech of yours hath moved me, / And shall perchance do good" (203)—but at the same time it defers the reprieve until it is too late to save Cordelia. Edgar's disastrously time-consuming reportage of "the worst" helps bring on the "worser worst" of Lear making his howling entrance with Cordelia's body.

Thus the next-to-last act of uncreation in *King Lear* is Shakespeare's stripping the play of report and forcing us to confront its final moments in their naked immediacy. We are not compelled to see Cordelia hanged, as we saw Gloucester blinded, but that is small comfort since Shakespeare inflicts a worse experience upon us: Lear's pathetic struggle to understand that most arbitrary of all differences—

> Why should a dog, a horse, a rat, have life,
> And thou no breath at all?

—as he seeks to discover in Cordelia the breath that represents both the immediacy of life and the mediacy of human speech. Lear's frantic searching of Cordelia's face for signs of life—the face he once said he would never see again (1.1.265)—suggests the emphasis given in these final moments of the play to uninterpreted seeing. In the last forty-five lines, amid other references to the visual, the words *sight*, *see*, and *look* appear eleven times. Even Edgar, inveterate interpreter though he is, ends the play with the words "we that are young / Shall never *see* so much, nor live so long."

The audience is similarly reduced to the status of onlookers obliged to make what sense they can of what they only see. Because Shakespeare refuses to make meanings manifest, our questions hang in the air. At what point should we realize Cordelia is dead? Or, rather, at what point should we interpret the unspoken behavior of the other characters as indicating that what we actually *see*—a boy actor's breathing body—is the arbitrary theatrical sign of a breathless Cordelia? Who does Lear mean when he says "And my poor fool is hanged"? Whose button—his or Cordelia's—does he want undone? Does he die from the knowledge that Cordelia is dead or from a surging belief that she lives? And does the departing Kent intend suicide or merely know that he is dying? These questions would have troubled Shakespeare's original first-night audience more than they do us, because we know what is coming. For them immediate experience, stripped of interpretation, would randomly arouse fear, pity, grief, and hope as they attempt moment by moment to discover what they should feel. The notion that what we feel is prior to what we say ("Speak what we feel") is confused here by the fact that the Jacobean audience could not know what to feel until they knew what was happening, until some rudimentary act of interpretation had taken place. Thus for much of this latter part of the scene the audience's feelings are in painful suspension as they attempt to interpret the naked "it is" of drama. This unenviable plight of the audience is analogous to that of the playwright who, having uncreated the familiar meanings of his linguistic and literary sources, is left with the raw unformed materials with which he must create *King Lear*.

We look in vain, then, for closures of form and meaning, and cathartic consolations. The irresolution and Manichaean conflict that characterize for Murray Krieger the "tragic vision" are not reassuringly contained by the austerity of tragic form but burst through it and persevere to the end.[5] Or, rather, to the un-end—because in a sense the play has not ended but merely stopped. When Lear enters with Cordelia, Kent's anguished "Is this the promised end?" underscores the failure of the play to fulfill its implicit promise of a just and satisfying conclusion in keeping with the religious character of the old *King Leir*. Earlier in the scene, with Edgar triumphant over Edmund, the evil daughters dead, and Lear and Cordelia about to be rescued, the Apollonian form of tragedy has seemed on the verge of enclosing the Dionysiac turmoil. As Edmund says, "The wheel has come full circle," and Albany fills in the just details:

> All friends shall taste
> The wages of their virtue, and all foes
> The cup of their deservings.

At a similar moment in *Hamlet* the hero is reconciled to heaven and the playwright to his generic form, the one honoring his father by revenge, the other honoring the form of revenge tragedy by depicting that revenge. But now the playwright ostentatiously subverts his generic form. Edmund's wheel of fulfilling form becomes Lear's wheel of fire: the theatrical screw is given another twist, Lear stumbles on stage with Cordelia, and we are worse than e'er we were.

The play "un-ends" on the same theme of abdication with which it began. Albany bows out with the words "you twain / Rule in this realm"; Kent demurs, "I have a journey, sir, shortly to go"; and Edgar becomes king by default, thereby earning the right to deliver the perfunctory four-line closing speech, which he places on the play like a Band-Aid on a gaping wound.

4. Saying the Worst

When Edgar ends the play by saying "Speak what we feel, not what we ought to say," we can hardly help hearing an echo of his earlier statement "The worst is not / So long as we can say 'This is the worst.'" It is the "saying" that counts. Whether Edgar sincerely says "what we feel" or more properly "what we ought to say," he must still "say." So must Shakespeare. Despite the intensity of his concern with immediacy in *King Lear*, his play remains unavoidably a saying—not the agonizing "it is" itself but a mediated representation of the worst. Perhaps in reminding us of this Shakespeare offers us a kind of catharsis in which our anxiety is relieved by his placement of fictional brackets around our suffering. If so, would that not mean that this painful play is in the last analysis merely a play and thus unreal? Precisely. Reality is worse.

From one perspective Shakespeare has done all he can do to us: the worst is over, we are released from his theatrical rack. From another, however, the worst he can do to us is to inform us that this is not the worst after all, only a saying of the worst. By this time we should know what that entails. Other racks.

The principle on which *King Lear* proceeds, that "the worst is not," implies that the play is not mimetic in the usual sense of that term. It does not hold the mirror up to nature, as Hamlet recommends. Instead of beginning with nature and adding art, it begins with art—with the ordered, ritually stylized, word-dominated world of its opening scene and, before that, with the created forms of *King Leir* and the *Arcadia*—and subtracts from it toward nature as the chaotic immediate, the nothing to which the verbal artist reduces all prior forms and meanings in order to begin again. Thus if the play begins with an uncreating act of abdication, it ends with another—uncreating its own fictional reality by abdicating to a sterner successor outside. Setting the audience free from the theatrical rack of this tough world is, however, no act of kindness by this unkind playwright. What we had been led to regard as the worst is seen now as merely a temporary shelter against hard weather. We are thrust out of the Globe onto an even greater stage of fools, and where thunder is not made by rolling cannon balls and the cold rain it raineth every day.

However, this despairing vision does only partial justice to Shakespeare's dramatization of "The worst is not / So long as we can say, 'This is the worst.'" For the saying is as incorrigibly ambiguous as the play itself. In the sense in which Edgar means the lines, "saying" always heralds a greater worseness to come. And that is surely the case. Repeatedly we see that "saying" or "report" is not as discretely secondary to immediate experience as we might think, for immediate experience can be, and very often is in this play, a commentary on prior sayings. When Albany cries "The gods defend her!" Lear's howling entrance with Cordelia's body is a visual report on the mediations not only of the gods but of Albany's statement about the gods. Or, to reverse the order, Edmund's protracted story about his father's death is not merely a verbal report but an immediate and primary event in its own right. As such it consumes time, and hence contributes to Cordelia's death by postponing her rescue. In both instances "saying the worst" forecasts a worser worst, and in the latter case it helps create it. Report then is not necessarily, as we tend to think of it, an ending, a formal narrative closure of a primary experience.

Still, we cannot fail to see another meaning coexisting in Edgar's lines about saying the worst: that the act of saying transcends and staves off the worseness it announces. *King Lear* says "This is the worst" at great and unrelieving length. That means, as I've said, that it forecasts a greater worseness awaiting us outside the theater. But it also means that so long as the play can say the worst we have not reached the worst. Thus the lines have something of the self-annulling quality of the statement "I cannot speak." As long as saying is possible "the worst is not," for the act of saying presupposes an existing order and a community of meaning, however diminished and naked to the world it has become. If *King Lear* has returned very nearly to the nothing of its own origin, it has done so by employing words and theatrical forms that inevitably imply a hierarchy of values and acts of ordering. Shakespeare's divestiture of his theatrical art is itself artful. That is, after all, the only way the worst can appear in the theater. Outside the theater we will all experience the worst in it special forms, customized to our individual displeasure. But if we are to encounter the worst itself, Shakespeare tells us, it will be because we shall have lost the capacity to say, with *King Lear*, "This is the worst." When that time comes—and these late eclipses in the sun and moon portend no good to us—wheels of fire will not be metaphors, and those whose tears do scald like molten lead will not cry "Howl" but howl in earnest.

Part 3
Immortality and Art

XV   Immortalizing Art

Shakespeare and immortality seem to have been made for one another. The man himself may no longer be among us in the flesh, but bound in calf he seems a good bet, as he himself predicted, to outlive brass and stone and gilded monuments, even in an age when last year's Chevrolet is as obsolete as the pharoah's chariot and the phrase *new and improved* is the secular equivalent of *hallelujah*. My intent here, however, is not to marvel at Shakespeare's ability to survive in the kingdom of the fashionable but rather to suggest various ways in which immortality not only characterizes his art but is an abiding subject within it.

Apart from being sung by flights of angels to an ethereal resting place, the most obvious method of immortalizing ourselves is by begetting children—so obvious indeed that we almost always discover how it is accomplished. For the poet, however, conceiving words may seem as likely a means of immortalizing oneself as conceiving children. Hence we find Shakespeare in the sonnets proceeding almost uninterruptedly from urging the self-centered young man to marry and through the alchemy of sex to distill his beauty into the essence of children, to reassuring him that in any event he will be preserved in the ambergris of art. For a while the two modes are played off against one another. Thus on the one hand—

> . . . nothing 'gainst Time's scythe can make defence
> Save breed, to brave him when he takes thee hence.
>   (Sonnet 12)

But on the other hand—

> And all in war with Time for love of you,
> As he takes from you, I engraft you new.
>   (Sonnet 15)

Still—

> But wherefore do not you a mightier way
> Make war upon this bloody tyrant, Time?

> And fortify yourself in your decay
> With means more blessed than my barren rhyme?
>
> (Sonnet 16)

However, more deeply considered—

> But were some child of yours alive that time,
> You should live twice, in it and in my rhyme.
>
> (Sonnet 17)

It comes out even then. Or almost even, since from this point on genetic immortality, having had its say, yields to poetic immortality, whose say is more lasting. The young man will shine less brightly and durably in his offspring, even in brass and stone, then in "black ink" (Sonnet 65) and in the eyes and voices of those who read these poems (Sonnet 81).

For of course the very act of writing implies a reader and a bridging of the time/space between writer and reader, and hence a momentary or in Shakespeare's case a not so momentary conquest of death. Surely it's no accident that so many of Shakespeare's sonnets about the impermanence of time are themselves couched in the present tense, as in Sonnet 18—"Shall I compare thee to a summer's day?"—with its conclusion "So long as men can breathe or eyes can see, / So long lives this, and this gives life to thee." Such a sonnet—and this one is not atypical—is less a narrative remembrance of things past than a recording of the present process of writing a sonnet. Shakespeare can say "Your name from hence immortal life shall have" (Sonnet 81), but the young man of London town, with all his particular Alcibiades-like doings, is never named: his personal identity disappears into the "you" of pronominal address. As such he is preserved not biographically but poetically, as an element in this enduring poem.

This present-tense reflexivity causes the act of writing to fuse with the act of reading, as though writer and reader are simultaneously figuring out how this poem should go. When Shakespeare says

> Your monument shall be my gentle verse,
> Which eyes not yet created shall o'er-read,
> And tongues to be your being shall rehearse
> When all the breathers of this world are dead
>
> (Sonnet 81)

it is not the young man's "being" that the eyes and tongues shall rehearse but Shakespeare's words. What is preserved, then, is not so much the young man as Shakespeare's speaking voice. As long as he goes on speaking, even in the voice and accent of his readers, he is still alive.

In a sense this implies that Shakespeare kills the young man off as a creature of flesh and blood by reducing him to words on a page. Is writing a life-taking as well as a life-giving activity? Shakespeare suggests as much when he claims (as in Sonnet 103) that he no longer writes about the young man because dull verse cannot capture his living graces and gifts:

> Were it not sinful then, striving to mend,
> To mar the subject that before was well?
> For to no other pass my verses tend
> Than of your graces and your gifts to tell;
>> And more, much more, than in my verse can sit
>> Your own glass shows you when you look in it.

Of course Shakespeare *is* writing about him in the process of explaining why he cannot; but even more, he is writing about writing. That is, while admitting that verse cannot rival life, cannot even rival a mirror in reflecting life, he writes a nonmimetic poem that suppresses the young man and exalts writing. As a result the young man dies out of art, back into life, and Shakespeare's poem rises from his ashes, lamenting its inadequacies but still speaking.

1. The Body and Breath of Words

If you are still speaking you are still alive. By another token, if you are being spoken *about* you are also still alive. Words may be, as they so often are in Shakespeare, mere breath, evanescent puffs of air; but they also inherit something from the old Greek notion of breath as soul or vital spirit (*pneuma*): your spirit lives on if your word, your name, survives. This survival need not be poetic as in the line quoted above—"Your name from hence immortal life shall have"; it may also take the memorial form of fame, name, report, or public esteem. The Elizabethan faith in the death-defying virtues of posthumous reputation underwrites the actions and attitudes of many of Shakespeare's characters. Henry V is mindful of this as he prepares to invade France and put his kingship to the mortal test:

> Either our history shall have full mouth,
> Speak freely of our acts, or else our grave,
> Like Turkish mute, shall have a tongueless mouth,
> Not worshipped with a waxen epitaph.   (1.2)

This passion for posthumous reputation accounts for Hamlet's anxiety that his story be told properly by Horatio, for Ulysses' urging Achilles to keep Time's wallet full of "alms for oblivion" by continuous heroism, for Othello's wish to be spoken of as one who loved not wisely but too well, and for Coriolanus's fatal forfeiture of his Roman conquest for fear his name would remain "to the ensuing age abhorred." If death with honor keeps one's name alive, death without it is a ghastly form of extinction—the kind of death Claudio speaks of in *Measure for Measure*, the body rotting in cold obstruction, the spirit whirled invisibly within imprisoning winds or, worse yet, howling with sinners around Satan's great bonfire (3.1).

Anything that keeps you from this sort of end is to be treasured, and if words can do it then words are to be treasured. Yet words are not altogether or even mainly reliable; they are after all breath, and hence betoken not only continuing life (verbal fame) but also evanescence and death. In this latter sense, as exhalations of mortality, words are hard put to preserve themselves, let alone impart immortality to anything else. This is especially true of the theatrical word as opposed to the literary word because in the theater the word dies aborning, evaporating into thin air the moment it is uttered. How is the playwright to deny these exhalant deaths, this sad consequence of all corporeal beings?

Paradoxically a major way is by asserting the corporeality or materiality of words. What makes words evanescent in ordinary logocentric usage is that they become bodiless conveyers of meaning. Their signifiers evaporate even before their signified content makes an appearance. That is just as it should be for Platonists and Christians; the Logos, whether in men's mouths or on the Cross, must suffer a bodily defeat before its divine meaning—its immortal part—can become manifest.

Poets, however, cannot afford to be Platonists or Christians in this sense; their calling is more worldly. To begin with, at any rate, they deal in the bodily stuff of speech, or speech invested with body. Enduring speech is memorable speech, and it is memorable because it is in some degree formal, whether as simply formal as "Sticks and stones may break my bones" or as complexly so as "The Canonization." Formalizing means materializing or embodying, a compacting of language. In Japanese, as Gary Snyder points out,[1] the word for song is *bushi* or *fushi*, literally a whorl, like a knot in the grain of a board or a whirlpool in a stream. Poems are such whorls. Ordinary language flows unimpeded, carrying its cargo of cliché, jargon, and other forms of verbal debris. The poet would like to dam it up, but the only material he has are words, and they are part of the stream. So he uses what he has. He creates a linguistic turbulence, a dense centripetal whorl of words and meanings.

The verbal equivalent of this watery process is an exploitation of the sonant properties of words to mitigate the evanescence of speech. The poet hardens breath the way a knot hardens the grain of a board. Puns, metaphors, rhyme, meter, ambiguity, negation: all drive a wedge between signifier and signified, giving "the word as entity primacy over the word as sign."[2] Materialized thus, the poetic word resists evaporating into prosaic meaning, the breathy loss of soul that attends its expression.

This shifting of stress within the sign from signified to signifier—the same shift that takes place, as Jacques Derrida argues, when speech gives way to writing—might seem to immortalize meaning by generating an endless play of signification. But Shakespeare implies rather that it embeds meaning within words of unalterable constancy. For in the antiplatonic process of corporealizing words the poet achieves a higher Platonism. The poetic word "gives life to thee" because the poet insists that all casual ungoverned meanings must yield to the rigorous sovereignty of his poem, which can at times be impossibly strict—as in Sonnet 116 where the word *love* becomes "an ever-fixed mark," the polestar by which wandering sublunary language should steer its course, or in *The Merchant of Venice* where the words of the law must be applied with scrupulous exactitude. The astral word of the sonnet is so removed from the wear and tear of slovenly daily usage as to become immortal; and the legal word of Venice is, by virtue in its unalterable exactness, proof against malicious interpretation, and hence transposes death into life.

We seem, then, to have two immortalizing tendencies as poetry either materializes or dematerializes breath and meaning, platonizing it upward or incarnating it downward. The platonic removal of the word from time would seem the likelier way to immortalize the work of art. Because the ambitious scholars in *Love's Labour's Lost* take this view, let us see how well Plato fares in that play.

2. *Love's Labour's Lost*

Immortality is clearly at issue when the misogynistic would-be scholars decide to found their version of Plato's academy. As the King says:

> Let fame, that all hunt after in their lives,
> Live registered upon our brazen tombs
> And then grace us in the disgrace of death;
> When spite of cormorant, devouring Time,
> The endeavor of this present breath may buy

> That honor which shall bate his scythe's keen edge
> And make us heirs of all eternity. . . .
> [Therefore] our court shall be a little Academe,
> Still and comtemplative in living art.   (1.1)

This heady prospect is to be achieved by making a three-year philosophical retreat during which, as Longaville says, "the mind shall banquet, though the body pine." Like monastic contemplation, these philosophic devotions entail a dying to the world. "To love, to wealth, to pomp," Dumaine pledges, "I pine and die, / With all these living in philosophy." They take the gnostic view. The world is a den of evil, replete with money, pomp, cuisine, and worst of all, women. But the study of esoteric truths will prove redemptive, elevating the soul beyond the talons of cormorant, devouring Time. In this comic version of Platonic pietism, however, immortality resides not in the realm of Ideas but in the more worldly zone of fame. The scholars will take refuge from the army of the world's desires—prudently for only three years—in order to make Navarre (and themselves) "the wonder of the world."

Metadramatically, we would note that whereas for the King "breath" means "life," and the "endeavor" is the founding of Academe, "breath" also means words, and "endeavor" includes Shakespeare's endeavor too. As the scholars seek to be "still and contemplative in living art" (the art of living), so Shakespeare seeks to create an ever-living art—to shape out of verbal breath a play that will somehow triumph over time and make the playwright an heir of all eternity.

What happens is complex, inasmuch as one thing happens to the scholars and another to Shakespeare's play. Within the play philosophy's labor is lost before love's: fame fails, the ignominies of courtship ensue. Pitting Platonism against the army of feminine desires, Shakespeare creates a metaphor that equates excessive verbal abstraction with celibacy and excessive verbal worldliness with promiscuity.

What predictably follows upon the nobles' commitment to antifeminist learning is that just as Costard in the opening scene is "taken with a wench"—the voluptuous Jacquenetta—so they are taken in more genteel fashion with the French ladies. Jacquenetta, Costard, and the amorous Don Armado engage in a promiscuous expense of spirit in a waste of shame and laughter, while the celibate academicians represent the male equivalent of virtue-hoarding virginity. In a word-dominated play like *Love's Labour's Lost* it is not surprising that these two sexual extremes are emblematized in the two sets of vows the nobles make—the first, in Act 1, virginizing speech and the second, in Act 4, wantonizing it. The first set of vows establishes

Academe; it binds the scholars to the study of words by binding them to the words of the statute that defines their obligations. Enjoining speech with women, this vow deprives language of its public life, sequestering it in the cloister of philosophy.

The second set of vows arises from the demise of the first. The love-smitten scholars must degrade their original vows in order to sally forth from their fortress of words and wage aggressive love. To this end words are now held to be "but breath, and breath a vapor is" (4.3), which means, happily, that promises can be created and uncreated at will: "O, who can give an oath?" Berowne cries, "Where is a book?" The would-be lovers have no trouble finding books or words for new oaths; but they are unable to locate the right words to persuade the ladies of their love. Whether as pseudo-Muscovites supposedly capable only of Russian speech or as Petrarchan sonneteers stacking sighs in space, they do not speak the ladies' language; and the climax of this wantoning with words occurs when they all swear a third set of oaths, each to the wrong lady.

Thus verbal and sexual purity yields to verbal and sexual license; the mind to the body, the spiritual to the corporeal, the immortal to the mortal. Given this final verbal and sexual failure—the inability of the scholars to discover a language or style that will persuade the ladies that they are genuinely loved and not merely lusted after—it is appropriate that the play should not so much end as fade into an ellipsis of unfulfillment. The scholars' failure, it seems, is a failure of knowledge—not a failure to know platonic abstractions but to know living and dying realities. Philosophy is, alas, sterile; and at this point the nobles are a kind of collective version of the young man in the sonnets who, for some self-absorbed reason, refuses to commit himself to life by marrying and begetting children. Even later, when the scholars abandon their academic pose and take up the hunt, they still have little contact with reality, as their inability to tell one masked lady from another indicates. Their pendular infatuations swing too far in both directions, from a celibate and barren intellectuality to a promiscuous and equally barren sexuality.

All of this is a matter of words, not deeds—a "converse of breath." Promiscuity is merely a metaphor for a Petrarchan style that plays fast and loose with language and vows, and hence fails to unite lover and beloved when "honest plain words" might have done the deed. The descent from Platonic altitudes still leaves the scholars suspended well above earthy realities. That is apparently why the play ends with the strangely sudden arrival of Mercade bringing news of the French king's death, an arrival that prompts Berowne's command, "Worthies, away—the scene begins to cloud," in a gesture that anticipates Prospero's abrupt dismissal of the masque when reminded of mortal matters. The sobered scholars make one final effort to court the ladies, but the arrival of death has reinstituted the constraints of time, leaving no room for immortality or even for the enduring bliss of a "world-without-end bargain."

Through their failures the scholars define by negation the unattainable bargain that would bring them to nonplatonic terms with death: marriage and procreation. Don Armado shows the way. For if he, a man of most altitudinous vocabulary, can be haled before an altar with Jacquenetta, then he will become immortalized by the child that "brags in her belly"—a prospect for somewhat dubious rejoicing.

Mercade's entrance also shatters the brittle structure of *Love's Labour's Lost* by introducing a dimension of reality the play cannot absorb. Shakespeare seems well aware that his own endeavor is plagued by the ambiguity of the "breath" that composes it; its "life" is as mortal as its airy speech. Thus the last act is full of metaphors and metaphoric actions that connect situations within the play to the play itself. The Muscovite merriment is dashed by the ladies "like a Christmas comedy" (5.2), and with the arrival of Mercade the pageant of the Nine Worthies begins to cloud. The pageant of *Love's Labour's Lost* begins to cloud also, falling at last into total shadow when Berowne acknowledges—

> Our wooing doth not end like an old play—
> Jack hath not Jill. These ladies' courtesy
> Might well have made our sport a comedy.

When the King replies "Come, sir, it wants a twelvemonth and a day / And then 'twill end," Berowne (and Shakespeare with him) says drily "That's too long for a play."

This reflexive announcement condemns not merely the sport of lovers but Shakespeare's theatrical sport as well. And rightly so: the history of its nonstagings attests to the fact that *Love's Labour's Lost* died theatrically long ago, somewhere in the seventeenth century. As a script-poem, however, it perhaps exceeds all other Shakespearean plays in the density of its verbal whorlings. Language materializes here. Words take on body and structure in such ramshackle shapes as honorificabilitudinatatibus, in syntactic reversals, repetitions, redundancies, and elegant variations, in punning splits of meaning, metaphorical far-fetchings, the play with vowels and consonants, the verbal doodling, all the interior poems, rhymes, measures. Measures perhaps most of all, for Shakespeare truly measures out speech the way a tailor measures cloth, to produce taffeta phrases, silken terms precise, and three-piled hyperboles.

Such material keeps words warm enough in the study, but a rougher cloth—russet yeas and honest kersey noes—is required if they are to wear well in the theater. For words in the study are physical marks on a page, but in the theater they are breath. To succeed on stage, linguistic play must graduate into dramatic play, which means that words must be wedded to actions to form the kind of marriage the scholars could not bring about. Only when anchored within a context of action, deriving from it and contributing to it, are words safe from cormorant, devouring Time. But that would take too long for this play.

3. Death in the Dramatic Mode

In the previous sections I have suggested some ways in which art can be construed as a denial of death. The materializing of language at a stylistic level and the metadramatizing of experience at a theatrical level are akin in this regard. However, this process is liable to differing interpretations. On the one hand we can say that when signifiers are foregrounded at the expense of their signifieds—when the evanescent breathiness of words is made to materialize in visual and sonic shapes—the poem or play is lent a substantiality that makes it seem if not immortal at least resistant to temporal erosion. From this standpoint the recalcitrant youth of the sonnets is preserved in rhyme and metaphor like Keats's bold lover frozen in the cold pastoral of his urnlike poem, never to kiss yet forever to love, just as the scholars of Navarre are eternally suspended twelve months shy of marriage.

On the other hand this foregrounding can be regarded as a mortification of art by art. That is, the poem's pretensions to immortality, its claims to erect a self-preserving structure of meanings, are deconstructed by its own corporealizings, which remind us that as long as urns and poems are embodiments of meanings they are subject to the common fate of bodily objects. Hence a play like *Love's Labour's Lost* deconstructs its own verbal pretensions by exposing the fragility of the formal barriers it has put in time's path—nets to catch the wind.

For that matter all of Shakespeare's plays deconstruct the seeming immortality of art, merely by being plays. One of the reasons Shakespeare can talk about immortalizing the youth in the sonnets is because sonnets are written and bound in quartos, not recited in the parlor or even trumpeted in the streets. Poetry dipped in black ink is more durable stuff than verse vaporized in air. It is also more durable than the Shakespeare who writes it and the youth he writes about. I mentioned earlier that the sonnets kill off their youthful subject even as they claim to immortalize him—they drown him in ink.

The sonneteer suffers the same fate, the fate of all writers. Some recent critics—Roland Barthes, Maurice Blanchot, Michel Foucault—have argued that writing is closely associated with death because instead of informing the work with his presence, as a speaker seems to do, the author succumbs to the necessity of disappearing from the scene.[3] That the disappearance of the author is a kind of death is no doubt a loose metaphor—we could as justly call him a child abandoner because he deposits his orphaned text on our doorstep and hastily makes off—but it is an ancient and familiar one: the dead "have gone away," they are, like Eliot's infamous cat Macavity, "not here." On such a view, then, we could say that very shortly after Shakespeare's sonnets sacrifice the youth who is their subject they turn viciously about and do in the author as well—though an autopsy would reveal that the author either committed suicide or was an accomplice in his own murder. In any event, by the time we read his text, he is, unlike a speaker, well beyond earshot of our questions, and we are left to trace what meanings we can on a slate of signifiers.

Plays are similarly homicidal, or playwrights similarly suicidal. At any rate the playwright is no more present on stage than the novelist is between the covers of his book. In fact, we could claim that the playwright is even deader than the poet, the novelist, and other artists of the printed page. For despite Shakespeare's absence from his quarto of sonnets, when we read them (or *Crime and Punishment* or *Nostromo*, etc.) we cannot help gaining a sense of his absent presence; we register a voice, a way of perceiving, an imagined "I" behind all the "he's" and "she's." But of course this "I," someone will object, is not really Dostoievski or Conrad; it is a narrative fiction, almost a character, at most a tangential projection of the writer. But by the same token what are the histrionic "I's" we real people use when we address a class, a chancellor, a colleague, a child, our dog, a tennis opponent, or an irate motorist? Are these not fictions also, projections, ventriloquisms, histrionic voices? We all have a repertory theater of "I's" in us, and the true "I" is more elusive than Kant's noumenal *Ding an sich.*

Just which "I" we hear within a text, then, may be debatable, but it is whatever we refer to when we speak of the Conradian or Dostoievskian or Shakespearean style. Shakespeare was somewhat glumly conscious of this when he wrote Sonnet 76, asking

> Why write I still all one, ever the same,
> And keep invention in a noted weed,

> That every word doth almost tell my name,
> Showing their birth and where they did proceed?

And yet the "I" of the playwright is more noumenal and remote than that of the lyric or narrative writer, as Stephen Dedalus implies in *A Portrait of the Artist as a Young Man* when he argues that the playwright disappears not like the dead but like the God of the Creation.

Stephen's equation of the absent author not with the dead but with the *deus absconditus* has the virtue of acknowledging the playwright's creativity, a talent notoriously lacking among the dead. But is has the disadvantage of implying that the playwright remains a kind of ghostly presence in or around or above his play. For of course though the God of the Creation withdraws, he remains, unlike the dead, transcendently present and subject to appeal, paring his fingernails perhaps, as Stephen claims, but still hovering in the wings as the performance rolls on or knocking about under the stage like the Ghost in *Hamlet*.

But Stephen's metaphor is misleading; if the playwright cannot live within his play, neither can he live outside or divinely above it. Far more than the poet or novelist, he deliberately writes himself out of existence. If he does his job properly nobody in the audience will hear his voice speaking through the throat of Richard III or Rosalind or Caliban. The poor poetic fool will be dead.

In fact doubly dead. Dead, first, as the novelist is dead, because he too is a writer of texts (scripts) that are mailed to distant readers—distant whether they live a hundred years hence or next door to the Globe. And doubly dead because his text reaches his audience not in its pristine form like a poem or novel but by way of the stage. Like a Platonic idea descending to earth, it enters a cave of shadows and suffers the material distortions of the mimetic stage where clowns, as Hamlet complains, speak "more than is set down for them" and players strut and bellow and saw the air and offend the modesty of both nature and the playwright. All of these theatrical villainies remind us that the speeches of players are not true speech but speech delivered, a text interpreted. And that means that the playwright is a kind of Duke Frederick leaving his domain in the keeping of an Angelo who stages things much differently than expected, sometimes better, sometimes worse. A Duke Frederick, however, who does not return.

But staging, whether done well or ill, is a mortal thing. That is, you could dispute the view that writing implies death by claiming just the reverse, that speech implies the death of the speaker whereas writing lends a kind of immortality to the author. The reason for this is that the speaker is present in the flesh, with all his mortal failings visible, whereas writing expunges the body. *Remembrance of Things Past* does not record Proust's asthmatic wheezing, or *The Dunciad* exhibit Pope's tiny body racked on its tubercular spine. Of course *Hamlet* does not show us a Shakespeare doubled over with kidney stones either, any more than *The Praise of Folly* did Erasmus, who died of them, but it shows us its hero's body in the mortal shape of Burbage or Booth or Gielgud in a way that we can never see that of the Redcrosse Knight or Raskolnikov. Theater is implicit with death because it is full of life, because it features not merely voices chattering, intoning, and screeching but also bodies dancing, drooping, embracing, battling, and of course dying. Indeed dying in fact as well as fiction, Olivier proceeding at life's slower pace while Hamlet makes haste toward his stage grave.

At the same time, theater shares the capacity of writing to transcend mortality by transcending the body. We cannot help realizing that Iago has a life independent of Burbage and Olivier, that he is playing them as much as they are playing him. Like the devil he implies he is, his spirit possesses them nightly and can be exorcised only by applause and a falling curtain. From actor to actor, from Burbage to Garrick to Olivier, Iago's restless spirit transmigrates eternally. So it is with the play *Othello*, the spirit of which possesses the mortal theatrical body of the Globe or Drury Lane or the Old Vic but, like a thing immortal, refuses to die when they do.

And yet of course the play dies every night. At the end of each performance the curtain descends like a shroud, even though tomorrow it will rise again with a prestolike flourish to reveal the same play miraculously reborn. The same play perhaps but not the same performance, since even successive performances by the same players in the same theater cannot be the same. Yet they are performances of the same play. The play outlives all of its mortal performances and thus lays claim to a kind of platonic immortality. Yet though the play outlives its performances, it can have no life without them. Without them it shrivels into a script. Then it is truly dead as a play, though perhaps wonderfully alive as a dramatic poem.

Even during its performance, when it is most alive, the play has an ambiguous relationship with death. On the one hand it seems to transcend death by transcending time. The written poem or book implies death by virtue of the pastness of its narrative mode; it may live as a poem or novel, but the events it depicts are no longer with us. The events of *Henry IV*, however, take place in an eternal present. The theater is Falstaff's natural habitat because it has no past; it "presents" a performance in both senses, creating a seemingly impromptu experience in which the audience rides moment by moment on the tip of time. On the other hand no sooner does each of these moments flare up than like Macbeth's brief candle it goes out again. The events of the play are present now, and will be so tomorrow, but each performance trails its past behind it as an ever lengthening shadow. Theater, it seems, is a kind of Coleridgean death-in-life.

A play, then, would seem an unlikely medium in which to preserve the past. But let us take a look at several plays in which Shakespeare seems unusually conscious of this unlikeliness, because his view of the matter appears to evolve in an interesting fashion.

4. *Julius Caesar*

The metadrama of *Love's Labour's Lost* addresses only the verbal and formal frailties of art. A more dangerous self-indictment occurs when the preservative virtues of drama itself are cast in doubt. That is, if in the familiar view fame, report, and reputation imply that when your name survives, you survive, we can regard a play as a kind of naming of the experience it presents, a dramatized narrative that, in the case of history plays, pockets up some portion of the past to keep it from oblivion. If words can do this then they must be instinct with sacred power. Yet Shakespeare is suspicious of verbal mana both early in his career ("Any godfather can give a name," Berowne says) and late ("What cares these roarers for the name of king?" demands the Boatswain in *The Tempest*). And he is also suspicious of drama as naming, in the sense of mimetic record keeping. If the poetic or dramatic word can preserve the past intact it must be possessed of a constancy denied the speech of ordinary mortals. In fact it must be very much like the word *love* as Shakespeare defines it in Sonnet 116. Whereas in its daily traffic with libertines, lovers, and infatuates, love's meaning is bent and altered beyond recognition, in the austere employ of the poet it is enshrined in platonic heavens where in its immutability it serves as "the star to every wandering bark." Unfortunately, as love withdraws to this grand height it leaves mortal lovers behind. Perhaps the poetic word can aspire to this sort of immortality, but the theatrical word cannot. Its marriages are not of true and distant minds but of close and present bodies; it is bound to the flesh and blood of the stage.

The difference between the poetic and the dramatic word is indicated in *Julius Caesar*. Just before the assassination Caesar speaks as if he were the poet of Sonnet 116. Rejecting the pleas of his senators to repeal his banishment of Cimber, he declares his word inviolable:

> I could well be moved, if I were as you;
> If I could pray to move, prayers would move me;

> But I am constant as the northern star
> Of whose truefixed and resting quality
> There is no fellow in the firmament.   (3.1)

Like *love* in the sonnet, Caesar's unfellowed word stands aloof from the vagaries of lesser speech and the prayers of lesser men; it too is the northern star "to every wandering bark."

Rebuffed so absolutely, the conspirators call upon a different form of speech. "Speak, hands, for me!" Casca cries, and in a moment all their hands speak forcefully indeed. What they say is that the word of Caesar resides not in the heavens above but in an inconstant sublunary body that can be hacked and rent. Where then is Caesar's word? Totally corporealized. It is embedded in those gashes that Antony calls "dumb mouths [which] ope their ruby lips / To beg the voice and utterance of my tongue" (3.1). Even if we think of Caesar's word as living on in Antony's voice, it is a great descent from language "constant as the northern star" to language up for political grabs in the turbulence following Caesar's death.

The fall of Caesar's word from the celestial to the corporeal is paralleled by another fall, that of Brutus's plot. As originally designed, Brutus's plot called for the assassination to be staged as a noble sacrifice, a clean classical killing:[4]

> Let's kill him boldly, but not wrathfully;
> Let's carve him as a dish fit for the gods,
> Not hew him as a carcass fit for the hounds.
>   (2.1)

But the actual event is a melee of hewing in which, as Antony later depicts it (3.1.204–10), Caesar is bayed and savaged by hounds. The hands that were to have spoken against him with restraint and nobility—the manual equivalent to his own celestial word—speak a language so bloody that even Brutus seems embarrassed and defensive:

> Though now we must appear bloody and cruel,
> As by our hands and this our present act
> You see we do, yet see you but our hands
> And this the bleeding business they have done.
> Our hearts you see not. . . .   (3.1)

As *Titus Andronicus* and *Hamlet* testify, tragedy is not always a sacrificial rite that dignifies the slayers and the slain. Brutus's high intentions, as usual, have little contact with low realities.

If neither Caesar's word nor Brutus's plot can achieve ethereal constancy, what does this say about Shakespeare's words and plot in *Julius Caesar*? How constant are they? We are given a clue when the murderers, dipping their hands in Caesar's blood, speak about survival. Casca says,

> Stoop, then, and wash. How many ages hence
> Shall this our lofty scene be acted over
> In states unborn and accents yet unknown!
> BRUTUS: How many times shall Caesar bleed in sport,
> That now on Pompey's basis lies along
> No worthier than the dust?

These are daring speeches. Not for Casca and Brutus but for Shakespeare. Exactly at the moment when the audience is most deeply involved in the "reality" of the action—when we are "seeing through" the actors and the stage to register the great action in ancient Rome—Shakespeare breaks the illusion of reality and obliges us to acknowledge that we are not on the steps of the Roman capitol but on our chairs in the Globe theater. The blood on the hands of Casca and Brutus came not from Caesar's heart but from the throat of a pig some hours before the Globe performance. Truly, then, a mortifying metadramatic moment. Mortifying both because it robs the assassins of the deathlessness their words lay claim to and because it transforms the spirit of historical action into the body of theatrical performance. As such it is a true corporealizing; it foregrounds theater as theater—and theater is nothing if not corporeal, an incarnation of human action in the bodies of actors and the stuff of the stage. The theater is antiplatonic by nature; it yanks immutable words like Caesar's down out of the heavens and puts them in the mouths of players who make them hiss and caress and bellow and brawl with other words. And it converts the fine abstract design of imagined plots like Brutus's into what Horatio shall soon call "carnal, bloody, and unnatural acts . . . accidental judgments, casual slaughters."

In a historical play like *Julius Caesar* this foregrounding of theater as theater both demystifies and mystifies the events depicted. On the one hand the grand Roman capitol dissolves into a London theater; and Caesar, Casca, and Brutus lose their Roman integrity and become mere players performing in what the Chorus of *Henry V* calls a mockery. All is made manifest and present. But not all. For if Caesar bleeds here only "in sport," if what we have just seen is not what actually happened but only a theatrical performance, then what did happen? Alas, who knows? Like Troilus complaining "This is and is not Cressid," Shakespeare says "This is and is not Caesar."

That is an acceptable admission in something like the show of the Nine Worthies in *Love's Labour's Lost*, where Costard's announcement "I Pompey am—" is interrupted by Berowne's "You lie, you are not he" (5.2). But it is disconcerting in a Roman play at a moment of such high seriousness.

But perhaps I have exaggerated the metadramatics of the moment. Isn't it more likely that the reference to theater is designed to aggrandize the historical occasion in its transcendence of time, not consign it to the lost past? Certainly that is what Casca and Brutus mean. But how much do they know about the action that is to be immortalized? Not much, as Casca's final remark on the subject suggests. As long, he says, as this scene shall be acted over, "So often shall the knot of us be called / The men that gave their country liberty." From the perspective of Elizabethan England, such a remark has to be regarded as ironic. For the monarchy the conspirators saved Rome from did not lead to "liberty," to a republic of the sort Brutus's ancestor established; it led first to the triumvirate composed of Antony, Lepidus, and Augustus and then to the imperializing of Rome by Augustus. Given those untrammeled consequences of the killing of Caesar, none of the conspirators can be said to know what it is he really does when he lets his hands speak for him. Nor does anyone else. It is all guesswork and interpretation.

And as far as interpretation goes, we in the theater are, as Shakespeare cannot help being aware, at four removes and three "accents" from the mysterious events themselves. To get back to the capitol steps in Rome we would have to regress from the poetic English of Shakespeare's play, to the English narrative of James North's *Plutarch* which he based the play on, to the French narrative of James Amyot's *Plutarch* which North translated, to the Greek narrative of Plutarch himself which Amyot translated, to the lost Latin historical studies and records from which Plutarch worked, and finally to the words of those who were audience to or actors in the scene itself. In its transmigration through so many and such various literary bodies, the soul of Caesar's word would have hard work remaining as constant as the northern star.

5. *Antony and Cleopatra*

Nothing on the surface of *Antony and Cleopatra* suggests that Shakespeare feels any differently about drama than he did in *Julius Caesar* or for that matter in *Henry V*. In fact one of Cleopatra's most memorable speeches near the end of the play invites comparison to that of Casca and Brutus in *Julius Caesar*. Conscious that Caesar wants her to think she will be treated

with care and pity—"He words me, girls, he words me, that I should not /
Be noble to myself"—and receiving confirmation from Dolabella that Caesar
intends to take her with him to Rome, she describes to Iras their coming fate:

> Saucy lictors
> Will catch at us like strumpets, and scald rhymers
> Ballad us out of tune. The quick comedians
> Extemporally will stage us and present
> Our Alexandrian revels. Antony
> Shall be brought drunken forth, and I shall see
> Some squeaking Cleopatra boy my greatness
> In the posture of a whore.   (5.2)

Here of course is Shakespeare's *Antony and Cleopatra*, even down to the child
actor in whose squeaking voice Cleopatra's greatness is being boyed. Unlike
its counterpart in *Julius Caesar*, however, this speech does not declare that
"this lofty scene," as Casca called it, will be captured again and again on
the stages of the future. It says, rather, what Shakespeare said metadramatically by means of Casca's and Brutus's speech: that the truth and (in
Cleopatra's case) splendor of what really happened will be lost, but also
strangely found again, in the mockery of its dramatization.

The great difference lies not in the speeches themselves but in their
contexts and speakers. Casca and especially Brutus aspire to a Caesarian
constancy, an implacable stoic governance of the emotions and the body.
Thus they misjudge the nature of theater as much as they misjudge the
audience before which their own sacrificial tragedy is enacted. They fail to
realize that the theater is the last place in which to enshrine their deed; it
is far too secular, too common, too changeable. There, you are made a
motley to the view, not a cynosure of greatness. So their speech exposes
the discrepancy between what they aspire to be and what they theatrically
become.

But Cleopatra seems to have been born on stage, in midperformance.[5]
Though she has "immortal longings" she is incorrigibly corporeal and infinitely various, by turns jealous, deceitful, beguiling, cruel, and riggish.
Unlike Bottom, she not only wants to play all roles but does, and compels
Antony to play them with her. As a result their Alexandrian revels flow into
Shakespeare's London revels without so much as a ripple of resistance. No
sooner has she complained about being staged in Rome than she herself
sets about staging a queenly death: "Go fetch / My best attires; I am again
for Cydnus / To meet Mark Antony." This means of course that we have lost
the historical Cleopatra no less than we have Caesar and Brutus. But this
play defines that loss as Antony defines his abdication from Roman reality:

> Let Rome in Tiber melt, and the wide arch
> Of the ranged empire fall! Here is my space.
> Kingdoms are clay; our dungy earth alike
> Feeds beast as man; the nobleness of life
> Is to do thus, when such a mutual pair
> And such a twain can do it, in which I bind,
> On pain of punishment, the world to weet
> We stand up peerless.   (1.1)

Which prompts Cleopatra's "Excellent falsehood!" Later, however, when
Dolabella demurs from her vision of the dead Antony as one who stood up
supernaturally peerless, she cries "You lie, up to the hearing of the gods!"
(5.2). Cleopatra is like Falstaff rising from his counterfeit death at
Shrewsbury to say

> Counterfeit? I lie, I am no counterfeit. To die is to be a counterfeit, for
> he is but the counterfeit of a man who hath not the life of a man; but to
> counterfeit dying, when a man thereby liveth, is to be no counterfeit,
> but the true and perfect image of life indeed. (1HIV 5.4)

Counterfeiting death may be a lie, but to *be* dead is, at least in Falstaff's
logic, an even greater lie. Cleopatra's logic is similar. If the "nobleness" of
their Alexandrian revels is an excellent falsehood, reality itself is no less a
falsehood, merely a drabber, less excellent one. Reality takes Enobarbus's
view of Antony, and dies shamefully in a ditch.

However, in her famous speech about her dream of Antony, Cleopatra
first condemns Dolabella for taking the Enobarbus view and then qualifies
her claims for the Antony she dreamed of:

> You lie, up to the hearing of the gods!
> But if there be or ever were one such,
> It's past the size of dreaming. Nature wants stuff
> To vie strange forms with fancy; yet to imagine
> An Antony were nature's piece 'gainst fancy,
> Condemning shadows quite.

Despite nature's short supply of creative "stuff," the Antony *she* has imagined into life is more splendid even than the Antony that Cleopatra
dreamed of, condemning her shadows quite. Though at first glance this
argument seems to dismiss shadows, in fact it enlarges their domain to
include nature's imaginings, very much as Prospero's "Our revels now are
ended" speech ends the revels by projecting them into the great globe itself.
And just as the great globe inevitably evokes the great Globe theater, so

Cleopatra's *shadows* evokes the players in the Globe, one of whom is even now delivering her words. Thus Cleopatra's speech does not play off the lies of fancy against the truths of nature and defer to the latter; it presents the audience with a series of imaginative envelopments as Cleopatra's dream yields to the imaginings of nature which yield to the staged dream of Shakespeare.

In the midst of so many dreams and images the historical Antony and Cleopatra are, as I said, as lost to us as Caesar and Brutus. In the earlier play, where constancy was such a grand deluded virtue, that loss might seem significant; but in *Antony and Cleopatra* it is a world well lost. These lovers, somewhat like Shakespeare's model for Falstaff, Sir John Oldcastle, have died historically in order to live theatrically, which means subduing themselves like the dyer's hand to what they work in and are worked into: grand shows and trivial deceits, self-stagings, studied entrances, lies, trickery, indignities, exposures. Even death must be taken from the hands of a clown and enacted as a nursery scene. Yet this is death of a most undeath-like variety. Although we see Cleopatra commit suicide we also see her immortal longings fulfilled, not in a heavenly reunion with Antony, but in the staginess of the act itself, which implies that she cannot wholly die because she must die again in tomorrow's performance. By means of such paradoxical undyings she and the play she is in acquire everlasting life not by denying death but by means of it.

Thus it is wonderfully appropriate that the Clown should warn Cleopatra against touching the "pretty worm of Nilus" because "his biting is immortal" (5.2). The malapropism brings into divided focus the mortality the Clown means and the immortality he says. The effect is to render unto the historical dimension of the play the mortality of its unrecoverable pastness and unto the theatrical dimension of the play its immortal presence. In the most practical of senses, the Clown—whose provenance is exclusively the theater; there was none such in Plutarch—tells the truth. For the biting of stage snakes is theatrically immortal in the sense of not being mortal in the least, as Cleopatra's reappearance tomorrow will prove. *Antony and Cleopatra* is the Clown's malapropism writ large; it too has transformed the mortal into the immortal.

6. *The Tempest*: Death and Drama

Julius Caesar and *Antony and Cleopatra*—and for that matter all the plays based on history—preserve the past only in roughest outline. At some point or other they even announce that fact, as the Chorus does in *Henry V*:

> O for a Muse of fire that would ascend
> The brightest heaven of invention,
> A kingdom for a stage, princes to act,
> And monarchs to behold the swelling scene!

In the absence of such muses and actors, however, the stage is a petty place whose imperfections can be amended only by the author and his audience in a collaborative act of imagination. But of course what is lost in the way of history is won back in other ways by the quick historians of the stage.

It's hardly surprising that theater should be inhospitable to history, because history is a story, whereas drama is an act. By its performative nature drama owes fealty to the present, not the past. Not that the past cannot, as we say, come alive on stage, but that it can do so only in the flickering transience of performance—now you see it, now you don't. The proper medium of the past is not drama but narrative.

Narrative need not but normally does appear in written form; and writing, as I said earlier, entails the disappearance and hence metaphorically the death of the author. The author dies, but as if in compensation for his loss his text lives; and within his text the past lives or more accurately re-lives, assuming we have a reader to revive it. Of course the playwright also disappears, even more thoroughly than the writer, but instead of compensating his survivors with an immutable text and a preserved past he abandons his audience to the mortal present-tense illusions of the stage, where acts of speech and body die away the instant they come alive. How can they be retrieved? Not by drama. Drama simply sheds itself and goes on. What is dead in it has truly passed away.

The only way for drama to fill time's poke with alms for oblivion is to wrap them in narrative. Thus most of Shakepeare's plays move like *Hamlet* toward a theatrical ending that promises a postdramatic narrative, a Horatian story that will recollect the events of the play in a coherent and ordered form. *The Tempest* itself begins in the most dramatic fashion with shipwreck and imminent death and ends with Prospero offering the weary nobles his cell for the night, some part of which, he says

> I'll waste
> With such discourse as, I not doubt, shall make it
> Go quick away—the story of my life,
> And the particular accidents gone by
> Since I came to this isle.   (5.1)

This promise of a narrative preservation of the past combines with Prospero's following words about the forthcoming nuptials of Ferdinand and

Miranda to lend the end of the play a sense of death denial that runs contrary to the dramatic impulse itself. That impulse is better represented by Prospero's remark about retiring to Milan "where / Every third thought shall be my grave."

But despite its time-bound nature *The Tempest* by no means dwells on death—not when it presents us with Stephano and Trinculo singing drunkenly and wrestling with the island's four-legged monster, or with Ariel flitting about and Ferdinand and Miranda mooning at one another and Caliban cavorting in newfound freedom. Even in the opening scene death is painted in the liveliest colors. For that matter even in the most death-ridden of Shakespearean scenes the Gravemaker in *Hamlet* speaks with more vitality about death than the Prince does about life. Which is simply to say that as long as the stage is inhabited by human bodies there's life in it. Which also means, however, that there's dying in it. Coleridge's death-in-life or Shakespeare's life-in-death, one or the other.

In fact in *The Tempest* there is more than life in it, since some of its appeal would seem to be its willingness to indulge our death-denying impulses. Implicit in the play's oft-noted efforts to impose nurture on nature is an attempt to transcend the human condition and hence death. Gonzalo's half-playful evocation of an island commonwealth is as idyllic and supernatural in its way as the masque-vision that elides winter and leaves only an everlastingly bountiful spring and summer. The play overall repeats this soft-pastoral theme. The opening scene presents us with a real world in which ships sink and men drown and no one has "authority" over nature. But then for the next "three glasses" we are conducted into a timeless world of imagination where "no harm is done" either to characters within or audience without.

But of course this world cannot last. While the masque is in progress Ferdinand murmurs "Let me live here ever"; and no doubt a hollow place in everyone echoes his wish. "Let me live in *The Tempest* ever" is simply art's refinement on our more fundamental wish, "Let me live ever." Even Prospero is so absorbed in the masque-vision that he nearly forgets the death-dealing intents of Caliban and crew. But he remembers in time to return to time. Shakespeare never allows us to forget that time is the spider in the cup of our illusions, spinning death even for Prospero, certainly for us.

7. *The Tempest*: Art and Nature

When Lear accuses women of being centaurs, he indicts homo sapiens in general. For the human animal is a creature half in and half out of nature—bodily in and mentally or spiritually out—and for thousands of years human progress was measured by the extent to which man kept nature at bay. Beneath all the reassuring talk about beneficent and orderly nature lay a dread of its hostile otherness. Religion, law, government, art, all the social and economic forms of order, were so many blocks in the wall that kept external nature from overrunning us; and repression and sublimation played a similar role against our own wayward impulses. The most persistent assaults of nature took the form of sex and death, sex threatening from within, death from without. Every effort had to be made to minimize the danger. Sexual taboos, marriage laws, and courtship rituals were designed to keep sex in restraint. The violence of death was controlled by peace treaties and laws, and the fear of death was assuaged explicitly by religious rituals and implicitly by the kinds of social and psychological death denial discussed throughout this book.

Among other things, *The Tempest* writes in miniscule this vast human effort to repress and civilize nature. By means of his art Prospero attempts to discipline those two threats to human complacency—sex and death— which are the tempest tossed up by rebellious nature. In the present context the point of interest is not politics or morality but theatrical art and the denial of death.

Prospero spends much of his time warding off death. After the supposed shipwreck we discover that he has the power to make death disappear. Later he sends Ariel to blunt Antonio's death plot against Alonzo and then Caliban's against Prospero himself. In a sense his every third thought throughout the play has been of death. But this is death from without. At the end, when he speaks of returning to Milan, it is death from within— death bred in the bone, not in conspiratorial minds—that he will think about. The stage direction in act 1, scene 2—*Resumes his magic robes*— suggests not only that Prospero's art is supernatural but that, so robed, he is himself immortal. In which case it is no great feat to fend off Antonio and Caliban. But when Prospero breaks his staff, drowns his book, and casts away his magic c' ,ak, he submits himself to mortal perils that no magic can avert. Prospero is an inverted Christ figure, etherealizing himself in divinity instead of incarnating himself in mortality. His Passion leads not to an ascension but to a descension.

The metadramatic parallel to this is the fall of Shakespeare's play from island fantasies to theater realities. The imagination cannot cheat so well as she is famed to do. Still, in a sense Shakespeare has not asked the imagination to cheat at all. The masque of the goddesses may have excluded winter and death from nature's seasons, but *The Tempest* does not. Ariel is obliged "to run upon the sharp wind of the north" and to do Prospero's business "in the veins of the earth / When it is baked with frost" (1.2.254 ff.). The space between Alonzo asleep and Alonzo dead is but three inches of obedient steel (2.1.285), and for Prospero the same distance is measured by the length of the nail Caliban would like to knock into his head. The island is hardly a wish-fulfillment pastoral paradise. Death abounds in prospect if not in fact.

In this sense, then, the imagination, which is normally antithetical to death, is kept tethered to the mortal condition, so that the dispersal of illusions at the end is well anticipated. In another sense the descent of island illusions to stage business was accomplished almost from the beginning. But let me defer that for a moment in order to attend to Antonio's dramatic doings.

Dramatic doings because Prospero explains Antonio's usurpation as a kind of staging come true. Left in command of Milan by Prospero's abdication, Antonio played the role of duke so passionately that he thought he *was* "absolute Milan," and as absolute Milan he then presumptuously "new created / The creatures that were mine, I say, or changed them, / Or else new formed them" (1.2). Two points of metadramatic interest fuse in this account: the question of human identity in relation to role-playing and the Machiavellian nature of Antonio's playwriting. For Antonio, role and identity are indistinguishable; in his passion for power he becomes absolute Milan. In pursuit of further power he imposes new roles upon Prospero's subjects.[6] That is, he "new created" or he "changed" or he "new formed" them. Prospero's quick tour here through the verbs of poiesis raises the issue of what it is that a playwright does to (human) nature when he creates dramatic roles. In effect Antonio applies Hamlet's advice to Gertrude about assuming a virtue if she has it not, for that monster custom enables behavior to reform character—for the good in Gertrude's case, for the bad in Antonio's. If that is so, then acting is a dangerous business.

In this play we have at least three versions of human nature or identity. Gonzalo is unchangeable; the company of bad men cannot alter his natural goodness. Alonzo, on the other hand, can assume an evil role, but also can divest himself of it. For him "heart's sorrow" can produce "a clear life ensuing" (3.3); and Prospero takes care to leave plenty of heart's sorrow in his way. Antonio is a more difficult project. Because the end of the play provides no evidence that he feels either regretful or repentant, we are left wondering if in his case the evil role has, like a parasite, eaten up its host. Finally there is Caliban, a kind of reverse Antonio, upon whose natural evil Prospero has unsuccessfully sought to graft an unnatural goodness. Unlike Antonio, he makes repentant gestures and promises to "be wise hereafter," but we are more than free to doubt.

All of this gives special point to the epilogue, in which the actor who plays Prospero begs release from his role, and Prospero the character begs release from the actor who has played him. For at this point, in contrast to all earlier epilogues, the actor has not fully doffed his role and come forth as himself, but remains in bondage to "Prospero," caught there by the spell of the audience's imagination.[7] The question is whether the audience will tyrannously keep the actor penned in his role, as Sycorax kept Ariel penned in the tree, or imitate Prospero's mercy and release him into the real world. Behind all this is the suggestion that like actors we are not possessed of a unified self but are a complex product of our own and others' imaginings. There is no final release from these spells and roles. With the help of the audience's good hands, Richard Burbage is released from his role as Prospero—since we clap for actors, not for characters—only, however, to resume his real-life role as Richard Burbage the actor.

The mercy the audience shows Prospero is in keeping with the mercy he shows them. I mentioned a while ago that the demystification of theatrical illusion implied by Prospero's "Our revels now are ended" speech is actually performed much earlier—in act 1, scene 2, when Miranda says "If by your art, my dearest father, you have / Put the wild waters in this roar, allay them." Miranda's remark, and Prospero's revelation that he has indeed raised the tempest, make us realize that in the opening scene Shakespeare has victimized us somewhat as Antonio did Prospero's subjects when he forced them to play a role in his political play. For if the storm deceives the nobles, the storm scene deceives us. For a few moments Shakespeare flourishes over our heads the staff of his theatrical power, raising a tempest in our imaginations just as he made the cliffs of Dover fall away before our feet in *King Lear*. Then like Prospero he relents, lays down his robe and staff, and says "There's no harm done."

From the beginning, in other words, he tenders us the kind of mercy it takes Prospero the entire play to muster toward the nobles and Ariel. In a sense Shakespeare forswears his art—breaks his staff and drowns his book—by revealing its presence to us. Thus when Prospero dons his magic robe again after Miranda falls asleep, Shakespeare dons his as well, in full view of his audience. From this time forth he will make no pretense to a deceiving realism. His art will be open and apparent, not hidden, an art of presence; and Shakespeare will not be a *deus absconditus* but an intrinsic deity, a playwright immanent within his art.

Thus almost from the start Shakespeare splits the pine and frees us from our captivity to mimetic illusion. He will not work his arts on us as Prospero does on the Italians. By letting us in on the illusion-game, he elevates us to Prospero's level where we can share with him the exercise of power. Our magical powers reside in the imagination, in our ability to transform actors into characters as the sea transforms eyes into pearls, as Prospero momentarily transforms nature into fantasy.[8] But if we are allowed to share Prospero's transformative power, we must also share in his abdication of power. Thus in the epilogue we are asked to show the actors that same mercy that Prospero showed his servants and victims, releasing actor from character and character from actor. Our part too requires saying "These our actors . . . are all spirits."

8. Dissolving Art

The metadramatic passages of *Julius Caesar, Henry V,* and *Antony and Cleopatra* raise the issue of art's truth to history. *The Tempest* raises the same issue about art's truth, only not with respect to history. With respect to what, then? If anything, the play seems to advertise its fraudulence.

At the beginning we see reality dissolve into illusion when the storm is revealed to be a product of Prospero's magic. At the end, in the "Our revels now are ended" speech, we have intimations of illusion dissolving into reality. To complicate matters, Prospero tells Ferdinand that the reality into which illusion dissolves is itself but a larger illusion, or, rather, larger illusions. Prospero's artful masque must yield to exigent realities on the island—the political revolution of the low-life characters—but metadramatically these "realities" will in turn dissolve at curtain time into the artful illusion of a play called *The Tempest*—performed in a Globe theater where plays and actors and audiences all dissolve into the encompassing illusion of "the great globe itself," the theater of life. From this standpoint Shakespeare's is a true art. His theatrical illusions cannot falsify reality when reality is itself an illusion.[9]

Hence Shakespeare's demystification of theater is mortalizing but by no means mortifying; it confesses what the world must confess, to being a scene of illusions.[10] A tempest, after all, is an unbounded turbulence issuing indistinguishably from and merging with the rest of nature's ambient weather. So too *The Tempest.* At the end character fades into player, Globe into globe, groundling into citizen, and London playwright into Stratfordian man of property. And all of these in their turn, the playwright assures us, will fade as well, though whither and into what, he does not say.

If there is immortality in any of this, it is an immortality based not on immutability and timelessness but on change within time. The tempest and the sea keep churning; the illusions of art and life keep dissolving and reforming. *The Tempest* is mimetically nonmimetic—an icastic fantasy that mirrors not life's realities, since it has none, but life's illusions. The play of illusion is like the play of signification in language. In the latter, whenever we seek a terminal signified outside the play of signifiers—a nonverbal meaning—we encounter merely other signifiers. Similarly here, if we seek the originating transcendental signified—the nontheatrical reality which the play presumably represents—we shall find merely a further play of illusions, an infinite immortal regress from theater to theater, play to play, illusion to illusion.

As Ariel's song affirms, life does not lose by Shakespeare's transformative art. Like Prospero's tempest, Shakespeare's *Tempest* only seems to kill; in fact it confers on life a finer life, transforming it into something rich and strange. Nor does art lose by life. Through the reverse metamorphosis of their hand-clapping magic, the audience converts art's pearls and coral back into life's eyes and bones. In which case life takes redeemed life from art.

But redeemed or not, life is a mortal matter. What happens at the end of this final play is essentially what happens at the end of a very early play like *Love's Labour's Lost*; time and mortality call an end to the holiday of art.[11] Which is to say that *The Tempest*, like the other plays I have discussed here, dramatizes what is implicit in Shakespeare generally: the fact that his art is not really an attempt to deny death, however much it may in a sense do so. He does not seek to create disembodied worlds without end but dips his art in the watercolors of human action and paints time where she stands. Eternity has to stoop to make an entrance on his stage, because the only immortality we are promised is a performance again tomorrow and, if we are lucky, tomorrow and tomorrow and tomorrow.

Supplement

Supplement.
The Anti-Immortalists

1. Villains

The vast majority of Shakespeare's characters deny death in some positive manner. They deify something and identify with it: a hero, a king, a beloved, the nation, money, knowledge, virginity, honor, and so forth. By so doing they tuck themselves into a niche in the social order and become defiladed against death's arrows. If they cannot survive because they are powerful enough to conquer death on the battlefield, then they will do so because they are good, and God loves the good, or because they are patriotic, and God loves England, or because they are men, and God has strong reservations about women.

On the other hand there are some characters who come upon the stage not to praise immortality but to bury it. I have in mind Shakespeare's villains and fools. By the villains I mean Aaron the Moor, Richard III, Iago, and Edmund; by the fools I mean the Fools—the allowed ones, not the natural ones. Let us study villainy first.

The villains are anti-immortalists of course because their business is to reduce the spiritual to the corporeal. They are all naturalists and skeptics who perceive a half-truth concealed from their victims—that man's devotion to the good, the true, and the beautiful is often merely the lip service of a creature whose most basic instinct is to seize and devour—and elevate it to the status of a universal law which they as realists and honest men feel obliged to honor. For them man is primarily an actor—the animal that pretends to be more than it is, and almost never fails to convince itself. Knowing this ("Virtue, a fig!"), the villains become consummate actors themselves, the difference being that they rarely confuse role with reality:

> Indeed, 'tis true that Henry told me of,
> For I have often heard my mother say
> I came into the world with my legs forward.
> Had I not reason, think ye, to make haste,
> And seek their ruin that usurped our right?
> The midwife wondered and the women cried
> "O, Jesus bless us, he is born with teeth!"

> And so I was; which plainly signified
> That I should snarl and bite and play the dog.
> Then, since the heavens have shaped my body so,
> Let hell make crooked my mind to answer it.
> I have no brother, I am like no brother;
> And this word "love," which greybeards call divine,
> Be resident in men like one another
> And not in me. I am myself alone.   (3 HVI 5.6)

If ordinary men pretend to be more than human, to be what "greybeards call divine," the villain pretends to be more than a beast, to be a man. His humanity, however, consists in a transparent patina of motives laid over the impenetrable blackness of a nature whose evil has no basis in reality. Trip the proper switch on Aaron the Moor and whatever the circumstance he will roar "Vengeance is in my heart, death in my hand, / Blood and vengeance are hammering in my head" (TA 2.3). And if you try to find reasons for these pulsations of bloody passion you will experience a bit of hammering in your own head too. For there is no apparent cause either in nature or in the play that makes these hard hearts; blood, vengeance, and death, like Aaron's black skin, simply come with the role.

Aaron stands on the bottom rung of villainy. Because he will not even trouble himself to concoct reasons for his behavior, he seems very nearly an allegorical embodiment of blood, vengeance, and death. Richard III, on the other hand, though still out of reach of ordinary humanity, stands a few rungs higher. Unlike Aaron, who is too engrossed in evil to take account of the audience, Richard has a dual identity. He is something of a phenomenologist: his realistic self, in brackets, performs his villainous deeds while his transcendental theatrical self stands at the edge of the apron interpreting to the audience like a proud parent. He thrives on explanations, but they all reduce to the blank fact that he is to the manner of villainy born, and self-bred a bit too. Hence as Richard Moulton held, "villainy has become an end in itself needing no special motive."[1] Which of course echoes Coleridge's famous attribution of motiveless malignity to Iago—so impressively documented later by Robert B. Heilman, Bernard Spivack, and Stanley Edgar Hyman.[2]

The best explanation of the Janus nature of the Shakespearean villain is Spivack's claim that his evil side has no convincing basis because it is a prefabricated import from the Vice of the Tudor moral plays. The Shakespearean plays in which he appears, that is, represent a point of transition between old-style allegory and a more realistic drama yet to come. Hence the villain, as opposed to the criminal (Claudius or Macbeth for instance), is a theatrical misfit, no longer allegorical but not yet fully human either; and perhaps for that reason, because of the friction between his two incomplete identities, he is a misfit possessed of tremendous stage life. Indeed one could say that the theatrical vitality of this monstrous creature lends him a certain deathlessness, as though part of him somehow protrudes above or below the realistic dimension of the play where death occurs. He who kills off immortality in others seems himself to transcend death.

There are some textual grounds for saying the villain is symbolically immortal. At the end of *Titus Andronicus*, though Aaron is scheduled for death, the perpetuation of his evil is suggested by the survival of his and Tamora's son. More than that, however, the very viciousness of his punishment—

> Set him breast-deep in earth and famish him;
> There let him stand and rave and cry for food.
> If any one relieves or pities him,
> For the offence he dies

—implies the kind of despairing overkill that comes from an attempt to destroy something more, or less, or at any rate other than human, something that does not die like us. And, to be sure, whatever it is that pulses in Aaron pulses so strongly that his end is by no means certain. For in his cornered, hissing defiance he positively swells with malignant life:

> Ten thousand worse [evils] than ever yet I did
> Would I perform if I might have my will.
> If one good deed in all my life I did,
> I do repent it from my very soul.

You have to wonder if there are enough crosses and sharpened stakes in Transylvania to harry this monster to its grave. And surely there is something ominously ambiguous about his being "buried alive," especially when his interment has yet to be accomplished before the play ends.

On the other hand, Richard III does die rather conclusively before our eyes—most villainously indeed, because his doing so seems inconvenient for my argument. However, let us attribute this to his being all along more human than Aaron, and to his being in a history play where convention demands a convincing exorcism of evil in the interests of national redemption, and especially to his being in a Tudor history play in which Queen

Elizabeth's grandfather must be shown to stand with his foot on the boar's body to properly emblematize the ushering in of the Tudor dynasty.

Nevertheless, villainy itself endows Richard, not with actual, but with symbolic immortality. He is a kind of deity of evil, utterly unique. His birth was inhuman—legs thrust ambitiously forward and teeth gnashing; his mother repudiates him; and he himself repudiates the human ("I that have neither pity, love, nor fear"). All he has, it seems, is the desire to aggrandize himself by sacrificing others. He wants to be meaningful. He wants to wear a crown. But so, for that matter, do most heroes. And most heroes also sacrifice others. Witness Henry V. Heroic sacrifice, however, serves the perverted cause of innocence. The French must die in order to divert not only death but guilt from the English—the political guilt of Henry IV's reign as a usurper, the moral guilt of his killing Richard II. English souls, especially King Harry's, can be washed as clean in the blood of the French as in that of the Lamb. Richard entertains purgative notions too; however, his means of purifying his soul is to pumice away every taint of goodness lurking within. Then, cleansed of humanity, he can stand forth and announce "I am myself alone."

It is arguable that because of this purification of good, Shakespeare's villains give us, or at least give the groundlings, a false picture of evil as the product of maverick individuals. That is, we now know that the greatest evils are performed not by Machiavels and criminals, those who defy cultural norms, but rather by those who too readily accept such norms, those on whom culture imprints itself as indelibly as a greylag goose on its goslings. Possessed of the holiest of unexamined motives—crying "God and England!" (or "Gross National Profit!" "Medicine!" or "Technology!")—they go forth with missionary zeal to fell the forests and the seal pups, maim laboratory animals to see if they heal, and, if all else fails, to depopulate the planet. "Men never do evil so completely and cheerfully," Pascal observed, "as when they do it from religious conviction."[3]

The usual assumption is that the villain illustrates Shakespeare's negative capability, the idea that he humanizes his villains a bit in order, presumably, to villainize his audiences a bit—that is, to force us to recognize the Iago in ourselves as well as the one on stage. But I suggest that the villain's role is not that of the scarecrow whose hideous evils fright us into goodness but that of the sacrificial victim whom Shakespeare drags on stage and pinions, or buries chest deep like Aaron, and in his role as high priest of theater says to the audience "Have at him! You will be the better for it afterward." And indeed we do feel better, because through Richard we have purged ourselves of our lesser evils, the random wild evils we repressed in the process of acquiring some of the great communal evils that pass for Good. Not that Shakespeare is himself a villain for doing this. After all, insofar as Aaron stands in for the Jews, the Irish, the New World savages, the Toms of Bedlam, and the Abraham men, among other outcasts and subhumans, he serves as a theatrical lightning rod absorbing evil not merely from Shakespeare but from an audience in search of scapegoats.

The worst thing about villains is that they so often tell the truth, or at least an impressive part of it. In their devilish way they know that devils never get their way. Blake knew this perhaps even better than Pascal. As he indicates, if you want to steal peaches or lie with lithe ladies, you need only appear costumed as an angel. And to appear as an angel you must hide your body. That is what villains and devils find contemptible about the world; everyone is got up in the sublimated garb of an angel. So their own strategy is, on devilish principle, to do very much what the Protestant preachers did: insist that man is a bolting hutch of beastliness and excremental filth. Quintessential materialists, they represent the foul claims of the body that reduce love to the sexual congress of a two-backed beast and virtue to a fig.[4]

For this reason villains, like saints, must be killed. We kill saints because they set impossibly high standards and hence imply that we are not sufficiently saintly ourselves. We kill villains because they tell us an even worse truth, that most of the time we are, like them, not even human. Joan of Arc must be killed for something of both reasons. To be accurate, however, no one ever kills saints, because before they are killed they must be desanctified—degraded to the status of impostors. That is, we must make them unpleasantly like ourselves so that their deaths will purify us. For instance, in 1 *Henry VI* Shakespeare not only desanctifies Joan but villainizes her. She is triply dangerous, being not merely a villain but a feminine villain and, worse yet, a French feminine villain. Clearly she must be done away with. Otherwise she may do to us what she does to the great warrior Talbot. After the battle of Bordeaux Sir William Lucy looks about for Talbot, "the great Alcides of the field," and, invoking the titles of his greatness at some length, asks where he is. Joan replies "Here is a silly stately style indeed!" and pointing says "Him that thou magnifiest with all these titles / Stinking and fly-blown lies here at our feet" (1 H VI 4.7). This stripping away of the symbolic dimension of Talbot leaves a fly-blown body but also leaves only half of the truth, for Talbot's titles, we know, have been earned.

And of course Joan's are not. Cynically got up (by Shakespeare as much as by herself) in the apparel of saintliness, when she is captured she claims an even greater title than any of Talbot's because she is

> . . . issued from the progeny of kings;
> Virtuous and holy; chosen from above
> To work exceeding miracles on earth.
>
> (5.4)

The vessel in which God confides must be angelically devoid of bodily stuff. But of course Joan's supernatural connections are diabolic, not divine; and although the Devil may covet souls he seeks them first in their corporeal lodgings. Hence even the maid, stripped of her saintliness, not merely acknowledges but proclaims her body when all else fails: "I am with child, ye bloody homicides!"

Pleading her belly does not save Joan, except theatrically: like Aaron she does not die on stage. Villains, as I say, are hard to kill; because they stand for the body, their own bodies are in a sense indestructible. Thus when Othello says

> I look down towards his feet; but that's a fable.
> If that thou be'st a devil, I cannot kill thee,
> (*Wounds Iago*)

the blade of his skepticism shatters against Iago's impenetrable reply: "I bleed, sir, but not killed." Iago seems plugged into a current of evil whose source lies beyond Venice and the Globe theater and even London itself. Othello does not kill him, nobody kills him. Who would dare? He burns with the kind of chilling diabolical flame that makes ordinary men fall back in fear.

By despiritualizing others, then, by reducing the fair Lavinia to a mass of bleeding stumps and the Othello music to incoherent ranting, Shakespeare's motiveless villains immortalize themselves, or at least immortalize the principle of evil they embody. Aaron may be embedded chest deep in the earth, but he rises again, washes the charcoal from his face, contorts his body, and limps forward to say "Now is the winter of our discontent." And Richard the mad boar may fall under the sword of Henry Richmond, but he too rises again, straightens his crooked body, and tells Roderigo in an open, honest, fetching voice, "I am not what I am." If there are dying-and-reviving gods, there are dying-and-reviving devils too—not so much because of their devilish nature as because of our angelic need. Even when they finally die out of literature and mythology, they return as German Jews before the war and German Germans after it, as Vietnamese "slopes," or as Arab monsters like Arafat, Qaddafi, and Khomeini.

The villains, then, are men more destroying than destroyed. Destruction, after all, is their business, the exercise of power for its own sake. One of their ancestors, Machiavelli, regarded power as an evil but necessary means to the greater good of the state; but for the Shakespearean Machiavel, power serves neither good nor evil but only, like lust, its own pleasure. It consists in controlling people, and the only way to be certain you are controlling people is to make them suffer. It is not enough just to make them do what you want—to turn King Edward against his brother George or Othello against his lieutenant Cassio. You must gouge your way into their deepest desires, put their hopes and faiths on the rack, and wring their hearts until they confess themselves your creature, until they say "Now are thou my lieutenant" and you reply "I am your own forever." That is the moment of conquest, when you love the victim you torment, because without him you could never experience such intoxication, or know so surely that with this power you will live, if not as long as God, as least as long as Satan.

2. Fools

And what of the poor Fools? Such grand passions are not for them. They are hardly in the same league as the villains, and knowing this they keep their distance. Even so, their function is similar to that of the villains: to bring man down from spiritual heights to corporeal depths, not villainously to destroy but foolishly to diminish. To that end, they remind Petrarchan lovers that from hour to hour men ripe and ripe, but also from hour to hour rot and rot—because, as the smitten Touchstone says, man hath his desires (*AYLI* 2.7; 3.3). Or they suggest to the religious that under the vestments of mens' spiritual differences, as Lavache points out, beats a similar urgency of the flesh:

> If men could be contented to be what they are, there were no fear in marriage; for young Charbon the puritan and old Poysam the papist, howsome'er their hearts are severed in religion, their heads are both one: they may joul horns together like any deer in the herd. (*All's Well* 1.3)

But most of all, Fools like to insist that whereas they themselves are "allowed" or entitled, the titles of all the great ones who allow them—the dukes and earls and grand ladies—are artificial, except one: their natural title to folly: "That," as Lear's Fool says, "thou wast born with" (1.4). And if all men are fools then they end up where Fools end up, where all the whoreson mad fellows end up, grinning in the grave with Yorick.

Thus Fools, like villains, are anti-immortalists; they bring man down to earth, six feet of it eventually. But unlike villains, Fools are not exempt from their own law of reduction. Though they have skipping spirits, their bodies are prone to English agues and the Viennese bone-ache. The disappearance of the Fool in *King Lear* is a kind of death brought on by too much shivering and chattering in the storm; and even Feste, despite his name, concludes his play on a chop-fallen note, not with music that is the food of life but with a song that tells how the daily rain eventually wears away the lives of all who live in this aged world. Folly itself may survive forever, but even Fools cannot keep death distracted for long.

However, before quite leaving the field of folly and distraction, let me glance at a character who roundly embodies some of the aspects of both Fool and villain, that horseback-breaker Falstaff. That he competes with Fools needs no documenting here; he is as allowed by Prince Hal as Lear's Fool is by the old King, cutting his verbal capers throughout Parts 1 and 2 and then riding all night to thrust a fat palm in front of the new-crowned King at Westminster Abbey, only to find that his allowance is used up: he has been a natural fool all along. He is like the Fools, and villains too for that matter, in corporealizing the spiritual, most famously in his reduction of honor to a mere word, a slight commotion of the air, and most soberingly in his reduction of martial chivalry to his leading his hundred and fifty ragamuffins into a battle that leaves only three to beg through life.

Falstaff is like the villains also in that the immensity of his theatrical vitality causes him to exceed the girth of his realistic environment. This is especially true of the Falstaff of Part 1. In Part 2 he is held accountable to time both physically ("I am old, I am old") and financially ("Master Shallow, I owe you a thousand pound"). In Part 1 he scrambles for sack and capons as if his business were pure survival, and yet he possesses a rubbery invulnerability to mortal defeats. As official master of improvisation, he is simply too shifty for death to corner. Like the villains he exceeds his realisitic environment, as though he were dancing to a distant music. One reason is that like them he is nephew to the old Vice (his only relative, that is, is outside the play; he has none in England to bind him into the social world). At any rate in Part 1 he lives so thoroughly at the level of theater, entertainer par excellence, that to ask the reasons for his behavior is as beside the point as asking about those of the villains. Besides, even if you ask, he will not answer. Even when caught begetting lies as fast as men in buckram and Kendall green, he will not answer. It is not that he lacks reasons but that he will not give them upon compulsion:

> Give you a reason upon compulsion! If reasons were as plenty as blackberries, I would give no man a reason upon compulsion, I. (2.4)

In this last witty sentence Shakespeare has compacted the essence of Falstaff's vitality. The pun on reasons shrivels the rational spirit of that word into mere raisins, and at the same time transforms the work of the intellect into phallic raisings. On the one hand Falstaff is not answerable to the world; he will not on compulsion come up with a single reason, though they were as easily come by as raisins and blackberries. And on the other hand he will not—alas, cannot—come up with a raising on compulsion either, for such raisings have little to do with reason.

This homophonic harvest of meanings would be quite enough by itself, but Shakespeare as usual has planted far more than we can easily gather. For instance, the seeming contrast between shriveled raisins and virile raisings is called in question as we gradually realize that in Falstaff's employment raisins are as fertile as raisings. That is, to begin with, reasons and raisins are equally anathema to him—reasons because he operates as he claims by "instinct"; and raisins because as dried grapes they pervert the true purpose of grapes, to become wine, to become sherris-sack, to acquire the virtuous capacity to ascend into the brain and displace "reason," making the brain "apprehensive, quick, forgetive, full of nimble, fiery, and delectable shapes," as well as "warming the blood" and thereby banishing cowardice (2 HIV 4.3). But raisins have all these virtues squeezed out of them. Unlike blackberries, which flourish and multiply, whose very appearance is of burgeoning vitality, raisins are a shriveling of the ripeness of both grapes and plentiful reasons.

But if a raisin is a shriveled grape, what then is a shriveled reason? Presumably something very like a lie, the mere skin and semblance of a reason. And thus we get to the fertile center of all the puns, for Falstaff's raisin-reasonlike lies are indeed as plentiful as blackberries, as plentiful as men in buckram and Kendall green, and as wonderfully irrelevant to the world of true explanation as his forthcoming reason for his seeming cowardice:

> By the Lord, I knew ye as well as he that made ye. Why, hear me, my masters. Was it for me to kill the heir apparent? Should I turn upon the true prince?

Such "reasons" as this ascend like sherris-sack above the workaday world in which men are accountable for their actions, and in which actions can be accounted for by causes. Falstaff is as invulnerable to reason as he is to death.

And so, not much further on, we see him fall dead on stage, cut down by the wind of Douglas's sword at his backside, only to raise himself again to give reasons for his raising, and better ones for his falling. Unlike the villains who die and rise again in the shape of another villain, Falstaff comes to life as himself. Rising from death at Shrewsbury, he capers less and less vigorously in Part 2, making his gradual way to Westminster, where he receives a mortal wound from the abruptly dismissive King Harry. Such treatment is required from Hal's standpoint, since if he is to apotheosize himself in the English heavens, the Falstaffian body in him, with all its mortal demands, must be sacrificed. From our standpoint, however, we cannot help regretting this gross insult to a body whose desires and discomforts seem to transcend its mortality, a body whose girth contains an excess not only of capons and sack but of life and abundance. Surely such a body cannot die. However, Falstaff survives only long enough for Mistress Quickly to gather her rhetorical forces and report his dying moments in *Henry V* (2.3).

And yet he rises once again in the *Merry Wives*, aided by the Queen's hand, some say, or perhaps by the heart-warming properties of the sherris-sack Nym says he cried out for at the approach of death earlier. This time, however, he is not quite himself, nor is given the chance to be, what with being dunked in a ditch and beaten and pinched and burned with tapers for his lechery and even compelled to stand the taunting of a Welshman "who makes fritters of English" before he can be welcomed into society (5.5). It seems a fearful price to pay for a little roistering in the Boar's Head Tavern with a truant prince, and surely no one but the great bed-presser himself could have survived it. Yet there he stands at the end, at his old ward, his redoubtable body leaned hopefully in the direction of Mrs. Page's sideboard, ready as always to be replenished and revivified.

Notes

Introduction

1   See Erich Fromm, *The Sane Society* (New York: Fawcett, 1955), *The Heart of Man* (New York: Harper, 1964), and *The Anatomy of Human Destructiveness* (New York: Holt, Rinehart and Winston, 1973); Elias Canetti, *Crowds and Power* (New York: Continuum, 1978), originally *Masse und Macht* (Hamburg: Claasen Verlag, 1960); Arthur Koestler, *Insight and Outlook* (London, 1948), *The Act of Creation* (New York: Macmillan, 1964), and *Janus* (New York: Random House, 1978); Norman O. Brown, *Life Against Death* (New York: Vintage Books, 1959); Konrad Lorenz, *On Aggression* (New York: Harcourt Brace Jovanovich, 1966); Jacques Choron, *Death and Western Thought* (New York: Macmillan, 1963); Ernest Becker, *The Birth and Death of Meaning* (New York: Free Press, 1962), *The Denial of Death* (New York: Free Press, 1973), and *Escape from Evil* (New York: Free Press, 1974); René Girard, *Violence and the Sacred*, trans. Patrick Gregory (Baltimore and London: Johns Hopkins University Press, 1977); and Robert Jay Lifton, *The Life of the Self* (New York: Basic Books, 1983).

2   Sir Thomas Browne, *Religio Medici* (1635) (1906; London: J. M. Dent and Sons, 1956), p. 39. Regarding the general Renaissance divisions of spiritual and corporeal, see Patrick Crutwell, "Physiology and Psychology in Shakespeare's Age," *Journal of the History of Ideas* 12 (January 1951): 75–89, and Paul H. Kocher, *Science and Religion in Elizabethan England* (San Marino, Calif. Huntington Library, 1953), chap. 14. For an informative discussion of the "Real versus the Ideal" in Shakespeare, see Rolf Soellner's chapter of that title in his *Shakespeare's Patterns of Self-Knowledge* (Columbus: Ohio State University Press, 1972), pp.131–49.

3   Fromm, *Heart of Man*, p. 117. In minimizing man's instincts I hardly mean to endorse a tabula rasa or "black box" notion of human nature. A more comfortable position lies somewhere between neoinstinctivists like Freud, Konrad Lorenz, and Robert Ardrey and behaviorists/operationalists like John B. Watson and B. F. Skinner. For instance, in *The Anatomy of Human Destructiveness*, Erich Fromm distinguishes between "organic drives" (formerly "instincts") for survival (food, fight, flight, sexuality) and nonorganic drives, "which are not phylogenetically programmed and are not common to all men: the desire for love and freedom; destructiveness, narcissism, sadism, masochism" (p. 72), and emphasizes also certain existential "needs" of man—to feel oriented and devoted, to feel emotionally rooted, to feel at one with life, to feel effective, etc.—which can be satisfied in a variety of cultural ways (pp. 218–67). For instance, with regard to the need for devotion,

> The objects of man's devotion vary. He can be devoted to an idol which requires him to kill his children or to an ideal that makes him protect children; he can be devoted to the growth of life or to its destruction. He can be devoted to the goal of amassing a fortune, of acquiring power, of destruction, or to that of loving and of being productive and courageous.

> . . . yet while the difference in the objects of devotion is of immense impor-
> tance, the need for devotion itself is a primary, existential need demanding
> fulfillment regardless of *how* this need is fulfilled. (P. 232)

In short, as Mary Midgley says, "We are naturally culture-building animals. But what
we build into our culture has to satisfy our natural pattern of motives" (*Beast and
Man: The Roots of Human Behavior* [Ithaca: Cornell University Press, 1978], p. 29). This
is roughly the position taken by sociobiologists like Edward O. Wilson who argue
for a genetic groundwork on which all behavior is built. See his *Sociobiology* (Cambridge: Belknap Press, 1975), *On Human Nature* (Cambridge and London: Harvard
University Press, 1978), and (with Charles J. Lumsden) *Promethean Fire* (Cambridge
and London: Harvard University Press, 1983).

4   For an interesting definition of culture as a combination of "social
information"—i.e., guides to the "smart" behavior needed for survival—and "culture
information"—i.e., guides to the "proper" behavior that allows man to feel good—see
Morris Freilich's "Manufacturing Culture: Man the Scientist," in *The Meaning of Culture*, ed. Morris Freilich (Lexington, Mass. and Toronto: Xerox College Publishing,
1972), pp. 267–325.

5   Becker, *Birth and Death of Meaning*, p. 76.

6   The words of the Digger Indian are recorded by Ruth Benedict in
Patterns of Culture (Boston: Houghton Mifflin, 1934), pp. 21– 22, who adds: "The old
man was still vigorous and a leader in relationships with the whites. He did not mean
that there was any question of the extinction of his people. But he had in mind the
loss of something that had value to that of life itself, the whole fabric of his
people's standards and beliefs." The same sense of disillusion and loss of meaning
characterizes the feelings of many retirees in modern society. Alan H. Olmstead, a
former newspaper columnist and editor of the *Manchester Evening Herald*, writes in
his published diary *Threshhold* (as reported by Thomas Mallon in *A Book of One's Own*
([New York: Ticknor and Fields, 1984], pp.102–3):

> When I quit working in the idea factory I at first had the idea that nobody
> could replace me. That subsided, rather swiftly, in favor of the still comfort-
> ing conclusion that nobody could fill the place as well as I had. That in turn
> is now yielding to a new and much less comforting realization. I am begin-
> ning to think it would never have made any difference if my particular
> factory had not been operating at all.

Needless to say such a conclusion may be arrived at before retirement, even on rare
occasion and against all odds by scholars and literary critics.

7   Kenneth Burke, *Language as Symbolic Action* (Berkeley and Los Angeles:
University of California Press, 1968), p. 63. In the same book Burke speaks of man
as the inventor of the negative, and then observes that "so far as sheerly empirical
development is concerned, it might be more accurate to say that language and the
negative 'invented' man" (p. 9). Language is not truly language—does not graduate
from a collection of verbal indices to a system of symbolic signs—until it can refer to
that which is not present. The tremendous developments in cultural adaption during
the last 40,000 years are often attributed to the fact that at that time the human brain
reached its current average size of 1,500 cc and, with vast neocortexual areas unas-
signed to bodily tasks, both language and man became possible (see Morton Hunt,
The Universe Within [New York: Simon and Schuster, 1982], pp. 32–47).

8   See Becker's chapter on "Socialization: The Creation of the Inner

World" in *Birth and Death of Meaning*, pp. 38–53. Regarding "annihilation anxiety" see Rollo May, *The Meaning of Anxiety* (New York: Ronald Press, 1950); J. C. Rheingold, *The Mother, Anxiety, and Death: The Catastrophic Death Complex* (Boston: Little, Brown, 1967); and Dorothy Bloch's extraordinary *So the Witch Won't Eat Me: Fantasy and the Child's Fear of Infanticide* (Boston: Houghton Mifflin, 1978).

9 See Lucien Lévy-Bruhl, *Primitive Mentality* (London: Allen and Unwin, 1923), pp. 37–38; A. Gesell and F. Ilg, *The Child from Five to Ten* (New York: Harper, 1946), pp. 439–49; and Sylvia Anthony, *The Child's Discovery of Death* (London: Kegan Paul, Trench, Trubner and Co., 1940). In "The Child's View of Death," *Journal of Genetic Psychology* 73 (1948): 3–27, Maria H. Nagy records the interesting results of her studies concerning the meaning of death for children from three to ten. She summarizes:

> What does death mean to the child? The replies given can be categorized into three major developmental stages: (1) The child who is less than five years of age usually does not recognize death as an irreversible fact; in death he sees life. (2) Between the ages of five and nine, death is most often personified and thought of as a contingency. (3) Only at the age of nine and later does he begin to view death as a process which happens to us according to certain laws. (Pp. 4–5)

10 Ernst Cassirer, *An Essay on Man* (New Haven: Yale University Press, 1944), pp. 111–12. Such myths answer of course to the fact that though we accept death in the abstract, we all feel in the depths of our individual "I" that we are immortal and that death is an unpardonable violation of the cosmic law of self-esteem.

11 See Becker's section titled "The Larger View of Transference" in *Denial of Death*, pp. 139–58. (I am obliged to Kirby Farrell for bringing Becker's nonclinical sense of transference to my attention.) The quote from Camus is in *The Myth of Sisyphus and Other Essays*, trans. Justin O'Brien (New York: Vintage, 1955), p. 12; and that from Freud is from "Thoughts for the Times on War and Death," *Standard Edition of the Complete Psychological Works of Sigmund Freud*, ed. James Strachey (London: Hogarth Press, 1953–66), 14: 289. Lifton disagrees slightly with Freud's view that "each one of us is convinced of his own immortality":

> Rather, we have what some recent workers have called "middle knowledge" of the idea of death. We both "know" that we will die and resist and fail to act upon that knowledge. Nor is the need to transcend death *mere* denial. More essentially, it represents a compelling universal urge to maintain an inner *sense* of continuous symbolic relationship, over time and space, with the various elements of life. In other words, I am speaking of a *sense* of immortality as in itself neither compensatory nor pathological, but as man's symbolization of his ties with both his biological fellows and his history, past and future. (*Life of the Self*, p. 31)

12 Gerhart Piers and Milton B. Singer, *Shame and Guilt: A Psychoanalytic and a Cultural Study* (New York: W. W. Norton, 1971), p. 26.

13 William James, *Varieties of Religious Experience* (Cambridge: Harvard University Press, 1985), p. 119.

14 Canetti, *Crowds and Power*, p. 227.

15 Girard, *Violence and the Sacred*, p. 255.

16 See Arthur Schopenhauer, *The World as Will and Idea*, trans. T. B. Haldane and J. Kemp (1883; London: Routledge and Kegan Paul, 1948), vol. 3, p. 249;

Otto Rank, *Beyond Psychology* (New York: Dover, 1958), p. 64; Brown, *Life Against Death*, p. 284; and for a summary of this general position, Becker, *Escape from Evil*, p. 124.

17   In the following generalized account of death in the Renaissance I am much indebted to Philippe Ariès's chapter "The Final Reckoning" in his monumental *The Hour of Our Death*, trans. Helen Weaver (New York: Vintage, 1982), pp. 93–139.

18   Theodore Spencer, *Death and Elizabethan Tragedy* (Cambridge: Harvard University Press, 1936), p. 32.

19   Philippe Ariès uses these terms in *The Hour of Our Death*.

20   *The Complete Works of Montaigne*, trans. Donald M. Frame (Stanford: Stanford University Press, 1948, 1957, 1958), pp. 60, 64, 61.

21   Robert Penn Warren, *All the King's Men* (New York: Modern Library, 1953), p. 54.

22   Montaigne, "Apology for Raymond Sebonde," *Complete Works*, p. 414. Carl Gustav Jung, *Modern Man in Search of a Soul*, trans. W. S. Dell and C. F. Baynes (New York: Harcourt, Brace and Co., 1933), p. 229. A modern version of this has recently been called the "imposter syndrome"—i.e., the deep feeling of unworthiness and the consequent fear of exposure that afflict many highly successful persons.

23   Of course the Anglican compromise attempted to ameliorate these distresses by retaining the clergy, the ceremonies, and two of the sacraments of Catholicism. Nevertheless, the advent of Protestantism in general inevitably broke down old securities while opening up new freedoms. My new freedom to interpret the Bible by the flickering light of grace and immediate infusion entails my being disconcertingly responsible for my interpretations also. How reassuring simply to turn to Rome in such matters. And in a sense that is what the Anglican Church did, insofar, that is, as it became increasingly absolutist and "catholicized" under Archbishop Laud, to the infuriation of the Puritans.

24   For sustained documentation of the egocentric passion for greatness among the men of Shakespeare's generation, see Anthony Esler, *The aspiring mind of the Elizabethan younger generation* (Durham, N. C.: Duke University Press, 1966). Re. familial tyranny, see Lawrence Stone, *The Crisis of the Aristocracy, 1558–1641* (Oxford: Clarendon, 1965), pp.589–600—e.g., "England was particularly insistent upon the subordination of children to parents, emphasized by outward forms of respect" (p. 591)—and, for elaboration of the point, Carolly Erickson, *The First Elizabeth* (New York: Summit Books, 1983), pp. 43–44. In reaction to this, one would expect Elizabethan young men to strive desperately to assert their significance in the world, and at the same time perhaps to pay a high price in guilt for violating the patriarchal Superego.

25   See Stone's section on "Conspicuous Consumption" in *Crisis of the Aristocracy*, pp. 184–89.

1. Cannibalism

1   Rolf Soellner points out that "cannibalistic images were customarily applied to usurers in Shakespeare's time," and cites Gerald de Malynes's *Saint George for England* (1601), p. 47, and Arthur Warren, *The Poor Man's Passions and Poverty's Patience* (1605), sig. B3ᵛ—see Soellner *"Timon of Athens": Shakespeare's Pessimistic Tragedy* (Columbus: Ohio State University Press, 1979), pp. 47, 75. Yasuhiro Ogawa

tells me that Wilson makes the same comparison in his *Discourse Upon Usury*. For a good discussion of usury in the play and in England, see Lawrence Danson, *The Harmonies of "The Merchant of Venice"* (New Haven and London: Yale University Press, 1978), pp. 139–52; and regarding the "use/ewes" pun see—Sigurd Burckhardt's *"The Merchant of Venice*: The Gentle Bond,"* in his *Shakespearean Meanings* (Princeton: Princeton University Press, 1968) and Marc Shell's chapter "The Wether and the Ewe" in his *Money, Language, and Thought* (Berkeley and Los Angeles: University of California Press, 1982), pp. 47–83.

2 Shylock's practice is a reversal of that of the Kwakiutl Indians of the Pacific Northwest. He swallows his enemies by taking their money, the Kwakiutls do so by expending their own. Thus one old chief confounded his enemies by destroying his money in their presence, crying "Hap, hap, hap, now I've eaten you!" Cited by Eli Sagan, *Cannibalism* (New York: Harper and Row, 1974), p. 112, from Clellan S. Ford in *Indians of the North Pacific Coast*, ed. Tom McFeat (Seattle: University of Washington Press, 1966), pp. 131–33.

3 In connection with Coriolanus's fear of being devoured, see the brilliant article by Janet Adelman, "Feeding, Dependency, and Aggression in *Coriolanus*," which first appeared in *Shakespeare: Pattern of Excelling Nature*, ed. David Bevington and Jay L. Halio (Cranbury, N. J.: Associated University Press, 1978) and later in *Representing Shakespeare*, ed. Murray M. Schwartz and Coppélia Kahn (Baltimore and London: Johns Hopkins University Press, 1980).

2. Mana and Money, Feeding and Fasting

1 See Brown's extraordinary essay on "Filthy Lucre" in his *Life Against Death*, pp. 234–304. See also Becker's chapter on "Money: The New Universal Immortality Ideology" in his *Escape from Evil*, pp. 63–90.

2 Canetti, *Crowds and Power*, p. 229.

3 Michel Foucault, *The History of Sexuality*, trans. Robert Hurley (New York: Random House, 1978), p. 136.

4 Canetti, *Crowds and Power*, p. 219.

5 Ibid., p. 252.

6 For the identification of the banquet as the Communion table, see Robert G. Hunter, *Shakespeare and the Comedy of Forgiveness* (New York and London: Columbia University Press, 1965), pp. 233– 34. See also Donald K. Anderson, "The Banquet of Love in English Drama," *Journal of English and Germanic Philology* 63 (1964): 422–32

7 Canetti, *Crowds and Power*, p. 220.

3. Disguise, Role-Playing, and Honor

1 This view of the metamorphoses of female into male characters is proposed by William C. Carroll in an unusually insightful book on the comedies, *The Metamorphoses of Shakespearean Comedy* (Princeton: Princeton University Press, 1985)— see chapter 4, "Forget To Be a Woman," pp. 103–37. The notion that woman must be masculinized in order to acquire power and status in the community is not merely Shakespearean; it has theological precedents in the rhetoric of the church fathers and

most explicitly in the recently discovered Gospel of Thomas, which attributes to Simon Peter the belief that as a woman Mary is not worthy of spiritual life, and to Jesus the statement "Behold I will take Mary, and make her a male, so that she may become a living spirit, resembling you males. For I tell you truly, that every female who makes herself male will enter the Kingdom of Heaven." This appears in a fascinating article by Elaine H. Pagels, "What Became of God the Mother? Conflicting Images of God in Early Christianity" in *The Signs Reader*, ed. Elizabeth Abel and Emily K. Abel (Chicago and London: University of Chicago Press, 1983), pp. 97–108.

2   Regarding Death's inscription on pastoral tombstones—"I too am in Arcadia"—see Irwin Panofsky, "*Et in Arcadia Ego*: Poussin and the Elegiac Tradition," in his *Meaning in the Visual Arts* (Garden City, N. Y.: Doubleday, 1957), pp. 295–320.

3   Walter J. Ong, *Fighting for Life: Contest, Sexuality, and Consciousness* (Ithaca and London: Cornell University Press, 1981), p. 72.

4   In *Symbolic Wounds*, rev. ed. (New York: Collier Books, 1962), his remarkable study of male puberty rites, Bruno Bettelheim notes that the release of Halloween rites enables pubescent boys to act on their desire to experience femininity by dressing in girls' and women's clothing, often exaggerating the breasts and sometimes giving the appearance of pregnancy (pp. 35–36). His study in general argues that circumcision and similar rituals express a male fascination with and jealousy of female sexuality.

I suppose it could be argued that the psychological motive for the theological practice of having priests wear feminine robes is to suppress all signs of masculine aggressiveness, which would tend to repel those wishing to enter the Church, and to associate the clergy with the welcoming, nurturing motherliness of the Church.

5   Jonas Barish, *The Anti-Theatrical Prejudice* (Berkeley and Los Angeles: University of California Press, 1981), pp. 82–92.

6   For sustained treatments of the concept of honor in Shakespeare's time see Hiram Haydn's *Counter-Renaissance* (New York: Grove Press, 1950), pp. 555–636; Curtis B. Watson's *Shakespeare and the Renaissance Concept of Honor* (Princeton: Princeton University Press, 1960); Stone's chapter "The Inflation of Honors" in *Crisis of the Aristocracy*, pp. 65–128; and Esler's *Aspiring mind of the Elizabethan younger generation*.

7   Esler, *Aspiring mind*, pp. 123, 164. The widespread sacredness of honor and the court itself in Shakespeare's time could perhaps derive from the Reformation's having called true religion in doubt. Substitute religions spring up everywhere, characterized by fierce loyalties, narcissistic self-aggrandizement, and touchiness about status. If you challenge my honor, my lady, or my Queen, you challenge my life.

8   I should add, however, that codes of gallantry toward women—courtly love, Petrarchism, honor—even though often mere ornament, nevertheless gave women a certain cultural and ideological leverage in the struggle to civilize male savagery.

9   "Shame culture" refers to the distinction first made by Ruth Benedict in *The Chrysanthemum and the Sword* (1946) between cultures that monitor right- and wrong-doing primarily by public sanctions ("shame cultures") or by private conscience ("guilt cultures")—a distinction profitably applied to classical Greek literature by E. R. Dodds in *The Greeks and the Irrational* (Berkeley and Los Angeles: University of California Press, 1951).

10   For the convolutions of sex and death in *Measure for Measure* see two excellent discussions: Janet Adelman's "Mortality and Mercy in *Measure for Measure*" in *The Shakespeare Plays: A Study Guide* (Delmar, Calif.: University Extension, Univer-

sity of California, San Diego, and Coast Community College District, 1978), pp. 104–14, and Richard Wheeler's chapter in his *Shakespeare's Development and the Problem Comedies* (Berkeley and Los Angeles: University of California Press, 1981), pp. 92–153.

4. Death, Sex, and the Body

1 "Between death and burning," James Redfield says of funerary ritual in the *Iliad*, "the dead person is in a liminal condition; he is neither alive nor properly dead" — *Nature and Culture in the "Iliad": The Tragedy of Hector* (Chicago: University of Chicago Press, 1975), p. 179. Cited by Susan Letzler Cole, *The Absent One: Mourning Ritual, Tragedy, and the Performance of Ambivalence* (University Park and London: Pennsylvania State University Press, 1985), p. 27.

2 Plato, *The Republic* 9. 571, *Plato: The Collected Dialogues*, ed. Edith Hamilton and Huntington Cairus (Princeton: Princton University Press, 1963), p. 798.

3 See Marvin Spevack, *The Harvard Concordance to Shakespeare* (Cambridge, Mass.: Belknap Press, 1973), pp. 96–97.

4 See, re. the Wild Man as a basis for negative definition, Haydn White, "The Forms of Wildness: Archaeology of an Idea," in *The Wild Man Within*, ed. Edward Dudley and Maximillian E. Novak (Pittsburgh: University of Pittsburgh Press, 1972), pp. 3–38.

5 I am indebted to Marilyn Moriarty for reminding me about map-bordering monsters in the Renaissance.

6 Keith Thomas, *Man and the Natural World* (New York: Pantheon, 1983), p. 39.

7 Immanuel Kant, "Duties towards the Body in Respect of Sexual Impulse," *Lectures on Ethics*, trans. Louis Infield (London, 1930), p. 164; cited by Midgley, *Beast and Man*, p. 45.

8 See Browne, *Religio Medici*, p. 79.

9 In bestializing sex, of course, man again unfairly attributes his own undesirable tendencies to animals; "in all other primate species, females are sexually receptive only during a relatively short period of estrus, [and] primate males show no interest in sex when no females that are in estrus are about. Humans, on the other hand, exhibit an almost continuous interest in sex" (Richard Morris, *Evolution and Human Nature* [New York: Seaview/Putnam, 1983], pp. 135–36). The biological reason for this, according to Edward O. Wilson, is the need of the human female to bond with a male who can help protect and feed the infant through its long period of helplessness. Estrus is fine if your offspring leaps to its feet after birth and gallops off, but sexual receptivity and the love it may engender are better if you have weak offspring. In fact, Wilson argues that the Church, in ignorance of biology, has falsely regarded the primary role of sexual behavior as procreative, whereas from a biological standpoint "sexual practics are to be regarded first as bonding devices and only second as a means for procreation." See Wilson, *On Human Nature*, pp. 140–42.

10 As regards the violence of Claudio's response: Ernest Becker quotes Otto Rank's remark, "Every conflict over truth is in the last analysis just the same old struggle . . . over immortality." Becker continues: "If anyone doubts this, let him try to explain in any other way the life-and-death viciousness of all ideological disputes. Each person nourishes his immortality in the ideology of self-perpetuation to which he gives his allegiance; this gives his life the only abiding significance it can have.

No wonder men go into a rage over fine points of belief: if your adversary wins the argument about truth, *you die*. Your immortality system has been shown to be fallible, your life becomes fallible" (*Escape from Evil*, p. 64). Claudio is not engaged in an ideological dispute, but his immortality system is no less threatened and he responds no less violently.

11   Thomas, *Man and the Natural World*, p. 43.

12   Ong, *Fighting for Life*, pp. 70–71. For a discussion of the male's need both to reject and accept the female, see also Coppélia Kahn, *Man's Estate* (Berkeley and Los Angeles: University of California Press, 1981), esp. pp. 1–20, and her article "The Absent Mother of *King Lear*" in *Rewriting the Renaissance: The Discourses of Sexual Difference in Early Modern Europe*, ed. Margaret Ferguson, Maureen Quilligan, and Nancy Vickers (Chicago: University of Chicago Press, 1986), pp. 33–49.

13   In *Man and the Natural World*, pp. 41–50, Keith Thomas describes the English, but of course also the general European, practice of bestializing "inferior humans" in order to justify various kinds of domination, exploitation, and cruelty. That the strategy is still in force needs no documentation. Kurtz's "Exterminate the brutes!" (*Heart of Darkness*) echoes loudly from Auschwitz to Vietnam to U.S. border checkpoints.

14   Tertullian, *De culta feminarium*, libri duo I, 1; cited by Mary Daly in "Social Attitudes Towards Women," *Dictionary of the History of Ideas*, ed. Philip P. Wiener, 5 vols. (New York: Charles Scribner's Sons, 1973), 4: 524.

15   Quoted by Ariès, *The Hour of Our Death*, p. 111.

16   Laurie A. Finke, "Painting Women: Images of Femininity in Jacobean Tragedy," *Theatre Journal* 36, no. 3 (October 1984): 357–70. In this connection I should mention another fine article emphasizing how a fear of women mobilizes a kind of exaggerated masculinity in men that leads to their destruction—Madelon Gohlke's "'I wooed thee with my sword': Shakespeare's Tragic Paradigms," in *The Woman's Part*, ed. Carol Neely, Gayle Green, and Carolyn Lenz (Champaign: University of Illinois Press, 1980), and reprinted in Schwartz and Kahn, *Representing Shakespeare*, pp. 170–87.

5. Sacrifice

1   See Roland H. Bainton, *The Reformation of the Sixteenth Century* (Boston: Beacon Press, 1952), chap. 2; and Richard Marienstras, *New perspectives on the Shakespearean world*, trans. Janet Lloyd (Cambridge, University Press, 1985), pp. 48–49.

2   St. George Kieran Hyland, *A Century of Persecution under Tudor and Stuart Sovereigns from Contemporary Records* (London, 1920), p. 292; quoted by Carolly Erickson, *The First Elizabeth*, p. 337.

3   Otto Rank, *Will Therapy and Truth and Reality* (1936; reprint one vol. ed., New York: Knopf, 1945), p. 130. Cited by Becker, *Escape from Evil*, p. 108. Authorities on sacrifice are innumerable, but surely Kenneth Burke deserves mention as a pioneer explorer of the secular forms of victimage; see, for instance, *Permanence and Change* (1935; rev. ed. New York: Bobbs-Merrill, 1954). See also Becker, *Escape from Evil*, pp. 108–19; and Girard, *Violence and the Sacred*.

4   Canetti, *Crowds and Power*, pp. 67–73.

5   Samuel Beckett, *Waiting for Godot* (New York: Grove Press, 1954) p. 49B.

6   Girard, *Violence and the Sacred*, p. 255.

7   Blaise Pascal, *Pensées*, no. 144. The most obvious Shakespearean example of angelism begetting diabolism is the case of the aptly named Angelo in *Measure for Measure*, who finds in the libertarian Claudio a perfect *pharmakos* on which he can project his own repressed proclivities and then, in puritanical revulsion, sacrifice for the moral good of society.

8   H. M. Richmond makes note of this equation in *Shakespeare's Political Plays* (New York: Random House, 1967), p. 184.

9   Hugh Dalziel Duncan, *Communication and Social Order* (New York: Bedminster Press, 1962), p. 132.

10   Johan Huizinga, *Homo Ludens* (Boston: Beacon Press, 1955), p. 91.

11   In *The Metamorphoses of Shakespearean Comedy*, Carroll argues convincingly for an offstage sexual consummation between Titania and Bottom on the basis of 3.1.198–201 and, even more convincing, 4.1.43–46 (see his pp. 152–55). My interpretation here is generally consistent with his analysis of the play in terms of metamorphosis.

12   See René Girard, "Myth and Ritual in Shakespeare: *A Midsummer Night's Dream*," in *Textual Strategies*, ed. Josue Harari (Ithaca: Cornell University Press, 1979). My own argument is roughly in keeping with Girard's notion that mimetic desire produces undifferentiated animality that in turn necessitates a sacrifice in which "Theseus acts as the high priest of a benign casting-out of all disturbing phenomena under the triple heading of poetry, lunacy, and love" (p. 209)—though I might add that Girard seems oblivious to many prior discussions of Theseus in this role. My argument here is also in keeping with my earlier examinations of the play in *"A Midsummer Night's Dream*: The Illusion of Drama," *Modern Language Quarterly* 26 (1965) and in a chapter in my *Shakespearean Metadrama* (Minneapolis: University of Minnesota Press, 1971), pp. 120–48.

13   In *Shakespeare's Creation: The Language of Magic and Play* (Amherst: University of Massachusetts Press, 1975), Kirby Farrell writes, "Like the celebrated bear who welcomes Antigonus . . . the animal objectifies the violent anxiety which may prey on those who go unprepared (and perhaps, like Antigonus, unwillingly) into new, unknown territory. And there is a bear hunted out in the play" (p. 100). He continues with a perceptive analysis of how "the play uses its art to keep bugbears at bay" (p. 100 and following).

14   Freud's Id is of course consistent with Plato's Wild Beast; both are centers of irrational emotional energy under repression. Just as Freud famously says "Where Id is, let Ego be," which entails a relaxation of repression, so Jung maintains that the unconscious Shadow, which takes shape in his and European man's dreams as a small dark-skinned savage, must not be totally suppressed ("as little of a remedy as beheading would be for headache") but integrated with the Ego. See *The Essential Jung*, ed. Anthony Storr (Princeton: Princeton University Press, 1983), pp. 75, 87–89.

6. Clothing Mortality

1   Montaigne, "Of the custom of wearing clothes," *Complete Works*, p. 166.

2   Ibid, p. 356. In this connection Montaigne was in accord with the view, maintained for some fifteen hundred years by physicians and laymen, that the human body was best understood as being somewhat simian and porcine. Forbidden by Roman law to dissect human cadavers, Galen had anatomized monkeys to discover

man's external organs and pigs for the internal ones. Not until 1543, when Vesalius published his *De Humanis Corporis Fabrica*, did anatomical knowledge derive from the human anatomy and not a composite of other animals. See Daniel J. Boorstin, *The Discoverers* (New York: Random House, 1983), pp. 344–60.

3   Victoria Ebin, *The Body Decorated* (London: Blacker Calmann Cooper Ltd., 1979), pp. 22–23.

4   Peter Matthiesson, *At Play in the Fields of the Lord* (New York: Random House, 1965), p. 287.

5   Claude Lévi-Strauss, *Le Cru et la cuit* (Mythologiques I) (Paris, 1964).

6   Montaigne, "That to philosophize is to learn to die," *Complete Works*, pp. 56–67.

7   Stone, *Crisis of the Aristocracy*, p. 563.

8   Erickson, *The First Elizabeth*, p. 231.

9   Ibid, p. 223. The description by Anthony Wood of court manners and hygiene during the reign of Charles I is probably applicable also, though to a lesser degree, to the courts of Elizabeth and James. He says, "To give a further character of the court, though they were neat and gay in apparell, yet they were very nasty and beastly, leaving at their departure their excrements in every corner, in chimneys, studies, cole-houses, cellars. Rude, rough, whoremongers; vaine, empty, careless." Cited in *Aubrey's Brief Lives*, ed. Oliver Lawson Dick (1949; reprint ed., New York: Penguin Books, 1972), p. 24.

10   Erickson, *The First Elizabeth*, p. 224.

11   For a perceptive discussion of the variations of critical feeling about *Henry V* see Lawrence Danson's "*Henry V*: King, Chorus, and Critics," *Shakespeare Quarterly* 34, no. 1 (Spring 1983): 27–43. See also John Blanpied's chapter on the play in his remarkable study of the histories, *Time and the Artist in Shakespeare's English Histories* (Newark: University of Delaware Press, 1983), pp. 203–45.

12   See Stephen Orgel's article, "The Spectacles of State," *Papers of the Sixteenth Annual Conference of the Centre for Medieval and Early Renaissance Studies*, ed. Richard C. Trexler (1985), pp. 109–21.

13   Ibid, p. 109.

7. Mortal Clothing in *Hamlet*

1   See Maurice Charney, *Style in "Hamlet"* (Princeton: Princeton University Press, 1969), pp. 186–90.

2   Francis Berry, *The Shakespearean Inset* (London and New York: Theatre Arts Books, 1960), pp. 124–125.

3   The poet is Anthony Skoloker who, as Charney says (*Style in "Hamlet"*, p. 188), "tells us in his *Daiphantus, or The Passions of Love* (1604) that his male hero 'Puts off his cloathes; his shirt he onely weares, / Much like mad-*Hamlet*; thus a Passion teares.'"

4   William Poel, *Shakespeare in the Theatre* (London: Sidgwick and Jackson, 1913), pp. 173–74, and Harley Granville-Barker, *Prefaces to Shakespeare*, 2 vols. (Princeton: Princeton University Press, 1947), 1:233.

5   Charney, *Style in "Hamlet,"* p. 189.

6   Perhaps the gown also lends Hamlet the seagoing traveler an air of transience as he speaks of the travels of dead bodies through the soil; and it might

contrast him with Ophelia, who is about to begin her own subterranean journey and who died by water during the same dramatic period in which Hamlet saved himself at sea.

   7   George Puttenham, *The Arte of English Poesie* (1589), in *Elizabethan Critical Essays*, ed. G. Gregory Smith (London: Oxford University Press, 1904), pp. 142–43.

   8   See three excellent studies of the Graveyard Scene: Bridget Gellert Lyons, *Voices of Melancholy* (New York: W. W. Norton, 1971), p. 105; Walter C. Foreman, Jr., *The Music of the Close* (Lexington: University of Kentucky Press, 1978), pp. 83–95; and Susan Snyder, *The Comic Matrix of Shakespeare's Tragedies* (Princeton: Princeton University Press, 1979), pp. 125–130.

   9   The case of the mysterious Claudio is worried at some length in my *To Be and Not To Be* (New York: Columbia University Press, 1983), pp. 113 ff.

   10   *Hamlet*, ed. Harold Jenkins, Arden Shakespeare (London and New York: Methuen, 1983), p. 369.

   11   For a treatment of *Hamlet* keying on the theological implications of providence, falling sparrows, and God's judgments, see Robert G. Hunter's fine book, *Shakespeare and the Mystery of God's Judgments* (Athens: University of Georgia Press, 1976), pp. 101–26.

8. Immortal Money in *The Merchant of Venice*

   1   Kenneth Burke, *A Grammar of Motives and a Rhetoric of Motives* (Cleveland and New York: Meridian Books, 1962), p. 111.

   2   Cited by Brown, *Life Against Death*, pp. 221, 224.

   3   Ibid., p. 208. Brown sums up by saying "Hence Luther expresses his readiness to depart this world in the formula, 'I am the ripe shard and the world is the gaping anus.' The world's anus is the Devil's anus" (p. 226).

   4   See *King Lear* 3.4.35 — a passage discussed later in chapter 12. As regards the anal theory of money, see *The Psychoanalysis of Money*, ed. Ernest Borneman (New York: Urizen Books, 1976), esp. part 1.

   5   See Becker, *Escape from Evil*, pp. 82–83. Because an understanding of money develops about the same time as an understanding of death, an armchair psychologist might wonder if money comes to symbolize immortality for the child in compensation for the shock of knowing it will die.

   6   This transformative process would be abetted by the sense of guilt the child feels for producing and possessing feces. After all, he is rewarded with praise when he gets rid of it properly, so it (and he or she) must be bad; yet because it is also a means of acquiring approval, it is also a source of power, the coin of a kind of primitive economic exchange: the child gives, the mother praises. From this standpoint feces is valuable and can be associated with money. On the other hand, if it is thought of as bad and the child as guilty, the guilt can be assuaged by a reaction formation in which the repellent is transformed by sublimation into the desirable, feces into money. There is an analogy in the Protestant condemnation of the body and the consequent feelings of guilt about inhabiting such a vile structure. The way to assuage such feelings is to condemn oneself to hard labor, to adopt the Protestant work ethic. Work is tiring and painful, as repellent as feces, but because of that it is also sacred and purificatory, a daily sacrificial ritual designed to please the gods and ameliorate one's sense of worthlessness: "No rest for the wicked." The principle of

the scapegoat operates in both cases to generate virtue out of pollution—that is, the scapegoat is repellent because full of sin but also a source of sacred power because its sacrifice will prove redemptive.

7   As a matter of fact it has been argued that the capitalist has a right to earn interest on his capital because he might have achieved maximum pleasure and satisfaction by spending it all at once—see Paul Schilder, "Psychoanalysis of Economics" in Borneman, *Psychoanalysis of Money*, p. 300. According to this view, usury and profit taking represent a form of deferred gratification, a kind of Lacanian restraint on desire that sustains desire. Such an argument fails to take account of the symbolic value of money which makes possessing it gratifying in itself, quite apart from what it can purchase. The dedicated capitalist does not want to obtain instant and total gratification at the cost of yielding his money; he wants the money itself to keep multiplying toward an infinitely desirable but also undesirable (because terminal) state of financial fulfillment.

8   As Fernand Braudel mentions somewhere (though I cannot find where) in *The Wheels of Commerce*, trans. Siân Reynolds, 2 vols. (New York: Harper and Row, 1982).

9   *Shakespeare's Ovid: Arthur Golding's Translation of "The Metamorphoses"*, ed. W. H. D. Rouse (New York: W. W. Norton, 1961), p. 221.

10   Karl Marx, *Grundrisse zur Kritik der Politschen Ökonomie*, cited by Michael Schneider in *Neurosis and Civilization*, trans. Michael Roloff (New York: Seabury Press, 1975), p. 128. The abstract process whereby gold becomes money is the same as that whereby acreage becomes land, workers become labor, and properties become capital. As Robert B. Heilbroner points out in *The Worldly Philosophers*, 4th ed. (New York: Simon and Schuster, 1972), pp. 23–28, the concept of gain itself did not appear until roughly the sixteenth century because land and capital were not constantly for sale or workers constantly for hire until then. The profit motive had not been institutionalized.

Moreover, money could not transcend the body symbolically until use-value, which is geared to practical needs for bodily survival, was supplemented by exchange-value which, like interest rates, is arbitrarily established. The importance of exchange-value in what he calls "The Repression of Use-Value" is stressed by Schneider, *Neurosis and Civilization*, pp. 125–30. Exchange-value transcends the material (the realm of use-value) much as symbolic immortality transcends the expectation of bodily death. Thus Schneider says "Exchange-value consciousness is indifferent, even blind to the sensuous-concrete quality and diversity of the use-value; it 'transcends' constantly the sensuous-qualitative world of useful things so as to discover on their invisible ground their 'essence,' that is, their 'value.' For an exchange-value consciousness each thing is only the physical husk of its 'value substance'" (pp. 126–27).

Interestingly enough in regard to the money-religion, the commercialization of land owed much to the redistribution of monastic estates by Henry VIII, which inspired land-jobbers to buy and sell again as speculation—see L. C. Knights, *Drama and Society in the Age of Jonson* (1937; reprint ed., New York: W. W. Norton, 1968), pp. 100–103.

11   Sigmund Freud, "The Theme of the Three Caskets," trans. C. J. M. Hubback, *Papers on Metapsychology, Papers on Applied Psychoanalysis*, vol. 4 of *Collected Papers* (London: Hogarth Press and the Institute of Psycho-analysis, 1956), pp. 244–56.

12   Lars Engle, " 'Thrift is Blessing': Exchange and Explanation in *The Merchant of Venice*," *Shakespeare Quarterly* 37, no. 1 (Spring 1986): 32–33.

13   In *The Republic*, however, Plato uses the Moirai as a way of claiming that humans are responsible for their own fortunes because they have chosen their lot — see William Chase Greene, *Moira* (New York: Harper and Row, 1944), pp. 315–16.

14   This general thesis is maintained by Helmut Schoeck in *Envy: A Theory of Social Behaviour*, trans. Michael Glenny and Betty Ross (New York: Harcourt, Brace and World, 1969; first published in 1966 as Der Neid).

15   Ibid., p. 10.

16   Gerhard Piers and M. B. Singer, *Shame and Guilt. A Psychoanalytic and Cultural Study* (New York: W. W. Norton, 1971), pp. 28 ff.

17   Burckhardt, *Shakespearean Meanings*, pp. 215–16. In connection with "laws," see Danson, *The Harmonies of "The Merchant of Venice"* esp. chaps. 2 and 3 on divine law and on law and language.

18   See Danson's account of attitudes toward usury in Tudor England in *The Harmonies of "The Merchant of Venice*," pp. 141–48.

19   Shell, *Money, Language, and Thought*, pp. 61–64. See also on love, language, and usury, John Russell Brown, *Shakespeare and His Comedies* (London: Methuen, 1957), pp. 45–81; Burckhardt, *Shakespearean Meanings*, pp. 26–36; Danson, *Harmonies of "The Merchant of Venice"*; Carroll, *Metamorphoses of Shakespearean Comedy*, pp. 117–26; and, with special emphasis on business exchanges, Lars Engle, " 'Thrift is Blessing.' "

20   Stephen Gosson, *Plays Confuted*, cited by Barish, *The Anti-Theatrical Prejudice*, p. 94.

21   An analogous way of looking at it is from the perspective of metamorphosis, as Carroll does in *Metamorphoses of Shakespearean Comedy*; see pp. 117–26 re. Portia's metamorphoses.

9. Tragedy and the Denial of Death 1

1   Freud, *Collected Papers*, vol. 4, p. 201.

2   Brown, *Life Against Death*, p. 118.

3   George Santayana, "Reason in Religion" in *The Life of Reason* (London, 1905–6).

4   John Blanpied, "Absence and Heroic Presence in the Histories." This was a short paper delivered at the Nazareth Shakespeare's Conference in Rochester, N.Y., subsequently printed but only, I think, for limited distribution.

5   Ong, *Fighting for Life*, p. 194. I am indebted to Father Ong's sensitive discussion of the inwardness of the "I" as compared to conventional names.

6   Erik Erikson, *Identity, Youth, and Crisis* (New York: W. W. Norton, 1968), p. 220.

7   Farrell's chapter — "Love, Death, and Patriarchy in *Romeo and Juliet*" — was presented as a paper at the Conference on Shakespeare's Personality directed by Sidney Homan at the University of Florida in March 1985. My remarks here merely supplement and to some extent modify Farrell's much fuller analysis. He emphasizes the symbolic immortality to be obtained within the patriarchal system and the vulnerability of heretics who challenge or abandon it, and I stress the extent to which

those who abandon the system create compensatory substitutes, in this case a religion of love based on the immortality of "I" and "thee." In any event I am indebted to Farrell's perceptive analysis of the play.

8   Erickson, *The First Elizabeth*, p. 43. Stone comments to the same effect in *Crisis of the Aristocracy*, pp. 591–92:

> England was particularly insistent upon the subordination of children to parents, emphasized by the outward forms of respect. As Donne pointed out, "children kneele to aske blessing of parents in England, but where else?" Though he was 63 when he inherited the title in 1666, Sir Dudley North, eldest son of Lord North, "would never put on his hat or sit down before his father, unless enjoined to it." "Gentlemen of thirty and forty years old," recalled Aubrey, "were to stand like mutes and fools bareheaded before their parents; and the daughters (grown woemen) were to stand at the cupboard-side during the whole time of their proud mother's visit, unless (as the fashion was) leave was desired, forsooth, that a cushion should be given them to kneel upon, brought them by the serving man after they had done sufficient penance standing."

See also Coppélia Kahn, "The Absent Mother in *King Lear*," pp. 33–49.

9   Alexandre Kojève, *Introduction à la lecture de Hégel*, ed. Raymond Queneau (Paris: Gallimard, 1947), pp. 373–74; cited by Anthony Wilden in *The Language of the Self* (Baltimore and London: Johns Hopkins University Press, 1968), pp. 195–96.

10. Tragedy and the Denial of Death 2

1   Carl Jung, "The Relations between the Ego and the Unconscious," in *Two Essays on Analytical Psychology*, ed. William McGuire, trans. R. F. C. Hull (Princeton: Princeton University Press, 1966), par. 389 (vol. 7 of *The Collected Works*).

2   See Paul Roazen, *Freud and His Followers* (New York: New York University Press, 1984), p. 322.

3   In his discussion of "Life or Death" in *Hamlet*, Theodore Lidz makes my point about Hamlet's dependence on his father for a sense of symbolic immortality: "Persons often prefer to die rather than lose those who make life meaningful for them or even prefer death to surrendering the customs and value systems upon which they depend" (*Hamlet's Enemy* [London: Vision, 1976], p. 208). See also an interesting discussion of *Hamlet* from the standpoint of mourning rituals by Cole, *The Absent One*. This cherishing of the mana-personality can take a literary turn among biographers who preserve the life of the great man and in so doing preserve their own as well. However, sometimes it is the process of preserving that must itself be sustained. As a biographer I live most fully *while* writing my book, not after completing it. In fact completing a biography—somewhat like Hamlet's completing his revenge—may represent a burial of the mana-personality and, consequently, a form of authorial suicide. When I reach that final fatal sentence—"On April 23, 1616, Shakespeare died"—I die too. A good example of this is the would-be biographer of a famous modern writer who gathers materials for decades but, while the scholarly world holds its breath, fails to turn out the definitive study. The reason is suggested by a quote: " 'No, no,' he said, 'I've never tired of knowing [the great man]. My joy in the search is inexhaustible. Never been dull. The more you know, the more you

realize how divine he really was.'" Something very like Hamlet here perhaps, fearful of depriving his own life of meaning by performing the revengeful act that sets the Ghost to rest and terminates the past.

4   As Eleanor Prosser observes, the word *antic* was often used to refer to Death in its grotesque aspect—the capering leader of the Dance of Death, for instance (*Hamlet and Revenge* [Stanford: Stanford University Press, 1967], p. 149). From this standpoint Hamlet assumes Death's (not to mention Yorick's) role as jester, pointing out the absurdities of life to those who but sleep and feed.

5   My death-oriented reading of *Hamlet* here is implicit in the chapters on "The Life of Death" and "Beyond Negation" in my *To Be and Not To Be*, pp. 97–110.

6   That death gives birth to life is of course a recurrent theme in sermon after sermon in Shakespeare's time. Donne, for instance, never tires of depicting the nastiness of the body that rots toward death, or of adding that the death of the body is ultimately the birth of the spirit. Indeed, as he sets it forth in the sermon called "Death's Duel," life is nothing but a series of deaths and births, of births out of death and into death. We are dead in our mother's womb, and are born into a life that is a worse death, and even after we are dead to this world we must die again, when the corruptions of our moldering bodies are purified for Christ's Coming. Only then, after experiencing all these deaths, do we wake to eternal life. Shakespeare, somewhat more worldly than the Dean of St. Paul's, extrapolates Donne's eschatology backwards into life, condensing Donne's long-range adventure in soul-making (from conception to the Second Coming) into Hamlet's experiences in the graveyard.

7   Rank, *Will Therapy and Truth and Reality*, p. 130, cited by Becker, *Escape from Evil*, p. 108.

8   See Norman Rabkin, *Shakespeare and the Common Understanding* (New York: Free Press, 1967), pp. 57–73, for an equation of Othello's love with Christian faith.

9   Robert B. Heilman, *Magic in the Web* (Lexington: University of Kentucky Press, 1956), p. 105.

10   In an illuminating analysis of *Othello* as a tragedy focusing on "absent fathers and ambivalent heirs," Cole emphasizes the role of Othello's handkerchief in setting his and Desdemona's love within a familial context. I am indebted to Cole's study of the play, which appears in her remarkable book *The Absent One*, pp. 149–60.

11   Rabkin effectively argues for the mystery of motivation underlying love in this and other Shakespearean plays in *Shakespeare and the Common Understanding*, pp. 64–65.

12   In "Othello's Occupation: Shakespeare and the Romance of Chivalry" (*English Literary Renaissance* 15, no. 3 [Autumn 1985]: 293–311), Mark Rose brilliantly demonstrates that the loss of Othello's "occupation" is part of a more general loss of a chivalric ideal both in the play and in Shakespeare's England.

11. Tragedy and the Denial of Death 3

1   See my *If It Were Done* (Amherst: University of Massachusetts Press, 1986).

2   Fromm, *Heart of Man*, p. 40.

3   Christopher Lasch, *The Culture of Narcissism* (New York: W. W. Norton, 1978), p. 175.

4   See ibid., p. 172.

5   Brown, *Life Against Death*, p. 118.

6   See Janet Adelman's perceptive remarks about Coriolanus's relation to "mother Rome" in her "Feeding, Dependency, and Aggression in *Coriolanus*."

7   *Oedipus the King*, trans. David Grene, vol. 2 of *The Complete Greek Tragedies*, ed. David Grene and Richard Lattimore (Chicago: University of Chicago Press, 1959), p. 11.

8   Becker, *Escape from Evil*, p. 150.

9   Alan Harrington, *The Immortalist* (New York: Random House, 1969), p. 101. Cited in ibid., p. 148.

10   Ernst Kantorowicz, *The King's Two Bodies* (Princeton: Princeton University Press, 1957).

11   Robert Bolt, *A Man for All Seasons* (New York: Vintage, 1966), pp. 94–95.

12   See Snyder's fine book *The Comic Matrix of Shakespearean Tragedy* for a broader view of comic elements in tragedy.

13   Kenneth Burke, *Counter-Statement* (1931; reprint ed., Berkeley and Los Angeles: University of California Press, 1968), p. 31.

14   Tom Stoppard, *Rosencrantz and Guildenstern Are Dead* (New York: Grove Press, 1967), p. 83.

12. *King Lear* 1

1   See for instance Borneman, *Psychoanalysis of Money*, which includes "Studies on the Anal Theory of Money" by Freud, Ferenczi, Coriat, and Abraham.

2   See "Studies in Anality" by Brown in *Life Against Death*, pp. 179–306, and "The Meaning of Anality" by Becker in *The Denial of Death*, pp. 30–34. Brown discusses the excremental vision of Luther and Swift. A third example from among geniuses is Mozart, who rather perfectly illustrates the opposition between God and feces in his scatalogical letters to his cousin Basle, since these are the only letters in which he uses his middle name "Amadeus," as though flaunting his ethereal-nethereal schizoid nature. See Wolfgang Hildesheimer, *Mozart*, trans. Marion Faber (New York: Farrar, Straus and Giroux, 1982), pp. 105–18. This conjunction of the sacred and the profane in money works both ways: profane money has its sacred dimension, but the sacred has its monetary dimension too. Lear's "shaking the superflux" of wealth to the poor is a profane version of the Church's practice of distributing to the sinful the excess grace piled up in the treasury of the saints' virtue. Such virtue was of course for sale in the form of indulgences.

3   An article in the *Los Angeles Times* (September 16, 1985) reports the words of retired Major General John K. Singlaub, a leader of the World Anti-Communist League, which is raising funds to support the anti-Sandinista rebels in Nicaragua. As the article says:

> He gazed across a ballroom filled with Texas millionaires, Nicaraguan rebels, South American rightists and Chinese anti-Communists. To his surprise, he said later, a tear welled up in his soldierly eye. "President Reagan is our symbol of strength," he said, "the triumph of God's will against the evil of Communist tyranny." The audience stood up and cheered.

Somewhat more extreme was the claim made earlier this year by a member of the

Aryan League captured on suspicion of murder. Asked about the possibility of his being killed during the manhunt, he said "God protects me from bullets."

4   With regard to mediation in *King Lear*, see Burckhardt, "The Quality of Nothing" in *Shakespearean Meanings*, pp. 237–59; Terence Hawkes, *Shakespeare's Talking Animals* (London: Edward Arnold, 1973), pp. 167–78; Lawrence Danson, *Tragic Alphabet* (New Haven and London: Yale University Press, 1974), pp. 163–97; and Richard Fly, "Beyond Extremity: *King Lear* and the Limits of Poetic Drama" in his *Shakespeare's Mediated World* (Amherst: University of Massachusetts Press, 1976), pp. 85–116.

13. *King Lear* 2

1   Morse Peckham, *Man's Rage for Chaos* (Philadelphia and Toronto: Chilton and Ambassador Books, 1965).

2   William Elton, *"King Lear" and the Gods* (San Marino, Calif.: Huntington Library, 1966), p. 181.

3   See Burckhardt, *"King Lear"*: The Quality of Nothing," in *Shakespearean Meanings*, pp. 237–59. I should record my general debt to Burckhardt's analysis. Perhaps this is a good place also to acknowledge Robert B. Heilman's consistently insightful observations on "nothing"—and on a good many other somethings—in a book to which all students of the play are indebted, *This Great Stage* (Baton Rouge: University of Louisiana Press, 1948). In this connection I should mention "Shakespeare's Nothing," by David Willbern in Schwartz and Kahn, *Representing Shakespeare*, pp. 244–63. Thomas McFarland documents the pattern of "reduction and renewal" in his chapter of that title in his *Tragic Meanings in Shakespeare* (New York: Random House, 1966). For an analysis of this reductive process as a compromising of the tragic by comic conventions see Snyder's chapter on the play in her *Comic Matrix of Shakespeare's Tragedies*, pp. 137–79.

4   Burckhardt, *Shakespearean Meanings*; Emily Leider, "Plainness of Style in *King Lear*," *Shakespeare Quarterly* 21 (1970): 45–53; Anne Barton, "Shakespeare and the Limits of Language," *Shakespeare Survey* 24 (1971): 19–30; Jill Levenson, "What the Silence Said: Still Points in *King Lear*," *Shakespeare 1971: Proceedings of the World Shakespeare Congress*, ed. Clifford Leech, J. M. R. Margeson (Toronto: University of Toronto Press, 1972), pp. 215–29; and Danson, "King Lear" in *Tragic Alphabet*.

5   See F. D. Hoeniger, "The Artist Exploring the Primitive: *King Lear*," in *Some Facets of "King Lear": Essays in Prismatic Criticism*, ed. Rosalie L. Colie and F. T. Flahiff (Toronto and Buffalo: University of Toronto Press, 1974), pp. 89–102.

6   Robert B. Heilman briefly catalogs the references to Christian values (*This Great Stage*, p. 331n.); and William H. Matchett traces the rhythm of dashed hopes in his perceptive article on "Some Dramatic Techniques in *King Lear*" in *Shakespeare: The Theatrical Dimension*, ed. Philip C. McGuire and David A. Samuelson (New York: AMS Press, 1979), pp. 185–208.

7   For an excellently conducted discussion of how the play appears to, but then does not, complete its morality "pilgrimage," see Edgar Schell's chapter on the play in his *Strangers and Pilgrims: From The Castle of Perseverance to "King Lear"* (Chicago and London: University of Chicago Press, 1983), esp. pp. 181–95. See also Hunter, *Shakespeare and the Mystery of God's Judgments*, and Howard Felperin, *Shake-*

spearean Representation (Princeton: Princeton University Press, 1977), both of which contain analyses of the role of the morality play and its relation to "existential" issues in *King Lear.*

8 Bridget Gellert Lyons, "The Subplot as Simplification in *King Lear*" in Colie and Flahiff, *Some Facets of "King Lear,"* pp. 23–38.

9 In a very perceptive article Richard Abrams examines the theatrical implications of the Cordelia-Fool doubling; see "The Double Casting of Cordelia and Lear's Fool: A Theatrical View," *Texas Studies in Literature and Language* 27, no. 4 (Winter 1985) 354–68.

10 Lyons, "Subplot as Simplification," p. 24. On matters of form, for Shakespeare's use of fairy-tale elements in the play, see Katherine Stockholder's "The Multiple Genres of *King Lear*: Breaking the Archtypes," *Bucknell Review* 16 (1968): 40–63.

11 Harry Levin, "A Scene from *King Lear,*" in *More Talking about Shakespeare*, ed. John Garrett (London: Longmans, Green and Co., 1959) and reprinted in Levin's *Shakespeare and the Revolution of the Times: Perspectives and Commentaries* (New York: Oxford University Press, 1976), p. 180. Burckhardt (*Shakespeare's Meanings*); Matchett ("Some Dramatic Techniques"); and especially Robert Egan (*Drama Within Drama* [New York and London: Columbia University Press 1972, 1975]) and Foreman (*Music of the Close*) stress the fraudulence of Edgar's "miracle." On the other hand, in "Text as Theatricality in *King Lear* and *Macbeth*" in *Tragedy and Tragic in Western Culture* (Montreal: Determinations, 1982), Judd Hubert argues that Edgar "requires no justification, for only such dramatic trifling has the power to effect cures and restore order" (p. 92).

12 I follow the Folio in attributing the final speech of the play to Edgar, as David Bevington does in the text I am using: *The Complete Works of Shakespeare*, 3d ed. (Glenview, Ill.: Scott, Foresman, 1980).

13 Shakespeare's divestiture of Christianity from the pious *King Leir* is analogous to Montaigne's deconstruction of the "Natural Theology" of Raymond Sebonde in his famous "Apology for Raymond Sebonde." Montaigne's discursive indictment of human reason unaided by divine grace is virtually dramatized in *King Lear* as Shakespeare demonstrates what man and his life become without God. *Hamlet*, one could argue, dramatizes a similar plight. But there, at the end, Shakespeare calls on a "divinity that shapes our ends" and "a special providence" to suggest what Montaigne declares in the final lines of the "Apology": "Nor can [fallen man] raise himself above himself and humanity; for he can see only with his own eyes, and seize only with his own grasp. He will rise, if God lends him his hand; he will rise by abandoning and renouncing his own means, and letting himself be raised and uplifted by divine grace; but not otherwise" (*Complete Works of Montaigne*, p. 457).

In *King Lear*, however, Shakespeare omits this final palinode. See Elton, *"King Lear" and the Gods*, pp. 34–71 and Felperin, *Shakespearean Representation*, pp. 87–106 for perceptive discussions of Shakespeare's modifications of his sources.

14 Stephen Booth, *"King Lear," "Macbeth," Indefinition, & Tragedy* (New Haven and London: Yale University Press, 1983), p. 11. Booth stresses the "impossibility of finality in the play" (p. 13) as one aspect of an indefiniteness that characterizes the whole (or the not yet whole!). Several critics have found a similar quality about the language of the play, particularly its striving toward the inexpressible. See Norman Maclean, "Episode, Scene, Speech and Word: The Madness of Lear," in *Critics and Criticism*, ed. R. S. Crane (Chicago: University of Chicago Press, 1952), esp. p.

614; Barton, "Shakespeare and the Limits of Language"; and Fly, *Shakespeare's Mediated World*, pp. 87–115.

14. *King Lear 3*

1   See Michael Goldman's typically excellent "The Worst of *King Lear*," in his *Shakespeare and the Energies of Drama* (Princeton: Princeton University Press, 1972), pp. 94–108; and Matchett, "Some Dramatic Techniques."

2   See Burckhardt, *Shakespeare's Meanings*, pp. 253–54.

3   This principle of the "worst" is a dreary perversion of Jacques Derrida's concept of the "supplement," which paradoxically adds onto and replaces or fills up an apparently full presence (cf. Derrida, *Of Grammatology*, trans. Gayatri C. Spivak [Baltimore: Johns Hopkins University Press, 1976], pp. 144–45; and Derrida, "The Supplement of Copula: Philosophy *before* Linguistics," in *Textual Strategies*, ed. Josue V. Harari [Ithica: Cornell University Press, 1979], pp. 82–120). The most obvious reason for the supplement is need or desire, and thus the supplement may attempt to replace the prior "presence," as culture replaces nature for Lévi-Strauss. That is the case in *King Lear*, but with a difference. "The worst" is repeatedly represented as lacking, but it is supplemented not by something better but by something worse yet. What it is lacking, it seems, is "worseness." Thus the "worsening" process is a progressive degeneration—a perverse pursuit of the full presence of worseness that finally takes us beyond the play itself.

4   Levin, "A Scene from *King Lear*," and Matchett, "Some Dramatic Techniques." I should add that the "first nighter" view of this episode receives a persuasive justification by Booth in his essay "On the Persistence of First Impressions" in *"King Lear," "Macbeth," Indefinition, & Tragedy*, pp. 121–25. See also a particularly insightful article by Bert O. States, "Standing on the Extreme Verge: *King Lear* and Other High Places," *Georgia Review* (Summer 1982): 417–25.

5   Murray Krieger defines "the tragic vision" in his book of that title (Chicago and London: University of Chicago Press, 1960), pp. 1–21. In effect, the experience of the tragic visionary is characterized by an absence of Derrida's transcendental signified—a world temporarily given over to the free play and conflict of values, forms, and meanings. But whereas Derrida sees this absence everywhere in "discourse," Krieger regards it as encompassed by the (illusory) presence of the form of tragedy. In speaking of the Nietzschean balancing of the Dionysian with the Apollonian, Krieger says:

> But what if we should find the Dionysian without the Apollonian? Here we would have life unalleviated, endlessly unendurably dangerous, finally destructive and self-destructive—in short, the demoniacal. In effect it would be like tragedy without that moment in which the play comes round and the cosmos is saved and returned to us intact. It would be, in other words, the tragic vision wandering free of its capacious home in tragedy. (P. 10)

As my foregoing remarks on the play suggest, I find this an apt description of *King Lear*. However, as Krieger would no doubt observe, if the tragic vision in *King Lear* breaks free of its bondage within tragedy it does not break free of all form. As a self-annulling assertion that "This is the worst," the play simultaneously creates form while insisting it is but the illusion of form. Such a view is in accord with Booth's observation that

> the glory of *King Lear* as an experience for its audience is in the fact that the play presents its morally capricious universe in a play that, paradoxically, is formally capricious and *also* uses pattern to do exactly what pattern usually does: assert the presence of an encompassing order in the *work* (as opposed to the world it describes). (*"King Lear," "Macbeth," Indefinition, & Tragedy*, p. 27)

15. Immortalizing Art

1   Gary Snyder, *The Real Work*, ed. William Scott McLean (New York: New Directions, 1980), p. 44. I am indebted to Ian Calderwood for bringing this point to my attention.

2   Burckhardt, "The Poet as Fool and Priest," in *Shakespearean Meanings*, p. 25. Also for a sustained analysis of the illusory incarnation of words as they pass through the window of art into its house of mirrors, see Murray Krieger, *A Window to Criticism: Shakespeare's Sonnets and Modern Poetics* (Princeton: Princeton University Press, 1964). See also Farrell, "The Fierce Endeavor of Your Wit: Living Art in *Love's Labour's Lost*" in his *Shakespeare's Creation*; William Carroll, "Living Art," in what is far and away the best treatment of the play, *The Great Feast of Languages* (Princeton: Princeton University Press, 1976); and J. Dennis Huston, " 'Form Confounded' and the Play of *Love's Labour's Lost*" in his *Shakespeare's Comedies of Play* (New York: Columbia University Press, 1981).

3   See Roland Barthes, *Writing Degree Zero* (New York: Hill and Wang, 1968); Maurice Blanchot, *L'Espace littéraire* (Paris: Gallimard, 1955); Michel Foucault, *language, counter-memory, practice* (Ithaca, Cornell University Press, 1978), pp. 113–38.

4   See Brents Stirling's influential discussion of this in " 'Or Else Were This a Savage Spectacle' [Ritual in *Julius Caesar*]," in his *Unity in Shakespearean Tragedy* (New York: Columbia University Press, 1956), pp. 40–54. See also Ernest Schanzer, "The Tragedy of Shakespeare's Brutus," *English Literary History* (March 1955); Adrien Bonjour, *The Structure of "Julius Caesar"* (Liverpool: Liverpool University Press, 1958); Rabkin, *Shakespeare and the Common Understanding*, pp. 105–19; Burckhardt, "How Not to Kill Caesar," in *Shakespearean Meanings*; and James Siemon's remarkable chapter " 'Every like is not the same': Figuration and the 'Knot of us' in *Julius Caesar*" in his *Shakespearean Iconoclasm* (Berkeley and Los Angeles: University of California Press, 1985), pp. 114–82.

5   See in this connection Robert M. Adams, *Strains of Discord* (Ithaca: Cornell University Press, 1958), pp. 56–57; Burckhardt, *Shakespearean Meanings*, pp. 280–82; Phyllis Rackin, "Shakespeare's Boy Cleopatra, the Decorum of Nature, and the Golden World of Poetry," *PMLA* 87 (1972): 201–12; Foreman, *The Music of the Close*, pp. 175–201; Sidney Homan, *When the Theater Turns to Itself* (Lewisburg, Pa.: Bucknell University Press, 1981), pp. 177–91; and Jonas Barish in his illuminating study of *The Anti-Theatrical Prejudice*, pp. 129–31. Harold E. Toliver has written a superb essay on the elegiac aspects of the play—"Cleopatra's Phantom Marriage"—to appear in his forthcoming book *Transported Language in Shakespeare and Milton*.

6   Richard Abrams discusses the relation between Prospero's art and that of Antonio, with Shakespearean implications in the wings, in *"The Tempest* and the

Concept of the Machiavellian Playwright," *English Literary Renaissance* 8, no. 1 (Winter 1978): 43–66. In an insightful chapter on the play in *Drama Within Drama*, Egan points out that Prospero's magic lies not so much in a direct power over nature itself as in a masterful ability to imitate nature, to create and project mimetic images which can, in their fictive perfection, rival reality" (p. 93).

7   Egan argues that Prospero is depicted in the epilogue as still a character, not, as earlier epiloguists were, as an actor standing outside a completed fiction (*Drama Within Drama*, pp. 115–17).

8   For a discussion of metamorphosis in *The Tempest*, as well as in Shakespeare comedy generally, see Carroll, *Metamorphoses of Shakespearean Comedy*, pp. 225–43.

9   Critics like Stephen Orgel and Stephen Greenblatt, who emphasize the ways in which power is theatricalized in Shakespeare's time, give special point to Prospero's "Our revels now are ended" speech, for the visionary revels fade into theatrical revels which in turn fade into, among other things, state revels—what Orgel calls "The Illusion of Power" in his book of that title (Berkeley and Los Angeles: University of California Press, 1975). See also Greenblatt's highly influential book on *Renaissance Self-Fashioning* (Chicago: University of Chicago Press, 1980).

The fusion of illusion, reality, and art in *The Tempest* has been bruited about in so many quarters that it is impossible even to begin citing the authorities. Still, see Frank Kermode's introduction to the New Arden edition of the play (London: Methuen, 1954); Reuben Brower's chapter in his *Fields of Light* (New York: Oxford University Press, 1962); Anne Righter, *Shakespeare and the Idea of the Play* (London: Chatto and Windus, 1962); Northrop Frye, *A Natural Perspective* (New York and London: Columbia University Press, 1965); Rabkin, *Shakespeare and the Common Understanding*, pp. 224–26; A. D. Nuttall, *Two Concepts of Allegory* (New York: Barnes and Noble, 1967); Philip Edwards, *Shakespeare and the Confines of Art* (London: Methuen, 1968), pp. 151–52; Harry Berger, Jr., "Miraculous Harp: A Reading of Shakespeare's *Tempest*," *Shakespeare Studies* 5 (1970); Robert Egan, " 'This Rough Magic': Perspectives of Art and Morality in *The Tempest*," *Shakespeare Quarterly* 23 (1972): 171–82, and *Drama Within Drama*, pp. 90–119; Sidney Homan, "*The Tempest* and Shakespeare's Last Plays: The Aesthetic Dimensions," *Shakespeare Quarterly* 24 (1973): 69–76; Joseph Summers, "The Anger of Prospero," *Michigan Quarterly Review* 12 (1973); Douglas Peterson, *Time, Tide, and Tempest* (San Marino, Calif.: Huntington Library, 1973); Marjorie B. Garber, *Dream in Shakespeare* (New Haven and London: Yale University Press, 1974), and also "The Eve of the Storm: Structure and Myth in Shakespeare's *Tempest*," *Hebrew University Studies in Literature* 8, no. 1 (Spring 1980): 13–43.

10   For a discussion of the play as a self-conscious "release from the theater," see the chapter of that title in Homan, *When the Theater Turns to Itself*, pp. 192–211.

11   In "Why Does Prospero Abjure his 'Rough Magic'?" *Shakespeare Quarterly* 36, no. 1 (Summer 1985), Cosmo Corfield discusses Prospero's abandonment of his art as a stripping to essential humanity.

Supplement. The Anti-Immortalists

1   Richard Moulton, *Shakespeare as a Dramatic Artist* (Oxford, 1885), p. 93; cited by Bernard Spivack, *Shakespeare and the Allegory of Evil* (New York and London: Columbia University Press, 1958), p. 36.

2   Heilman, *Magic in the Web*, especially the section entitled "Iago: The Grievance Game"; Spivack, *Shakespeare and the Allegory of Evil*; and Stanley Edgar Hyman, *Iago: Some Approaches to the Illusion of his Motivation* (London: Elek Books, 1970).

3   Blaise Pascal, *Pensées*, no. 813. In this regard Pascal anticipates the findings of Dr. Stanley Milgram of Yale, in whose well-known experiments, subjects, who as individuals did not want to, would inflict "severe" pain on laboratory "victims" (actually actors) under the auspices of "science" and "education." See, for example, Milgram's, "Nationality and Conformity," *Scientific American* 205 (1961).

4   For the Protestant, and especially the Lutheran, identification of the Devil with the excrementary body, see Brown, *Life Against Death*, pp. 202–34.

Index

Abrams, Richard, xi, 224 n.9, 226 n.6
Adams, Robert M., 226 n.5
Adelman, Janet, 211 n.3, 212 n.10,
    222 n.6
Anderson, Donald K., 211 n.6
Anglican compromise, 210 n.23
Annihilation anxiety, 208 n.8
Anthony, Sylvia, 209 n.9
Ardrey, Robert, 207 n.3
Ariès, Philippe, 9, 210 nn.17,19, 214 n.15
Aryan League, 222 n.3

Bacon, Sir Francis, and bestiality, 46
Bainton, Roland H., 214 n.1
Barish, Jonas, 38, 212 n.5, 226 n.5
Barthes, Roland, and authorial death,
    178, 226 n.3
Barton, Anne, 223 n.4, 224 n.14
Becker, Ernest, xi, 5, 8; and money, 89;
    and symbolic power, 129, 208 nn.5,8,
    209 nn.11,16, 213 nn.1,10, 214 n.3,
    217 n.5, 222 nn.2,9
Beckett, Samuel, 59, 214 n.5
Benedict, Ruth, 208 n.6, 212 n.9
Berger, Harry, Jr., 227 n.9
Berry, Francis, 216 n.2
Bestiality: and death, 46–51; and
    Genesis, 48
Bettelheim, Bruno, 212 n.4
Blanchot, Maurice, and authorial death,
    178, 226 n.3
Blanpied, John, and H5, 105–6, 216 n.11,
    219 n.4
Bloch, Dorothy, 208 n.8
Bolt, Robert, A Man for All Seasons, 131,
    222 n.11
Bonjour, Adrien, 226 n.4
Boorstin, Daniel J., 215 n.2
Booth, Stephen, 224 n.14, 225 nn.4,5
Borneman, Ernest, 217 n.4, 222 n.1

Braudel, Fernand, 218 n.8
Brower, Reuben, 227 n.9
Brown, John Russell, 218 n.19
Brown, Norman O., 8; and Luther, 89;
    and Oedipal complex, 105, 127,
    207 nn.1,2, 209 n.16, 211 n.1,
    217 nn.2,3, 219 n.2, 222 nn.2,5, 228 n.4
Browne, Sir Thomas: and human na-
    ture, 4; and sex, 49–50, 213 n.8
Burckhardt, Sigurd, and MV, 96, 210 n.1,
    218 nn.17,19, 223 nn.4,3,4, 224 n.11,
    225 n.2, 226 nn.2,4,5
Burke, Kenneth, 5; and form, 134; and
    money as God, 87–88, 208 n.7, 214 n.3,
    217 n.1, 222 n.13

Calderwood, Ian, 226 n.1
Campion, Thomas, 58
Camus, Albert, 6, 209 n.11
Canetti, Elias, 8, 25, 59, 207 n.1,
    209 n.14, 211 nn.2,4,5,7, 214 n.4
Carroll, William C., xi, 211 n.1, 214 n.11,
    218 nn.19,21, 226 n.2, 227 n.8
Cassirer, Ernst, and myth 6, 8, 209 n.10
Charney, Maurice, 81, 216 nn.1,3,5
Choron, Jacques, 207 n.1
Cole, Susan Letzler, 213 n.1, 220 n.3,
    221 n.10
Conrad, Joseph, 5
Corfield, Cosmo, 227 n.11
Corporeality of speech, 172–73
Cruttwell, Patrick, 207 n.2

Danson, Lawrence, xi, 210 n.1, 216 n.11,
    218 n.17, 223 n.4
Dedalus, Stephen, and dramatic mode,
    179
Derrida, Jacques, 225 nn.3,5
Digger Indians, 5, 208 n.3
Dodds, E. R., 212 n.9

Donne, John, 8; and the body, 69; and
  women's souls, 50, 221 n.6
Duchess of Malfi, 70
Duncan, Hugh Dalziel, 63, 214 n.9

Ebin, Victoria, 216 n.3
Edwards, Philip, 227 n.9
Egan, Robert, 224 n.11, 226 n.6, 226–
  27 n.7, 227 n.9
Elton, William, 223 n.2, 224 n.13
Engle, Lars, and *MV*, 93, 219 nn.12,19
Erickson, Carolly, and Elizabethan
  family, 108, 210 n.24, 216 nn.8,9,10,
  220 n.8
Erikson, Erik, 219 n.6
Esler, Anthony, and courtly narcissism,
  41, 210 n.24, 212 nn.6,7
Excremental vision, 222 n.2

Farrell, Kirby, and *Rom*, 108, 209 n.11,
  215 n.13, 219 n.7, 226 n.2
Felperin, Howard, 223 n.7, 224 n.13
Finke, Laurie A., and idealization of
  women, 56, 214 n.16
Fly, Richard, 223 n.4, 224 n.14
Ford, Clellan S., 211 n.2
Foreman, Walter C., Jr., 217 n.8, 226 n.5
Foucault, Michel, 24, 211 n.3; and autho-
  rial death, 178, 226 n.3
Freilich, Morris, 208 n.4
Freud, Sigmund: and casket theme in
  MV, 92; and self-fathering, 105; and
  shelving death, 6–7, 207 n.3, 209 n.11,
  215 n.14, 218 n.11, 219 n.1
Fromm, Erich, 4–5; and force, 125,
  207 nn.1,3, 221 n.2
Frye, Northrop, 227 n.9

Galen, 215 n.2
Garber, Marjorie, 227 n.9
Gesell, A., 209 n.9
Girard, René, 8, 60, 207 n.1, 209 n.15,
  214 nn.3,6, 215 n.12
Gohlke, Madelon, 214 n.16
Goldman, Michael, 225 n.1
Gosson, Stephen, 38, 219 n.20
Granville-Barker, Harley, 216 n.4
Greenblatt, Stephen, 227 n.9

Greene, William Chase, 218 n.13
Guilt culture, 212 n.9

Hamartia, 130
Hampton Court, 70
Harding, Thomas, 58
Harrington, Alan, and mana personal-
  ity, 129, 222 n.9
Hawkes, Terence, 223 n.4
Haydn, Hiram, 212 n.6
Hegel, Georg Wilhelm, and symbolism,
  111, 220 n.9
Heilbroner, Robert B., 218 n.10
Heilman, Robert B., and *Oth*, 119, 198,
  221 n.9, 223 nn.3,6, 228 n.2
Hoeniger, F. D., 223 n.5
Holbein, Hans, 10
Homan, Sidney, 226 n.5, 227 nn.9,10
Honest Whore, 70
Honor, concept of, 212 n.6
Hopkins, Gerard Manley, 6
Hubert, Judd, 224 n.11
Huizinga, Johann, 214 n.10
Hunt, Morton, 208 n.7
Hunter, Robert G., 211 n.6, 217 n.11,
  223 n.7
Huston, J. Dennis, 226 n.2
Hyland, St. George Kieran, 214 n.2
Hyman, Stanley Edgar, and Iago, 198,
  228 n.2

Ilg, F., 209 n.9
Impostor syndrome, 210 n.22
Instincts, 207 n.3

James, William, 7, 209 n.13
Jenkins, Harold, and Lamord, 85,
  217 n.10
Jewel, John, 58
Joyce, James, and dramatic mode, 179
Jung, Carl Gustav, 11–12, 210 n.22,
  215 n.14, 220 n.1
Junot, Androche, and self-fathering, 105

Kahn, Coppélia, 214 n.12, 220 n.8
Kant, Immanuel, and sex, 49, 213 n.7
Kantorowicz, Ernst, 222 n.10
Kermode, Frank, 227 n.9
Knights, L. C., 218 n.10

Kocher, Paul H., 207n.2
Koestler, Arthur, 207n.1
Kojève, Alexandre, and symbolism, 111, 220n.9
Krieger, Murray, 225n.5, 226n.2
Kwakiutl Indians, 13, 211n.2

Lacan, Jacques, 218n.7
Lasch, Christopher, and fathering, 126, 221n.3, 222n.4
Laud, Archbishop, 210n.23
Leider, Emily, 223n.4
Levenson, Jill, 223n.4
Levin, Harry, 224n.11, 225n.4
Lévi-Strauss, Claude, 69, 216n.5, 225n.3
Lévy-Bruhl, Lucien, 209n.9
Lidz, Theodore, 220n.3
Lifton, Robert Jay, 207n.1, 209n.11
Liminality, 212n.1
Lorenz, Konrad, 207nn.1,3
Lumsden, Charles J., 208n.3
Luther, Martin, 11, 12; and devilish money, 88–89
Lyons, Bridget Gellert, 217n.8, 224nn.8,10

Maclean, Norman, 224n.14
Mallon, Thomas, 208n.6
Malynes, Gerald de, 18, 210n.1
Mana-personality, and biography, 220n.3
Marienstras, Richard, 214n.1
Marx, Karl, 218n.10
Matchett, William H., 223n.6, 224n.11, 225nn.1,4
Matthiesson, Peter, 69, 216n.4
May, Rollo, 209n.8
McFarland, Thomas, 223n.3
Midgley, Mary, 208n.3
Milgram, Stanley, 228n.3
Moiria, and MV, 93–94
Money: and the body, 218n.10; and deferred gratification, 218n.7; and feces, 217n.6
Montaigne, Michel de, 10–12; and clothing, 68–69; 210nn.20,22, 215nn.1,2, 216n.6, 224n.13
Moriarty, Marilyn, 213n.5

Morris, Richard, 213n.9
Moulton, Richard, 227n.1
Mowat, Barbara A., xi
Mozart, Wolfgang Amadeus, 222n.2

Nagy, Maria H., 209n.9
Negation, 208n.7
Nicaragua, 222n.3
North, Sir Dudley, 220n.8
Nuttall, A. D., 227n.9

Odilon of Cluny, and sex, 53
Oedipal complex, 6
Oedipus, 222n.7
Ogawa, Yasuhiro, 210n.1
Olmstead, Alan H., 208n.6
Ong, Walter J., and gender, 51, 212n.3, 214n.12, 219n.5
Orgel, Stephen, 216nn.12,13, 227n.9
Ovid, 218n.9

Pagels, Elaine H., 211n.1
Panofsky, Irwin, 212n.2
Pascal, Blaise, 215n.7, 228n.3
Peckham, Morse, 223n.1
Peterson, Douglas, 227n.9
Piers, Gerhardt, and MV, 95, 209n.13, 218n.16
Plato, and bestiality, 47, 65, 213n.2, 215n.14, 219n.13
Poel, William, 216n.4
Prosser, Eleanor, 221n.4
Puttenham, George, and stylistic clothing, 81–82, 217n.7

Rabkin, Norman, 221nn.8,11, 227n.9
Rackin, Phyllis, 226n.5
Rank, Otto, 8, 13, 118, 209n.16, 213nn.10,3, 221n.7
Reagan, Ronald, 222n.3
Redfield, James, 213n.1
Reich, Annie, and phallic symbolism, 126
Revenger's Tragedy, 70
Rheingold, J. C., 208n.8
Richmond, H. M., 214n.8
Righter, Anne (Barton), 227n.9
Roazen, Paul, 220n.2
Rose, Mark, 221n.12

Sacraments, 210n.23
Sagan Eli, 211n.2
Santayana, Georges, 219n.3
Sartre, Jean Paul, 105
Schanzer, Ernest, 226n.4
Schell, Edgar, 223n.7
Schilder, Paul, 218n.7
Schneider, Michael, 218n.10
Schoeck, Helmut, and *MV*, 95,
    218nn.14,15
Schopenhauer, Arthur, 8, 209n.16
Shakespeare, William
    Ado, 18; and sensuality, 50; and sym-
        bolic rape, 43
    Ant, 184–87; and the comic, 133
    AWEW: and male bonding, 51–54;
        and sterility, 104; and symbolic
        rape, 44–45
    AYL, and disguise, 36–37
    Cor: and disguise, 34–35; and food,
        20–21; Volumnia, 39–40
    Cym: and clothing, 72; and symbolic
        rape, 43
    Ham, 17; and clothing, 76–86; and the
        comic, 132; and food, 30–32; and
        unfathering, 113–18
    1H4: Falstaff, 26–29, 33, 204–5; Hal,
        27–29; Hotspur, 23–25
    2H4, 18
    H5, 13; and ceremony, 73–76; and
        sacrifice, 62–64
    1H6: and sacrifice, 59–61; and villainy,
        201–2
    3H6: and acting, 197–98; and the
        comic, 131–32
    JC, 181–84
    Jn, and clothing, 71
    LLL, and immortality, 173–77
    Lr, 136–66
    Mac: and bestiality, 47; and clothing,
        71–72; and the comic, 133; and
        feasting, 30; Lady Macbeth, 38–39;
        and patricide, 122–25
    MM, and symbolic rape, 44
    MND, and sacrifice, 64–67
    MV: and cannibalism, 17–19; and
        money, 87–99; Portia, 35–36
    Oth, and fetishism, 118–21
    Per, and chastity, 43

    R2, and self-fathering, 109–12
    R3, 61; and demeaning death, 133–34;
        and villainy, 199–200
    Rom, and self-fathering, 105–9
    Tim, and cannibalism, 19–22
    Tit: and Aaron's villainy, 198–99; and
        cannibalism, 17–18; and rape, 43
    Tmp: and art, 187–94; and banquet,
        29–30; and clothing, 72–73
    Tro: and clothing, 72; and honor,
        40–41
    Venus, and male bonding, 51–52
    Wiv, 206
    WT, and clothing, 71
Shame culture, 212n.9
Shell, Marc, and *MV*, 97, 210n.1, 212n.9,
    218n.19
Siemon, James, 226n.4
Singer, Milton B., 209n.12, 218n.16
Skinner, B. F., 207n.3
Skoloker, Anthony, 216n.3
Snyder, Gary, 226n.1
Snyder, Susan, 217n.8, 222n.12, 223n.3
Soellner, Rolf, 207n.2, 210n.1
Spencer, Theodore, 10, 210n.18
Spevak, Marvin, 213n.3
Spiegelman, Willard, xi
Spinoza, Baruch, 105
Spivack, Bernard, and villains, 198
States, Bert O., 225n.4
Stirling, Brents, 226n.4
Stockholder, Katherine, 224n.10
Stone, Lawrence, 70, 210nn.24,25,
    212n.6, 216n.7
Stoppard, Tom, 134–35, 222n.14
Summers, Joseph, 227n.9

Tertullian, and sex, 53, 214n.14
Thomas, Keith, and bestiality, 49, 50,
    213n.6, 214nn.11,13
Toliver, Harold E., 226n.5
Transvestism, 38, 212n.4

Vesalius, 215n.2

Warren, Arthur, 18, 210n.1
Warren, Robert Penn, 11, 210n.21
Watson, Curtis B., 212n.6
Watson, John B., 207n.3

Weil, Simone, and force, 125
Wheeler, Richard, 212n.10
White, Haydn, 213n.4
Willbern, David, 223n.3

Wilson, Edward O., 208n.3
Wilson, Thomas, 18, 213n.9
Wittgenstein, Ludwig, 14
Wood, Anthony, 216n.9